An Inquiry into Analytic-Continental Metaphysics

Intersections in Continental and Analytic Philosophy

Series Editors
Jeffrey A. Bell, Paul Livingston and James Williams

Drawing on different traditions for new solutions to philosophical problems

Books in this series will bring together work in the analytic and continental traditions in philosophy. Although these traditions have until recently been thought of as separate, if not irreconcilable, these books will show how key philosophical problems can be addressed by drawing from work in both.

The intersections on display here will demonstrate the strength and vitality of a pluralist approach to philosophy, as well as its wide relevance to contemporary philosophical concerns.

Books available

Language and Process: Words, Whitehead and the World, Michael Halewood

Dynamic Realism: Uncovering the Reality of Becoming through Phenomenology and Process Philosophy, Tina Röck

An Inquiry into Analytic-Continental Metaphysics: Truth, Relevance and Metaphysics, Jeffrey A. Bell

Towards a Critical Existentialism: Truth, Relevance and Politics, Jeffrey A. Bell

Visit the Intersections website at edinburghuniversitypress.com/series-intersections-in-continental-and-analytic-philosophy

An Inquiry into Analytic-Continental Metaphysics

Truth, Relevance and Metaphysics

Jeffrey A. Bell

EDINBURGH
University Press

For Elizabeth, Rebecca
And to the Memory of
Leah Bell
Whose Life Will Always Inspire Me

Edinburgh University Press is one of the leading university presses in the UK. We publish academic books and journals in our selected subject areas across the humanities and social sciences, combining cutting-edge scholarship with high editorial and production values to produce academic works of lasting importance. For more information visit our website: edinburghuniversitypress.com

© Jeffrey A. Bell, 2022, 2024

Edinburgh University Press Ltd
The Tun – Holyrood Road
12(2f) Jackson's Entry
Edinburgh EH8 8PJ

First published in hardback by Edinburgh University Press 2022

Typeset in Bembo
by R. J. Footring Ltd, Derby, and
printed and bound by CPI Group (UK) Ltd,
Croydon, CR0 4YY

A CIP record for this book is available from the British Library

ISBN 978 1 3995 0828 5 (hardback)
ISBN 978 1 3995 0829 2 (paperback)
ISBN 978 1 3995 0830 8 (webready PDF)
ISBN 978 1 3995 0831 5 (epub)

The right of Jeffrey A. Bell to be identified as the author of this work has been asserted in accordance with the Copyright, Designs and Patents Act 1988, and the Copyright and Related Rights Regulations 2003 (SI No. 2498).

Contents

Acknowledgements	ix
Introduction	1
§1 Problem of the New	15
§2 Problem of Relations	16
§3 Problem of Emergence	17
§4 Problem of One and Many	18
§5 Plato and the Third Man Argument	19
1. Plato's Theory of Forms	19
2. Vlastos on the Third Man Argument	19
3. Gail Fine and the Imperfection Argument	21
4. The New and the Third Man Argument	22
5. The Imperfection Argument and Degrees of Being/Novelty	22
6. The Problem of Becoming in Plato	23
7. *Philebus* and the Method of Mixture	24
8. Relative and Absolute Relations	26
§6 Bradley and the Problem of Relations	28
1. TMA and Regress	28
2. Bradley on Relations	28
3. Bradley's Regress and the TMA	30
4. The Imperfection Argument and Bradley's Regress	31
5. Relative and Absolute Relations (Again)	32
§7 Moore, Russell and the Birth of Analytic Philosophy	34
1. Birth of Analytic Philosophy	34
2. Moore on Bradley	35
3. Moorean Brute Facts and End to Regress	36
4. Russell on Bradley	37
5. Moore/Russell and Brute Facts	41
6. Defending Bradley	41
7. Michael Della Rocca on the Method of Intuition	44

8. Della Rocca's Spinozist Solution to the Problem of Relations — 44
9. Method of Intuition and Analytic Philosophy of Time — 47
10. Monism or Pluralism? — 49

§8 Russell and Deleuze on Leibniz — 50
1. Russell on the Task of Analysis (and the Taste of Coffee) — 50
2. Russell on Leibniz — 51
3. Deleuze on Leibniz — 53
4. Clear and Distinct/Confused and Obscure; or, on Differential Unconscious — 60

§9 On Problematic Fields — 65
1. Plato, Leibniz and Problematic Fields — 65
2. Problematic Fields and Field Theory — 66
3. Bourdieu on Fields — 68
4. Russell on the Externality of Relations to Terms — 70
5. Problematic Fields and Bourdieu's Fields Contrasted — 71
6. Austin and Performatives — 72
7. Weimar Republic and 20 November 1923 — 74
8. Problematic Fields and External Circumstances — 75
9. On Learning — 76
10. Problematic Fields and Platonic Ideas — 78

§10 Kant and Problematic Ideas — 81
1. Kant and Plato — 81
2. Infinity and Antinomies — 82
3. Returning to Kant and Hume — 84
4. Unity of Consciousness — 86
5. Kant, Russell and the Otherness of the Given — 87
6. Kant, Infinite Regresses and Infinite Tasks — 89
7. Possible Experience to Real Experience — 92
8. Kant's Left-Hand Paradox — 93
9. Kant, Plato and Frege — 95
10. Kant and Problematic Ideas — 97

§11 Armstrong and Lewis on the Problem of One and Many — 99
1. Kant's Transcendental Illusion — 99
2. Frege and the Third Man Argument — 100
3. Armstrong on Universals — 101
4. Lewis on Universals and Natural Properties — 102
5. Classes and Individuals — 106
6. The Trouble with Singletons — 107
7. Lewis and Regresses — 108

  8. Natural Properties and Humean Supervenience 109
  9. Primacy of the Determinate 111
  10. *Philebus* and Lewis 112
  11. Problematic Ideas as Non-Mereological Parts of the Determinate 113

§12 Determinables and Determinates 115
  1. The Problem of Emergence 115
  2. Jessica Wilson and Fundamental Determinables 116
  3. Wilson and Deleuze 117
  4. Uexküll's Ticks 118
  5. Metaphysical Indeterminacy and the Primacy of the Determinate 119
  6. Determinables and Problematic Ideas 122

§13 The Limits of Representational Thought 124
  1. Predicates as Determinates or Determinables? 124
  2. Mark Wilson on Predicates 125
  3. Hasok Chang on Inventing Temperature 128
  4. Mark Wilson on Theory Façades 129
  5. Husserl and the 'constitutive becoming of the world' 131
  6. Husserl and American Neo-realism; or, Hook and Nagel Invent Analytic Philosophy 132
  7. Heidegger, Carnap and the Purification of Everyday Language 136
  8. Husserl's Humean Phenomenology 137
  9. Husserl and Regress of Consciousness 138
  10. Husserl and the Problem of Singletons 140
  11. Husserl and Lebensphilosophie 141
  12. Problematic Ideas and Singletons 142
  13. Deleuze's Transcendental Empiricism 144

§14 Learning from a Cup of Coffee 146
  1. Mark Wilson, Temperature and Theory Façades 146
  2. Transcendental Empiricism and Real Experience 147
  3. Adorno's Negative Dialectics 148
  4. Adorno's Non-conceptual Objectivity 152
  5. Ethnomethodology and the Taste of Coffee 155
  6. Objectivity and Problematic Ideas 157

§15 Carnap and the Fate of Metaphysics 160
  1. Carnap's 'Elimination of Metaphysics' 160
  2. Regresses and Logical Analysis 162
  3. Wilfrid Sellars and the Myth of the Given 165

4. McDowell and World-Disclosing Experience	168
5. Dreyfus on McDowell; or, on Non-conceptual Experience	169
6. McDowell Replies, and Jason Stanley on Skill	172
7. MacFarlane on McDowell; or, the Problem of Mathematical Experience	174
8. Lewis and Singletons, Again	177
9. Meillassoux, Contingency and Mathematics	178
10. Huw Price, Pragmatic Relevance and the Fate of Metaphysics	182
11. Monism or Pluralism?	190
§16 Truth and Relevance	192
1. Arbitrary Accounts and Infinite Regresses	192
2. Brute Facts or Spinozist Bullet?	192
3. Davidson's Coherence Theory of Truth	193
4. Davidson on Language	196
5. Problematic Ideas; or, Pluralism = Monism	197
6. Problematic Ideas and the Relevance of the Determinate	198
7. Living the Problem; or, the Inescapable Social Field	199
8. Meillassoux and the Primacy of the Determinate	200
9. Towards a Humean Political Theory	201
Conclusion	204
Bibliography	207
Index	226

Acknowledgements

There are many people to thank for the opportunities I was afforded that made it possible to write this book, as well as its companion volume (*Towards a Critical Existentialism*). I thank the Leverhulme Trust for having awarded me a Leverhulme Visiting Professorship that I served at Royal Holloway, University of London, during the second half of 2019. I also thank my Dean, Karen Fontenot, and Department Head, Bill Robison, for supporting the sabbatical leave that enabled me to serve my Visiting Professorship in London. Much of this book was written during an enjoyable stay in London, and in a wonderful flat (thank you Sarah). I especially thank Nathan Widder and Henry Somers-Hall for inviting me to come to Royal Holloway, for working tirelessly on my behalf to complete the Leverhulme application, and for all their helpful feedback and comments on rough drafts of these books. I must also thank James Williams and Paul Livingston for their invaluable comments on the books, and for enabling me to make them better than they would have been otherwise. Michael Della Rocca's encouraging feedback and comments let me know I was not chasing windmills; and Peter Gratton's perceptive comments and unequalled copy-editing skills helped me to clean up some bad writing habits and express myself more clearly. I also received invaluable feedback on drafts to chapters from these books that I gave as talks throughout the UK and in Europe during my stay in London. Many thanks are due for invitations from Frank Ruda and Dominic Smith at the University of Dundee; Chris Henry at the University of Kent; Christopher (Tiff) Thomas at Manchester Metropolitan University; Craig Lundy at Nottingham Trent University; Keith Ansell-Pearson and Stephen Houlgate at the University of Warwick; Eckardt Lindner at the University of Vienna; and Martin Procházka at Charles University, Prague. From them and their students and colleagues I received invaluable comments and suggestions, many of which ended up in what I wrote.

Both books have been long in the making, and many people have provided grist for the mill. Most important among these are my former colleagues at the NewAPPS blog, especially John Protevi, whose friendship before and since NewAPPS has been a treasure, and Eric Schliesser, whose omnivorous approach to philosophy has been an ongoing inspiration for my own work, and whose collaboration on posts at NewAPPS set into motion

ACKNOWLEDGEMENTS

many of the key themes that ended up in this book. John, Eric and the rest of the crew at NewAPPS – Mark Norris Lance, Edward Kazarian, Roberta Millstein, Catarina Dutilh Novaes, Jon Cogburn, Mohan Matthen and Eric Winsberg – provided me with many opportunities to engage in the type of analytic–continental crossover work that has come to fill the pages of these books. My colleague Peter Petrakis has had many long conversations with me on themes to be found herein as well, themes he will no doubt recognise.

I have also benefited from many informal conversations as I worked on parts of these books. The 'Communication Problems' chapter of *Towards a Critical Existentialism*, as well as some themes in this book, were prompted by a conversation I had in London with Brent Adkins. Andrew Cutrofello offered helpful guidance after reading an earlier version of this book, and his own work exemplifies how one can successfully bridge the divide between analytic and continental philosophy. Thanks to Dan Smith's invitation to speak at Purdue, and to the feedback from Dan and his colleagues (especially Michael Jacovides), I was given encouraging suggestions early in the process of writing. Craig Lundy, Paul Patton, Sean Bowden, Ian Buchanan, Dan Fineman, Audrey Wasser, among many others, have all provided helpful feedback along the way as the books came together.

I also want to thank Carol MacDonald at Edinburgh University Press for her support and guidance over the years, and especially for her efforts to see these books through the process of getting them to press. The anonymous readers, especially the second reader for *Towards a Critical Existentialism*, provided very helpful feedback and suggestions, most of which I acted on, and as a result the books are better for it. Tim Clark's perceptive and discerning copy-editing of these books has made them both better than they would have been otherwise. And most of all I want to thank my wife, Elizabeth, whose untiring support has been a continual source of strength for me in more ways than she can ever know.

Introduction

In his *Prolegomena to Any Future Metaphysics*, Immanuel Kant raises an important question about the status of philosophy: despite its long, illustrious history, why cannot philosophy, 'as other sciences, attain universal and lasting acclaim?' (Kant 2014, 5). Almost 130 years later, and after a century of impressive developments in the sciences, Bertrand Russell reaffirms Kant's observation, noting that '[i]f you ask a mathematician, a mineralogist, a historian, or any other man of learning, what definite body of truths has been ascertained by his science, his answer will last as long as you are willing to listen'. If you ask the same question of a philosopher, however, 'he will, if he is candid, have to confess that his study has not achieved positive results such as have been achieved by other sciences' (Russell 2001, 90). More recently, things have gotten arguably worse for philosophers, with some, such as Daniel Dennett, directing his fire at the continental tradition and blaming them for contributing to the cultural climate that allowed someone like Donald Trump to be elected as President of the United States. 'I think what the postmodernists did', Dennett claims, 'was truly evil. They are responsible for the intellectual fad that made it respectable to be cynical about truth and facts.'[1] In taking up the theme of truth and relevance, as this book will, and by drawing from the work of Gilles Deleuze in the process (a philosopher who could be grouped among the postmodern philosophers), it may appear that I am simply adding yet another work to the list of those that not only do not contribute to the 'definite body of truths', as Russell aspired to do, but even worse contribute to the contemporary cynicism 'about truth and facts' by watering down truth with discussions of relevance.

In discussing truth and relevance, however, the plan for this work is not to diminish the status of truth, or to provide support and comfort for post-truth relativism. Rather, we will begin with Kant and Russell, and in particular their recognition that philosophy pales by comparison to the sciences when

---

1. Interview with Carole Cadwalladr, *Guardian*, 12 February 2017, at <https://www.theguardian.com/science/2017/feb/12/daniel-dennett-politics-bacteria-bach-back-dawkins-trump-interview>. Michiko Kakutani's *The Death of Truth* (2018) and Lee McIntyre's *Post-Truth* (2018) are among a number of books that single out philosophers, or at least philosophers of a particular tradition – the continental, postmodern tradition – for rejecting truth and paving the way for the post-truth era of alternative facts.

it comes to attaining a 'definite body of truths'. Should this observation be taken as motivation to push philosophy towards an approach modelled on the sciences, and hence an approach that will enable it to achieve a 'definite body of truths', or should one accept that philosophy is concerned with matters other than attaining truth in the sense that the sciences pursue it? The underlying assumption behind the critique of postmodernism, Dennett's included, appears to be that philosophy ought to follow the first path rather than the second. For both Kant and Russell, however, the relationship between philosophy and science is more complicated than this. Immediately following his comment about the lack of 'positive results' that one can point to throughout the history of philosophy, Russell adds that once philosophical questioning gets to the point where 'definite knowledge concerning any subject becomes possible, this subject ceases to be called philosophy, and becomes a separate science'; thus philosophy is the place where one asks questions to which 'no definite answer can be given' (Russell 2001, 90). Philosophical questioning is thus an incubator of the sciences, and while the definite body of truths one finds in the sciences were not achieved by philosophy itself, it was philosophy that asked the questions that became those of science once 'definite knowledge' became possible.

Let us begin with Plato to clarify the nature of this process. In a typical Platonic dialogue, for instance, the guiding theme of each dialogue largely focuses on addressing a question, a 'What is X?' question: what is the nature of holiness (*Euthyphro*), justice (*Republic*), love (*Symposium*), the relationship between knowledge and pleasure (*Philebus*), and so on. In the *Euthyphro*, for example, Euthyphro will begin to list instances of what he takes to be holy, but Socrates is quick to remind him that 'this is not what I asked you, to tell me of one or two of the many holy acts, but to tell the essential aspect, by which all holy acts are holy; for you said that all unholy acts were unholy and all holy ones holy by one aspect' (*Euthyphro* 6d-e). Socrates is not interested in a list of determinate instances of acts that are holy, but rather in *what* it is that makes each of these instances holy, and thus makes it true to say of each of them that they are holy. In the *Republic*, as in many of the dialogues, Socrates finds an interlocutor who is willing to give him the type of answer he is looking for: the first person willing to share their truth is Cephalus, who claims that part of what it is that makes something just is being able to repay one's debts (*Republic* 330d-331b). In response to answers such as this, further questions arise, and Socrates is quick to raise them. Socrates asks Cephalus if it would be just to return a borrowed weapon if the person we are to return it to is not in their right mind and is a potential risk to themselves and others. Cephalus admits it would not be just to return the weapon in this case, and thus Cephalus had not found the 'essential aspect' that makes a particular action just. Returning to Russell, we could say that Socrates – who admits at his trial to having not definitively answered his ultimate questions, confessing as a result to knowing he knows nothing – may simply not have found a way to answer these questions in a definite way, and thereby transform them into questions that can be answered by science. But what does such a transformation consist of, and when, in what circumstances, can we mark the successful transition from philosophy to science? It is precisely here that I will introduce Deleuze's arguments into the mix, and more precisely the distinction he makes between two types of questions. In *Difference and Repetition*, Deleuze argues that the first type of question is the 'What is X?' question, or what I will call a truth question; the second type includes the '"How much?", "How?", "In what cases?" and "Who?" questions (Deleuze 1994, 188), or what I will call relevance questions. As Deleuze goes on to argue, it is to questions of the second type that philosophers turn, and '[i]t should be noticed', he adds, 'how few philosophers have placed their trust in the question "What is X?" in order to have Ideas' (188). To understand the nature of something, 'to have Ideas', it is not sufficient to answer a 'What is X?' question, for whatever answer we come up with will bring with it, as we flesh out the details of the answer, questions of the second type. We have already seen this process at work in Socrates' questioning response to Cephalus – who are you repaying the debt to, and in what case or circumstance is this being done?, etc. Stated differently, and as will be argued for in the pages to follow, both science and philosophy take up truth and relevance questions in their effort 'to have Ideas', that is, in their effort to understand the nature of things. But the key difference, I will argue, echoing Russell's sentiments, is that science tends towards truth questions, to the determinate entities that respond to a 'What is X?' question, while philosophy tends towards relevance questions, to those conditions that provide the significance, meaning and relevance for the determinate entity that can become the answer to a 'What is X?' question.

To begin to shed light on this difference and set the stage for the arguments to follow, let us return to Kant. In elaborating upon why philosophy 'cannot, as other sciences, attain universal and lasting acclaim' (Kant 2014, 5), Kant argues that, had philosophers truly asked whether or not the central task they had taken on is even possible, that task being metaphysics, then perhaps things might be different. The task of metaphysics, as Kant sees it, is to engage in a 'metaphysical cognition', whereby 'the principles of such cognition (which include not only its fundamental propositions or basic principles, but also its fundamental concepts) must … never be taken from experience; for the cognition is supposed to be not physical but metaphysical, i.e., lying beyond experience' (15). The task of metaphysics, in short, is 'to have Ideas', Ideas that are irreducible to the determinate content of experience. The problem with metaphysics from Kant's perspective, however, is that unlike the sciences and their effort to ground their claims on *what* is given to experience – in that which answers to a 'What is X?' question – philosophy had never truly reconciled its claims with experience, with *what* is given in experience, and this for the very simple reason that, by pursuing metaphysics, philosophers sought to ground their claims in principles that lie beyond experience. Philosophers, in short, and to anticipate arguments to be made below, sought to think the nature of things, 'to have an Idea', in a way that draws from relevance questions rather than 'What is X?' questions; and relevance questions, as we will see, are precisely what challenge the status and nature of that which answers to a 'What is X?' question, much as Socrates' questioning undermined Cephalus' claim regarding the nature of justice.

For Kant's efforts, we have Hume to thank for raising this challenge to philosophy, for questioning the possibility of metaphysics itself. As Kant reads him, the challenge Hume leaves us with gets to the metaphysical basis of the sciences themselves when he questions the '*connection of cause and effect*' (Kant 2014, 7). When the cue ball 'causes' the eight ball to roll into the corner pocket, what is not given to us in experience, Hume argues, is the *necessary connection* between the cue ball as *cause* and the rolling of the eight ball into the corner pocket as *effect*. 'May I not conceive', Hume asks, 'that a hundred different events might follow from that cause? May not both these balls remain at absolute rest? May not the first ball return in a straight line, or leap off from the second in any line or direction. All these suppositions are consistent and conceivable' (Hume 2005, 32). For Hume, therefore, reason alone (that is, *a priori*) does not provide the connection between cause and effect. Experience provides the connection, and to claim otherwise would be to go beyond experience and engage in metaphysics, which for Hume is not possible since the only knowledge we can attain is that derived from experience. A consequence of Hume's challenge to the sciences, according to Kant, is that it gives to philosophy the task of reconciling its own metaphysical principles – principles grounded in that which lies beyond experience, such as the principle of cause and effect, among others – with *what* is given to experience, and if it rises to this challenge then philosophy can provide a response to Hume's scepticism. Once this task is completed, which is just what Kant set out to do in the *Prolegomena* and in his *Critique of Pure Reason*, then philosophy may attain, in tandem with the sciences, a taste of 'universal and lasting acclaim' (Kant 2014, 3).

The result of Kant's efforts have been profoundly influential upon the subsequent course of philosophy. A key component of this influence has been the continuing tension between the two traditions Kant sought to reconcile – metaphysics (philosophy) and the sciences. On the one hand, the transcendental idealism Kant developed in order to justify the synthetic *a priori* concepts integral to the sciences, such as causation (to be discussed in §10), spawned a move among philosophers towards absolute idealism, with figures such as Fichte and Hegel claiming to be the true successors to Kant's project. On the other hand, by attempting to provide a proper foundation for the sciences, the contrasting tendency is simply to align philosophy with the work of the sciences and dismiss much of the philosophical enterprise that does not do so. For reasons that will be discussed in this work, the latter tendency has become the dominant focus of philosophers in the English-speaking world. G.E. Moore, Bertrand Russell and the American school of neo-realists (discussed in §13), for instance, all rejected the idealist and metaphysical tendency of Kant's project and explicitly embraced a method suitable to the sciences. This approach was endorsed most explicitly in the manifesto, 'The Program and Platform of Six Realists' (Holt et. al. 1910) and in Russell's 'On Scientific Method in Philosophy' (Russell 1917a), and it would remain the default assumption for most English-language philosophers throughout the twentieth century and into the twenty-first. Rudolf Carnap, to take just one prominent example, set out to eliminate metaphysics altogether (as discussed in §13), on the concern that 'metaphysicians seek their object behind the objects of empirical science … they wish to enquire after the essence, the ultimate cause of things' (Carnap 1984, 5). More recently, scientists themselves have piled on against philosophy. Stephen Hawking, for example, no doubt expresses the views of many when he argues that 'philosophy is dead' because it 'has not kept up with modern developments in science, particularly physics' (Hawking 2012, 5), and that had it done so it would realise that it is physics that best answers the questions that were once in the purview of philosophers. Coupled with the criticisms of philosophy with which we began, by Dennett and others, it would appear then that, as in Kant's day, philosophy has yet to achieve 'universal and lasting acclaim'.

What the tendency typified by Hawking, Carnap and others misses, however, and what will be a central concern of this work, is precisely the tension between metaphysics and science that Kant has left us with. In fact, Kant could well argue that Hawking has misunderstood the very problem Hume raises. In reference to Hume's opponents, of whom there were many, Kant argues that '*Reid, Oswald, Beattie,* and finally *Priestley*, missed the point of his problem … constantly taking for granted just what he doubted, and, conversely, proving with vehemence and, more often than not, with great insolence exactly what it had never entered his mind to doubt' (Kant 2014, 8). In particular, the question for Hume 'was not', Kant claims, 'whether the concept of cause is right, useful, and, with respect to all cognition of nature, indispensable, for this Hume had never put in doubt; it was rather whether it is thought through reason *a priori*, and in this way has an inner truth independent of all experience' (8–9). In other words, Hume is not questioning the *relevance* of the concept of cause; it clearly is an indispensable concept and has become integral to the success of the sciences. The pragmatic success and relevance of the concept of cause, however, does not mean that this concept is justified or grounded, or that claims that presuppose it can claim a truth independent of all experience. Scientists may be unconcerned whether their claims are true independent of all experience, and may simply be concerned with the predictive success of their hypotheses, hypotheses verified through experience and experiments. But this also misses Hume's point, because for Kant the very claims being tested through experiments and experience presuppose concepts that cannot be verified through experiments and experience – the idea and concept of necessary causal connection, for instance. Like metaphysics, therefore, the sciences also use and depend upon concepts that are not strictly empirical, so they must examine those concepts critically in order to avoid the very error they accuse the metaphysicians of making. In examining these concepts, which is what I will do in the pages to follow, we will find that metaphysics and the empirical sciences reflect contrasting tendencies in relation to the process involved in having an Idea – these being the tendencies towards truth questions ('What is X?') and relevance questions ('How much?', 'How?', 'In what cases?' and 'Who?').

In taking up relevance questions, I will pay heed to the lesson Kant drew from Hume – most notably, I will argue that the lesson to draw is that relevance questions are the proper metaphysical questions. The relevance of the concept 'cause', for instance, was embraced by both Hume and Kant, because of its place within the pragmatic and functional concerns of scientific practice, but they did both question the truth of the concept – that is, whether the concept 'cause' is metaphysically grounded. Should we even be worried about the truth of the concept 'cause'? Stephen Hawking, after all, does have a point regarding the success of the sciences, and pragmatist philosophers have long rejected the distinction we are making between truth and relevance, and will account for truth in terms of pragmatic relevance. Our reason for embracing the distinction between truth and relevance questions, however, is to avoid reducing truth to the pragmatic and functional concerns of a given context on the one hand, and to avoid eliminating pragmatic concerns by way of an appeal to a transcendent truth on the other. The contrasting tendencies of truth and relevance questions are integrally involved with both science and philosophy, I argue, although science stresses that which responds to truth questions while philosophy emphasises the response to relevance questions.

It is at this point that I will be arguing for a metaphysics of problems, or what I will call problematic Ideas. Problematic Ideas provide the conditions of relevance that motivate the questions of how, how much, who, and in what case, and more importantly they make possible the determinate realities that respond to the 'What is X?' questions. In these arguments I will thus be elaborating upon, and providing a detailed basis for understanding, Deleuze's claim that 'problematic Ideas are precisely the ultimate elements of nature' (Deleuze 1994, 165). Stated differently, and to rephrase Deleuze's point, the effort of philosophers 'to have an Idea' is best attained when one encounters and takes up the nature of a problem and the '"How much?", "How?", "In what cases?" and "Who?"' questions that come with this encounter (Deleuze 1994, 188). On the account offered here, then, problematic Ideas will be the ongoing response to these relevance questions, and it is this response that makes possible the determinate content of representational thought, and with that the possibility of addressing truth questions. Since problematic Ideas are precisely that which makes the determinate nature of representational thought and experience possible, we are thus following Kant in the spirit of his effort to address Hume's challenge by accounting for the determinate nature of experience by virtue of that which lies beyond experience, by the problematic Ideas that are irreducible to the determinate.

As we will see in the sections to follow, the nature of problematic Ideas as understood here could fall rather quickly to a Carnapian criticism. In the same manner that Carnap criticises Heidegger's statements about the 'Nothing that nothings' he could no doubt criticise problematic Ideas. Since problematic Ideas are irreducible to determinate experience, there appears to be no way to verify when one has or has not used the term 'problematic Ideas' correctly, much as was the case, according to Carnap, with Heidegger's use of the term 'Nothing'. There can be no criterion for correctly determining the nature of problematic Ideas since such a criterion can only be found within the determinate content of an experience that we can represent, and yet problematic Ideas are not to be confused with this determinate content. I will discuss the merits of Carnap's criticisms later (in §15), but first let us set the stage for what is to follow by offering a preliminary account of what is meant by problematic Ideas.

The first and most obvious thing to note is the use of the term Ideas, with a capitalised 'I'. As understood here, I am following Kant, who in turn admits to borrowing the term from Plato. The reason for Kant's use of the term, as he puts it, is because 'Plato made use of the expression "idea" in such a way as quite evidently to have meant by it something which not only can never be borrowed from the senses but far surpasses even the concepts of understanding ... inasmuch as in experience nothing is ever to be met with that is coincident with it' (Kant 1965, 310; A313/B370). When we discuss Kant's arguments (in §10), we will find that what provides the justification for Ideas that 'can never be borrowed from the senses' is the fact that experience itself would not be possible if these Ideas were not already at work and presupposed by every experience. What will become the focus of our attention will thus be the stress Kant places on the conditions of possible experience; more precisely for my purposes, problematic Ideas will be the conditions for the possibility of the determinate while at the same time there is nothing in them 'to be met with that is coincident with' the determinate. For Kant the task of justifying the use of Ideas that are not to be met with in experience consists of setting out the limits and framework of possible experience itself. Anything that transcends these limits can be relegated to the speculative metaphysics that Kant, along with Hume, would have been happy to consign 'to the flames' (Hume 2005, 213). The nature of God's will, for instance, is not something that falls within the realm of possible experience, and thus whatever one asserts to be the nature of God's will is purely speculative and beyond the limits of what would count as legitimate knowledge for Kant. What these limits consist of, for him, are rules which predetermine the limits and nature of any possible experience: 'experience is itself a species of knowledge which involves understanding, and understanding has rules which I must presuppose as being in me prior to objects being given to me, and therefore as being *a priori*' (Kant 1965, 23; Bxvii). The pure concepts of the understanding will be what provide these rules and they do so, by analogy, in the same way that the rules of chess predetermine what is possible in a game of chess. The rules of chess are conventional, which is part of Carnap's point, whereas the rules of the concepts of the understanding are, for Kant, necessary for the possibility of experience. It is no coincidence, as we will see, that Carnap will compare the logical analysis of the relations between propositions, or the task he thinks is appropriate for philosophers, with that of a chess player whose analysis of the position on a board involves a similar approach to 'chess figures … [that are] combined and manipulated according to definite rules' (Carnap 1984, 10). Ernest Nagel will echo this sentiment when, writing of his experience studying philosophy in Europe in the 1930s, he praised the work of Carnap and the logical positivists in Vienna, of which Carnap was a member, as being among the few places in Europe where there were 'quiet green pastures for intellectual analysis, wherein its practitioners can find refuge from a troubled world and cultivate intellectual games with chess-like indifference to its course' (Nagel 1936a, 9). As I will argue for here, the Ideas involved in problematic Ideas are not rules that predetermine possibilities, in the way the pure concepts of the understanding do for Kant; to the contrary, problematic Ideas will be the condition for the possibility of determinate rules. Thus the position I will argue for falls between Carnap's and Kant's – as with Kant, problematic Ideas are understood to be the condition for the possibility of the determinate, *and* as with Carnap the determinate includes determinate rules, and thus rules themselves are conditioned (if not conventional) rather than conditions as Kant argues.

This brings us to the other half of our concept, the *problematic* nature of problematic Ideas. We can find an emphasis on the problematic in Kant as well, most notably when he claims, in the *Critique of Pure Reason*, that with the advent of reason we naturally push our thought from one reason or condition to another up to that which is unconditioned, to the absolute whole, totality and Idea that includes the infinity of all conditions. This 'absolute whole of all appearances', however, is for Kant 'only an idea; since we can never represent it in image, it remains a problem to which there is no solution' (Kant 1965, 319; A328/B384). The idea that contains the 'absolute whole of all appearances' is thus not only an Idea of which nothing is to be met with in experience – 'we can never represent it in image' – it is also a problem 'to which there is no solution'. The task of Kant's critical project is to address the implications of this problem, by critically evaluating our claims to know in order to determine whether or not they hew to the rules of the pure concepts or transgress these rules and lead us to assert Ideas that are beyond the limits of possible experience. From the perspective taken here, Kant's critical project is not available to us since problematic Ideas are what make rules possible. Rules, therefore, cannot be used to stave off the problematic nature of problematic Ideas, or the tendency of thought to transgress the rules of legitimate thought, and thereby enforce a thinking that remains within the limits of possible experience.

This becomes clearer if we set out what it means for problematic Ideas not to be confused with their solutions. If we take a chess problem, for instance, such as a position on the board where there is a known set of moves whereby white can mate in six moves, then this problem is solved once one discovers the sequence of moves, at which point the problem disappears; though it is hoped a chess player will remember the steps to follow should the same position occur in a game. The problematic nature of problematic Ideas, however, is not exhausted by any determinate set of moves, and thus by any of the solutions that respond to the problem, or to the relevance questions, as we will see below. What we take from Kant's recognition of ideas as a 'problem to which there is no solution', therefore, is the irreducibility of the problem to the solutions it makes possible, or the irreducibility of Ideas to anything determinate, and thus the problem is that we continually encounter Ideas 'we can never represent … in [an] image'. Of the various ways we will set forth the nature of Ideas as problematic Ideas, one will be to argue that they are to be thought of as fundamental determinables that subsist in their determinate solutions, analogous to the manner in which the colour blue, as a determinable, subsists in a determinate shade of blue, such as navy blue (the determinable/determinate distinction will be discussed in §12); alternatively, they can be thought of as a problem that is a non-mereological part of its solution, meaning a part that cannot be separated and detached from that of which it is a part (to be discussed in §11), and this is a part, moreover, that is not exhausted by the determinate solution of which it is a part. Among the other examples to be discussed in the sections to follow will be predicates, which I will argue are solutions to the problem of objective thought (§13); and skills, which will be seen to be solutions to the problem that is learning (§9, §15). In a companion book to this project, *Towards a Critical Existentialism: Truth, Relevance and Politics* (hereafter, *TCE*), I will consider the nature of liberalism in politics as a solution to the problem of making sense of life, or the problem of household maintenance (οἰκονομία) in Aristotle's sense.

At this point a Carnap-inspired criticism might claim that we are engaging with metaphysics, and with a metaphysics of the worst type since we are not following Kant's call to remain true to the rules that limit us to possible experience. In response – and this is a theme to be developed in much detail in what follows – I will argue that this criticism is itself based on a metaphysical assumption, one that I will challenge. This is the assumption that affirms the primacy of the determinate, meaning the view that what ultimately accounts for and grounds the determinate nature of experience, and an experience that can then become the subject of representational thought, is itself determinate. Problematic Ideas, on the account offered here, are that which the determinate always presupposes; hence the determinate is the conditioned and it would be a mistake to confuse the conditioned (determinate) with that which conditions it (problematic Ideas).

In arguing against the primacy of the determinate and in defence of problematic Ideas, two main lines of argument will be followed, though there will be crossover and interaction between them as they unfold. In the first, we will show how problematic Ideas can be helpful in addressing a number of key metaphysical issues. We will limit ourselves to just four, though there are no doubt others, and perhaps some that should not have been ignored. These will be the problem of the new, the problem of relations, the problem of emergence and the problem of one and many. In various ways, these problems have been the concern of philosophers in both the analytic and continental traditions. As a result, I will draw from debates in both traditions and bring them to bear on these four problems as well as the implicit relations these debates may have with respect to the problematic Ideas we claim provide a fruitful way to address these problems. The second line of argument will develop an alternative to Kant's understanding of the conditions of *possible experience*, an alternative Deleuze gestures towards with his discussion of a transcendental empiricism that sets out the conditions of *real experience*. Problematic Ideas will be integral to this discussion, and a number of the sections to follow will detail the manner in which problematic Ideas serve as the condition for real or actual experience.

In addition to these two lines of argument, the following discussion will be guided by the thought of two philosophers who may seem to be at odds with one another rather than complementary – namely, Spinoza and Hume. As we will see, a number of the debates in philosophy with which we will be concerned hinge upon where one stands with respect to monism and pluralism. Michael Della Rocca, for instance, will follow Bradley's Spinozist move and argue that 'the only consistent form of rationalism is one that accepts a form of monism and denies any multiplicity of distinct objects' (Della Rocca 2017, 479). Bertrand Russell, by contrast, will launch a substantial campaign against Bradley's project, in no small part motivated precisely by a desire to accept a plurality of distinct objects. Russell will thus embrace a world of particulars, a world of simple, brute facts, in order to counter Bradley's claim that the minute we accept a relation among distinct objects we initiate a problematic, infinite regress. According to Russell (to be discussed in §7), 'whatever is complex is composed of related simple things, and analysis is no longer confronted at every step by an endless regress' (Russell 1907, 44). With this move to brute, self-sufficient simple things Russell believes he has rescued the real world of particulars from Bradley's monistic, absolute idealism. Russell, along with Carnap, Quine and others to be discussed below, will follow this Humean trajectory and affirm a multiplicity of distinct objects.

With our arguments for problematic Ideas, I will argue that the Spinozist and Humean tendencies are just that, tendencies – they are limits towards which processes tend but which they do not fully realise. There is a pluralist tendency, a differentiating tendency to the actualisation of a determinate plurality; and there is a monistic tendency, or a dedifferentiating tendency whereby problematic Ideas subsist in the determinate but are not to be confused with them. Problematic Ideas are thus not to be thought in terms of the one or the multiple, if either is taken to be determinate; or, as Deleuze puts it, 'Ideas are multiplicities ... "Multiplicity," which replaces the one no less than the multiple, is the true substantive, substance itself' (Deleuze 1994, 182). Substance, therefore, is neither one (Spinoza), nor multiple (Hume), but consists rather of the problematic Ideas (multiplicities) the determinate presupposes. The fairly common view that Spinoza and Hume are at odds with one another reflects, I shall argue, the continued prevalence of the primacy of the determinate. Once we see how problematic Ideas are the conditions for the determinate itself, and move away from the primacy of the determinate, we will find that Spinoza and Hume express two tendencies of the same dynamic process, a process that is irreducible to the determinate realities that are solutions to the nature of problematic Ideas.

This arguments of this book will develop along a continuous trajectory, and thus rather than developing along the more conventional chapter-by-chapter approach, where each chapter explores a largely independent or stand-alone theme, the argument here will develop in a sinuous fashion, beginning with the four metaphysical problems stated earlier and then drawing from multiple traditions and arguments as we move forward and as they become relevant to the developing argument. After the first four sections, which briefly lay out the four metaphysical problems of the new, relations, emergence, and one and many, the next six sections will draw on a number of debates in philosophy in order to motivate the concept of problematic Ideas. Section 5 will begin with Plato, and in particular with the implications the Third Man Argument has for Plato's theory of Ideas (or Forms). We will especially highlight Plato's *Philebus*, and his call there to avoid rushing to the One or the Infinite and to attend, rather, to the mixture that is between them, a mixture that is not, I will argue, a mixture of determinate entities but, as with multiplicities, a mixture that is the condition for the determinate one or multiple. Understood in this way, our understanding of problematic Ideas will be largely in line with Plato. Sections 6 and 7 will continue with the regresses of the Third Man Argument but will turn to explore how the history of analytic philosophy can be understood as the result of an effort to embrace pluralism and avoid the regress Bradley claims attends any attempt to account for the reality of relations between distinct objects. Section 6 will focus on Bradley's arguments, and section 7 will show how G.E. Moore and Bertrand Russell, in their attempts to counter Bradley, ultimately provided many of the methodological tools and assumptions that have become the largely unquestioned dogma of analytic philosophy, as Michael Della Rocca has recently argued. In section 8 we will turn to Russell's and Deleuze's readings of Leibniz. With his theory of the monads, Leibniz offers an early attempt to counter Spinoza's monism with a philosophy that embraces a pluralism of distinct objects (i.e., monads), a move Russell unsurprisingly supported. Deleuze also drew important resources from Leibniz, especially the concept of the differential unconscious that will, along with some other key concepts, provide the basis for Deleuze's arguments for Ideas as problems and multiplicities, or problematic Ideas. Section 9 will continue this discussion, and we will further elaborate our understanding of problematic Ideas by relating them to the notion of fields, both as understood in field theory and in the work of Pierre Bourdieu. In section 10 we will begin to clarify the manner in which problematic Ideas are the conditions of real experience by contrasting them with Kant's understanding of the conditions of possible experience. This section will evidence the indebtedness of this work to Kant's, but also the manner in which it sharply diverges.

The remaining sections will further clarify our understanding of problematic Ideas by showing how they can contribute to an understanding of the four problems with which this work begins. There will be overlap between our discussions of these problems. For instance, in section 11 we will focus on how D.M. Armstrong and David Lewis approach the problem of the one and many, with Armstrong favouring a theory of universals to address the problem, and Lewis turning to a theory of natural properties; but along the way these accounts overlap with the problem of relations (which will have already been the subject of sections 5 through 7) and the problem of emergence. Problematic Ideas, I shall argue, provide a way to reconcile key aspects of both Armstrong's and Lewis's work, especially the latter's account of singletons. Section 12 will turn to Jessica Wilson's work on fundamental determinables. Wilson provides us with powerful arguments against the primacy of the determinate, and her arguments for a non-reductive naturalism also provide a context where we can begin to see how problematic Ideas can address the problem of emergence. Section 13 will explore the relationship of problematic Ideas to representational thought and more precisely to the efforts of the sciences to provide accurate representations and descriptions of phenomena. By drawing on the work of Mark Wilson, Husserl and others, we will further motivate the concept of problematic Ideas, and in the process address the problem of the one and many, or in this case the problem of applying a single predicate to many properties that share this predicate. Section 14 will further explore the limits of representational thought by focusing on the work of Theodor Adorno, most notably his theory of objectivity and the negative dialectics of thinking that which cannot be thought. In this section we will see how problematic Ideas can address the problem of the new. Section 15 will revisit the problem of relations in light of the arguments put forward in this book – in particular, the focus here will be on the Myth of the Given and the debates this has generated in both analytic and continental philosophy, but most especially our focus will be on Wilfrid Sellars and John McDowell. In this discussion we will turn to McDowell's defence of the Sellarsian tradition against criticisms Hubert Dreyfus has made, a debate that will illuminate many of the issues at play in the current project. In the final section, section 16, we will return to a theme that will have been an immanent focus of much of this work – namely, the conditions of relevance. In other words, the relevance questions – the 'How much?', 'How?', 'In what cases?' and 'Who?' questions (Deleuze 1994, 188) – will become our more explicit concern at this point, even though problematic Ideas, I argue, involve the tendencies both towards relevance questions – towards further differentiating, amidst the determinate, the relevant from the irrelevant – and towards truth questions, or what accounts for the nature of the determinate, for the definite body of truths, but is itself irreducible to anything particular or determinate. By drawing from the work of Donald Davidson, we will be able to give further clarity to the manner in which problematic Ideas are neither One nor Plural, neither truth nor relevance, if by this is meant a determinate one and/or plurality. As the condition for the determinate, problematic Ideas consist of monist (Spinoza)–pluralist (Hume) tendencies, and Davidson's understanding of language sheds light on how this is so. In this section we will also highlight Huw Price's claim that much of recent analytic philosophy, especially the analytic metaphysics of David Lewis and others, has failed to recognise the important distinction between the relevance and indispensability of a claim and the independent reality that a claim asserts. In short, Price repeats the criticism Kant made of Hume's critics, though in this case it is directed towards the analytic metaphysicians' critique of Carnap. This section will lead us to recognise the political and social relevance of problematic Ideas, and will highlight the concerns that come with arbitrarily segregating the quiet pastures of intellectual game playing from the troubles of living in the world with others. What is needed as a result, I will argue, is a Humean political theory, which is the focus of *Towards a Critical Existentialism*. Whereas this book explores the various ways in which problematic Ideas can be used to address a number of the concepts and debates that have come to fill the pages of philosophy's history, *TCE* will begin by exploring the way in which problematic Ideas emerge as the problem of making sense, and in particular the problem of making sense of one's life with others – or the problem of caring for one's household within a broader community (οἰκονομία). Although *TCE* can be read independently of the present work, and this book can be read independently of *TCE*, it is hoped that what is done here will provide a metaphysical lens that helps to clarify the nature of the problems that become explicit concerns within political discourse, just as the political concerns discussed in *TCE* can help to elucidate a particularly important way in which problematic Ideas have had and will continue to have relevance to understanding the nature of life and the 'How much?', 'How?', 'In what cases?' and 'Who?' questions that confront us on a daily basis.

§1 Problem of the New

What is new, truly new? If we say that some event or phenomenon, A, is truly new, then by what criterion do we make this claim? The most immediate answer appears to be that what is new is unlike anything that preceded it, or there are no phenomena or events prior to A that include or harbour A, for if they did then A would not be truly new but would be simply the explication of what was already implicitly present. The problem of the new may therefore not even be a problem. One could echo the sentiments expressed in the book of *Ecclesiastes* and resign oneself to the view that 'what has been will be again, what has been done will be done again; there is nothing new under the sun' (*Ecclesiastes* 1:9, New International Version). If one does accept that there can be something that is truly novel, a reality irreducible to what has preceded it, then we have other problems that come along.

§2 Problem of Relations

If the new is new by virtue of its relation to that which precedes it, that which is not new, then we have a relationship that needs to be explained if we are to understand what it is that makes something new. We need to explain, for instance, the relationship between the phenomenon that is new, A, and the phenomenon or set of phenomena, let us call it B, that explains why A is new since A is unlike B but nonetheless related to B in some way. For instance, when Haydn first performed some of the pieces he composed while living in London, many considered them to be astonishingly new. In fact, a new category emerged in the wake of Haydn's compositions, the category now known as the Classical tradition in music, a tradition that is different from the Baroque tradition. At the time of his London performances, however, there was not yet the Classical label with which to identify Haydn's music, and yet this music was sufficiently unlike the music of his time (i.e., the Baroque music of his period) that it was considered new. What the new is new relative to, therefore, is important. Haydn's music was considered new not because of how it differed from the cuisine of his time, though that could play a role in creating the culture or world in which Haydn's music became possible, but primarily in how it related to other music. Even if we do not contest these points, however, we still have the problem of accounting for the relationship between A, Haydn's music in this case, and B, the Baroque music of his time. We cannot account for the novelty of A by simply focusing on A, for then we would neglect B, and it is the relationship between A and B that explains why A is new. We similarly cannot explain the relationship between A and B by just focusing on B, for then we ignore A, and it is the novelty of A we want to explain. We also cannot argue for another relationship, let us call it AB, between A and B that accounts for why A is novel in relation to B, because then we would need to account for the relationship between AB and A and B, and so on as we launch ourselves upon a regress of forever needing a relationship to account for relationships. This is the problem of relations, a problem that is generated, as F.H. Bradley argues, with any relation we may choose, not just the relation between a new phenomenon, A, and that which it is new in relation to, B.

§3 Problem of Emergence

Another way to account for a new phenomenon is as a property that results from the systemic interactions of elements that then give rise to a property that is irreducible to any of these elements. An art dealer opens a gallery in an undeveloped warehouse district of a city. In time the gallery becomes popular. A few other galleries open in the same area, and before long the 'warehouse district' becomes a new area of town that is known for its art and cultural activities. This new property of the city is irreducible to any one gallery or venue, but is rather a property that emerges if there is a sufficient number of galleries and cultural events. Once the emergent property emerges, it can in turn have effects independent of the individual elements. People may now be drawn to the warehouse district in order to participate in its art scene, or the city as a whole may become known for its art scene and attract more residents as a result. The behaviour of ant colonies, multi-celled organisms, conscious life, among many other phenomena, have all been explained in terms of emergent properties, properties that are new and irreducible to the phenomena from which they emerge, a *categorial novum* as Nicolai Hartmann (2012) put it. At this point a variation of the problem of relations appears, for we still have the problem of explaining the relation between the emergent property and the elements from which this property emerges. A consequence of this problem is that critics will argue, along reductionist lines, that there is no true distinction between emergent properties and their underlying elements. David Lewis, as we will see, will adopt a version of this criticism of emergent properties (see §11), while Jessica Wilson will argue for a non-reductive naturalism that embraces key aspects of emergentism (see §12).

§4 Problem of One and Many

A final problem that will occupy us in the pages to follow is the problem of the one and the many. In his final publication, Donald Davidson discussed a version of this problem as the problem of predication (see §16). The problem, in short, is how to account for the relation between a predicate, descriptor, or universal and the particular subjects that bear this predicate. This problem arises when we take up the Stranger's challenge in the *Sophist* (see Davidson 2005a, 80–1) and wonder how we can meaningfully make true and false statements, such as 'Theaetetus sits' or 'Theaetetus flies' (*Sophist* 260A-C), when, as in the case of false statements, there is no particular subject (Theaetetus) for whom the predicate (…is flying) applies. How can we meaningfully refer to or speak of that which does not exist? Davidson will chart the history of attempts to address this problem, beginning with Plato's, and he ends by offering his own suggested solution (to be discussed in §16). Long before turning to Davidson, we will begin with Plato's account of the relationship between the concepts and categories through which we think about the world and the many particulars that are identified by way of these concepts and categories. What is this relationship? Do we again have another version of the problem of relations, this time the problem of the relation between the *One* category, universal, or form and the *Many* particulars that share in this One form? It is to these questions that we now turn.

§5 Plato and the Third Man Argument

1. Plato's Theory of Forms

A version of the problem of relations (§2) that is found in Plato and Aristotle is most commonly known as the Third Man Argument, an argument that has been used against Plato's theory of Forms. We first find it in Plato's dialogue *Parmenides*, where Parmenides presents his understanding of Socrates' theory of Forms, suggesting that it consists of the fact that 'when there is a number of things which seem to you to be great, you may think, as you look at them all, that there is one and the same idea in them, and hence you think the great is one' (132a1–4). There is thus one idea (or Form) that accounts for the fact that many particulars, e.g., horses, are seen as horses, or great things are seen as great, in that they each share in some way in the nature of this one Form. Socrates replies that this is indeed the case; he understands the nature of Forms in this way. It is at this point, however, that the problem of relations enters the scene, for the question now arises as to the nature of the relationship between these Forms and the many particulars that in some way instantiate them.

2. Vlastos on the Third Man Argument

This problem of relations – that is, the regress problem commonly known as the Third Man Argument (or TMA) – directly follows from Plato's theory of Forms. As Vlastos (1954) shows in his classic paper, the TMA arises as a result of two implicit premises at work in the *Parmenides*. The first is what Vlastos refers to (following the lead of A.E. Taylor [1916]) as the Self-Predication Assumption (SP). What is assumed, in short, is that 'Largeness is itself large. F-ness is itself F' (Vlastos 1954, 323). Without this assumption, one would not be able to identify what the Form has in common with the particular, and hence see the particular as exemplifying or instantiating this Form. The second assumption is the Nonidentity Assumption (NI), whereby the characterising trait, F-ness, is taken to be nonidentical with the particular that has this trait. As Vlastos puts it, 'If x is F, x cannot be identical with F-ness' (325). From here we get what is necessary for the regress to get started, and this is precisely what Parmenides points out. Picking up where we left off in the previous section, Parmenides asks, 'But if with your mind's eye you regard the absolute great and these many great things in the same way, will not another great appear beyond, by which all these must appear to be great?' (132a6–9). In other words, if we look at the many things that are large (or great) and, in addition, look at the Form itself ('the absolute great') with the 'mind's eye', then all these things will be large. Since the Form of largeness ('the absolute great') is itself large (by SP), and since any particular which is large is not (by NI) identical to the Form by virtue of which it is apprehended as large, then there must be yet another Form that allows us to see the first Form and the many large things as all Large; and yet this second Form is itself large (by SP) and can thus be seen yet again by virtue of a third Form, and so on *ad infinitum*. As Parmenides concludes, by introducing the one idea or Form in relation to the many, as Socrates does, the result is that 'ideas will no longer be one, but their number will be infinite' (132b1–2). Since it is assumed that we cannot think through an infinite number of Forms in order to think a single thing, the conclusion is that thought and knowledge in accordance with the Forms is itself impossible.

There has been a tremendous amount of discussion of the TMA. This is unsurprising, given the centrality of the theory of Forms to Plato's philosophy. In defence of Plato, scholars will look for ways to minimise or outright neutralise the TMA, while Aristotle scholars may be prone to see the TMA as a pivotal point in the history of philosophy, the point when Aristotle most clearly broke from Plato and found his own philosophical voice. In defence of Plato, for instance, Vlastos argues that much of what is most troubling about the TMA for us would never actually come to 'the clear light of explicit assertion' for Plato (1954, 342). As a result, the problems the TMA poses for Plato's metaphysical project are for the most part 'hidden from his conscious mind' (343). What we have with Plato in the *Parmenides*, therefore, according to Vlastos, is a 'record of honest perplexity' (343), a record of a philosopher working through the implications of his theory and who would no doubt have addressed the problems we see had he been more explicitly aware of them. In particular, Vlastos argues that Plato is largely unaware that the two principles required to get the regress going (SP and NI), principles that are integral to Plato's metaphysical project, are in the end mutually inconsistent. For instance, if F-ness [Largeness] is itself F [large] (by SP), and if a particular F [large thing] cannot be identical to F-ness [Largeness] (by NI), then it follows that F-ness cannot be F-ness, which is contradictory. Had Plato explicitly considered the two premises as being necessary to get the regress going, and had he seen that they are mutually inconsistent, then, Vlastos believes, he would have had 'compelling reason to repudiate them both' (342), or at least would have constructed his theory in a way that escapes the regress argument while perhaps continuing to maintain premises that are central to his philosophy, premises such as SP and NI.

3. Gail Fine and the Imperfection Argument

In her book, *On Ideas*, Gail Fine argues that Plato does just what Vlastos suggests: that he does escape the regress argument while at the same time maintaining the SP and NI principles that are central to his philosophy. In short, Fine takes the bait and reads Plato as one who both recognises the problems involved with the regress argument and finds a way to address them. Key to her argument is her reading of Forms as paradigms, or perfect exemplars of which the many particulars are imperfect copies. Fine calls this the 'Imperfection Argument', whereby there is a perfect Form that accounts for our ability to apprehend the many imperfect manifestations of this Form. For Fine, Plato thus maintains SP since the perfect Form F is indeed F, or it 'is intrinsically F, F in virtue of itself' (Fine 1993, 229). The perfect F is also nonidentical to its imperfect manifestations. What is perfectly large is F synonymously, Fine argues, but not in the same way as that which is imperfectly large. As a result of the Imperfection Argument, or the paradigmatism of this argument, the TMA regress never gets started, as Fine puts it, for 'No group of F things that contains a form of F requires a second form of F, since the form in the group is not imperfectly F' (227). The need for the move to the Form F-ness that lies beyond the many things that are F was the result, as we saw, of NI, where if x is F then x is nonidentical to F-ness. For Fine, however, the Form is not F in the same way as every other x is F. It is perfect, or, as Fine argues, it is 'self-explanatory', meaning that '[a]ny form of F is F in virtue of itself' (234) and thus it does not need a move beyond itself to account for itself. We thus have the Form together with all that imperfectly resembles it without the need to move to a second form to account for the elements of this set, or to a third form as the second form becomes an element of yet another set, and so on. With the Imperfection Argument, moreover, Fine argues that we can rethink Plato's late dialogues. More to the point, Fine argues that the emphasis one finds in the *Timaeus* on paradigmatism provides evidence for the fact that Plato did indeed engage with the 'honest perplexity' associated with the regress arguments of the *Parmenides* and discovered, through this process, an escape route through paradigmatism. Fine thus opines that 'perhaps the Timaeus newly emphasises paradigmatism, after the criticisms of the *Parmenides*, to make it clear how to avoid the TMA' (229).

4. The New and the Third Man Argument

Needless to say, this is not the last word on the TMA. Before returning to the problems the argument raises, and their relevance to the themes being developed here, let us first return to the questions with which we ended §2. This will allow us to move more fully into the nature of the problem of the new. The most significant question of §2 has to do with the relationship between that which is new and that which precedes it. If something is too continuous with the past, if an updated version or cover song is not relevantly different from the original, then it would seem we are not entitled to call it new; similarly, just being different from any example of what has gone before is also not sufficient for being new. With the regress problem (or TMA) as laid out by Parmenides, we can see that if the new is a Form separate from that which is new, then the problem is that everything that is new is thought to be new by virtue of something else, by the Form of the new, and yet if this Form is itself something new (as it would be by SP) then it too would be understood to be new by virtue of another Form, and so on. Added to this problem is the common assumption that for Plato the Forms are eternal and unchanging, they simply are what they are, which is contrary to the very notion of the new, of something that *is not* reducible to that which precedes it, and thus the Forms are at odds with becoming, as has been widely noted. Wilfrid Sellars (1955, 430), among many others, argues that 'Plato didn't know quite what to say about the status of Becoming, for he had not yet resolved to his own satisfaction the puzzles relating to "is not".' In the *Republic* (478d), Sellars notes that Becoming is placed 'between' the unchanging reality or Being of the Forms and the nonexistent, though 'he could have viewed Becoming as somehow a mixture of Being (the Forms) and a Not-Being conceived as an ontological principle or, better, stuff' (1955, 430). This move to an understanding of Becoming in terms of mixture and degrees of existence will become, as we will see (in §5.7), a prominent theme in the *Philebus*, to which we can also add the paradigmatism of the *Timaeus*, as Fine has shown (as we saw in §5.3).

5. The Imperfection Argument and Degrees of Being/Novelty

Returning to Fine's reading of Plato, the move to paradigmatism offers us the beginnings of a solution to the problems regarding both the Form of Becoming (and hence the New as well) and the version of the TMA as found in the *Parmenides*. If Forms are to be understood as perfections that are self-explanatory, or F is F by virtue of itself, then the New (as well as Becoming) is not by virtue of something else but is so through itself, through its own nature. That which exemplifies the new, or becoming, does so to lesser or greater degrees, and hence some things are relatively newer than other things, or some events and phenomena mark a greater degree of becoming than others. These points need to be fleshed out, but at first blush we can see that this approach does avoid the problem whereby the New (and Becoming) is to be thought, as Form, as eternal and unchanging nature – which would undermine the very nature of the New, which is thought to be the very essence of change, or what change brings about – and is instead to be thought in terms of a mixture of Becoming and Being, a mixture that is always nothing less than an imperfect Becoming, for it is mixed with Being, with the unchanging. In itself, Becoming is perfect, or is to be understood through its own nature (it is self-explanatory), even if it is not unchanging. The Imperfection Argument, following Fine, thus enables us to think of degrees of the New as well as of Becoming, and conversely to think of degrees of Being and the unchanging as well. The Imperfection Argument also allows us to avoid the move to another Form, a Form that enables us to see the New as new along with all those things that may be imperfectly new (again, see §5.3). These moves, however, require clarifying the intrinsic nature of Becoming, or what it means for Becoming to be self-explanatory, and thus we need to flesh out the sense in which something can be understood to have a greater degree of Becoming than something else. It is to this that we now turn.

6. The Problem of Becoming in Plato

As Sellars notes in his discussion of Vlastos' analysis of the Third Man Argument in the *Parmenides*, part of Plato's problem in thinking through the nature of Forms was reconciling Being with Becoming, or resolving to his satisfaction 'the puzzles relating to "is not"' (Sellars 1955, 430). The most noteworthy of these puzzles, as Parmenides himself made famous, is that by thinking through the nature of 'is not', one thereby makes something of it, and suddenly that which 'is not' now 'is' something, if only as something that is thought. This puzzle will have a long legacy in the history of philosophy and influence philosophers such as Hegel and Heidegger, the latter thinking through its ramifications in his *Introduction to Metaphysics* (see Heidegger 1959 and our later discussion of Heidegger and Carnap in §13.7). Despite the puzzle, it nonetheless seems clear that becoming entails that which 'is not', for in becoming old, one becomes what one 'is not' now, and when one has become old then one 'is not' young anymore. Becoming thus seems to entail an inextricable relationship between that which 'is' and that which 'is not'. For this reason, thinking through the nature of things in the realm of becoming is a particular challenge of which Plato was well aware, as evidenced in the *Philebus* by the following comment: 'How can we gain anything fixed whatsoever about things which have no fixedness whatsoever?' (*Philebus* 59b). This problem is especially pressing since, as Plato puts it, the 'fixed and pure and true and what we call unalloyed knowledge has to do with the things which are eternally the same without change or mixture, or with that which is most akin to them; and all other things are to be regarded as secondary' (59c). How can that which has 'no fixedness whatsoever' come to be thought and acquire the fixedness that comes with knowledge? The solution emerges for Plato in the *Philebus* with what I will call the method of mixture. As Plato argues, 'we must seek the good, not in the unmixed but in the mixed life' (61b), by which is meant a life of virtue, whereby a virtuous life entails a mixture and measured proportion of wisdom (One) and pleasure (Infinite), or 'as it were an incorporeal order which shall rule nobly a living body' (64b; for more on virtue and mixture, see below §11.10). Understood in this way, a proper life will be a mixed life, a life in which knowledge and wisdom will always accompany, albeit in a mixed and imperfect manner, a life of transient pleasures – hence a mixture of unchanging and changing realities. Although the *Philebus* largely develops this solution as a theory of ethics compatible with a theory of Forms (see Davidson 1990 where he emphasises this reading), we want to understand the metaphysical and epistemological implications of the *Philebus*, for they seem to imply that the unchanging nature of Being or reality also ought to be understood as mixed with a reality that is transient and changing, but a changing reality that is accompanied, Plato hopes, by an inquiry that is guided by a desire for the eternal and unchanging – in short, by philosophy (*philo* [love]-*sophia* [wisdom]).

7. *Philebus* and the Method of Mixture

But how does this method of mixture as set forth in the *Philebus* help us to think through the nature of Becoming, or to think degrees of Becoming in light of the Imperfection Argument? In particular, if Becoming is to be understood as a Form that is perfect, whereby F is indeed F, or, as Fine argues, it is 'intrinsically F, F in virtue of itself' (Fine 1993, 229; see §5.4), then what is the *itself* in virtue of which F or Becoming is intrinsically F? This question is especially relevant given the Heraclitean claim that one cannot step into the same river twice (see Kirk and Raven 1984; also *Cratylus* 402a), or even, as Heraclitus' follower Cratylus would push the point, step into the same river once (see Aristotle's *Metaphysics* 1010a). The continual flux and becoming-other of reality is such that the river is never self-same to begin with, and thus there is no itself there in virtue of which Becoming is Becoming! It is at this point that we can adopt Plato's method of mixture, though perhaps not entirely with Plato's blessing. As Plato lays out the method, the guiding assumption is that there is something that is the result of the mixing process. Plato is quite forthright on this point when he has Socrates say that 'God revealed in the universe two elements, the infinite and the finite', and from here he has us assume that in addition to these two elements there is 'a third, made by combining these two' (*Philebus* 16c), and the resulting combination will be a bounded structure that is neither One nor Infinite. Unfortunately, as Socrates puts it, 'the wise men of the present day make the one and the many too quickly or too slowly, in haphazard fashion … they disregard all that lies between them' (17a). In other words, the wise men of Socrates' day rushed off either to embrace the One or the Infinite without looking to the proper structure or mixture that lies between the two elements. As to the nature of this mixture that lies between them, Socrates offers the examples of grammar and music to clarify how this might look. In the case of speech, the 'Sound, which passes out through the mouth of each and all of us, is one, and yet again it is infinite in number … but that which makes each of us a grammarian is the knowledge of the number and nature of sounds' (17b); similarly, for the musician

> Sound is one in the art of music … And we may say that there are two sounds, low and high, and a third, which is intermediate … [but] when you have grasped the number and quality of the intervals of the voice in respect to high and low pitch, and the limits of the intervals, and all the combinations derived from them … when you have thus grasped the facts, you have become a musician. (17c–e)

Of the infinite comparisons of more and less, etc., that can be made with respect to sounds and speech, the person with a grasp of the bounded structure and mixture of the One and the Infinite (e.g., grammar or music) will be able to identify the relevant comparisons, the differences and limits that matter. We could say that the grammarian and the musician each has a taste for the relevant.

We are now in a better position to see how Plato's method of mixture can help us to understand the nature of Becoming. The One, as Plato continues to understand it in the *Philebus*, is the One Form, the single Form that enables us to apprehend the determinate many that instantiate this Form, or the many that imperfectly resembles the Form, as Fine argues. The Infinite is that which is relative, for Plato, or that which is inseparable from processes of relative comparison and change, of more or less for instance. Plato is clear on this point: 'But always, we affirm, in the hotter and colder there is more and less ... [and] wherever they ["more" and "less"] are present, they do not allow any definite quantity to exist; they always introduce in every instance a comparison ... and thus they create the relation of more and less, thereby doing away with fixed quantity' (24b-c). Whenever we initiate a comparison, we enter upon the unbounded (*apeiron*, without limit or boundary in Greek), for by saying something is becoming hotter, this very process of becoming is continually changing, continually becoming more and less relative to the opposite (colder) with which it is relative. As Plato puts it, 'hotter and colder are always progressing and never stationary; but quantity is at rest and does not progress. By this reasoning hotter and its opposite are shown to be infinite [*apeiron*]' (24d). The same is true for pleasure, of which we can think in relative terms with respect to more and less – e.g., one beer is good, two is better, etc. What a proper mixture of the One and Infinite gives us is a bounded structure or grammar that is neither One nor Infinite, and it is this structure that leaves us aware of the relevant limits, or the limits relative to a particular something (sound or speech) – e.g., the musician, aware of the unbounded nature of sound, is able to sense the relevant limits of the musical intervals, the limits essential to being musical, and the person drinking beer will acquire a taste or knowledge for the relevant limits to pleasure in drinking beer, the limits within which the good life is maintained. Becoming, I will argue, is the pure relationship or relative without terms, without a more X or less Y; that is, it is the pure 'is-is not' relation that is presupposed in every comparative relationship among elements, such as in comparing hot and cold, where in determining that one is hotter than another, one is determining that one *is* what another *is not*. Becoming is thus the absolute infinite, and thus not the infinite relative to sound and pitch as in the case of the musician, or the infinite relative to how hot or cold something is relative to another, etc. Becoming is the reality these relative infinites presuppose.

8. Relative and Absolute Relations

We can arrive at this same hypothesis regarding the nature of Becoming, and hence of the New, by returning to the problem of relations. As Plato sets forth the task of mixing the One and the Infinite in the *Philebus*, it is exemplified by the grammarian, musician and the ethical person, among many others of course. In performing these mixtures, the problem is to find the relative and relevant limits and relations between already distinct things – e.g., the *One* Beautiful form that the *many*, infinitely comparable sounds of music instantiate. We can call this a relative relation. In the relationship between the

One and Becoming in its absolutely infinite nature, however, the One may be distinct and determinable – it is what it is in virtue of itself, its distinct and determinable self – but Becoming is not in itself distinct, determinable, or itself, as we have seen; it is rather the absolutely infinite nature that forever eludes identity, the reality that has 'no fixedness whatsoever' (*Philebus* 59b). We can call this relation between One and Becoming an absolute relation. With respect to relative relations, we will find, by turning to Bradley's famous regress argument, that they lead us to an absolute relation, much as we found Plato being led there. It is to this that we now turn.

§6 Bradley and the Problem of Relations

1. TMA and Regress

We can quickly bring Bradley's arguments into the discussion by way of the problem of regress (or TMA). As we saw (§5.2), in the *Parmenides* the regress gets started by way of processes associated with self-predication (SP) and non-identity (NI). If we take the One single Form, the Beautiful in the case of music as discussed above, then the Form of Beauty is itself beautiful. Plato is quite forthright in this regard when, in the *Phaedo* (100c), Socrates presumes that 'whatever else is beautiful apart from absolute beauty is beautiful because it partakes of that absolute beauty, and for no other reason'. The beautiful sounds of music are in turn beautiful because they partake 'of that absolute beauty', and thus the Form and the many sounds related to music all share in the same quality – they are all beautiful. Since a beautiful thing, however, is (by NI) not to be identified with the Form it partakes in, we need a higher form to account for the shared quality of beauty the many sounds and the first Form of Beauty all have. This higher Form is itself beautiful, and in turn capable of being seen as such by virtue of yet another Form, which initiates, as we saw, the regress. It is precisely the shared quality of beauty (F-ness [as in §5.2]), and the relationship it has to that which has the quality, that brings about (by NI) Bradley's famous (or infamous) regress argument.

2. Bradley on Relations

Bradley's arguments against the reality of relations can be found in many places, and we will discuss them at some length (in the next section for instance), but the third chapter of *Appearance and Reality*, 'Relation and Quality', is the most relevant for our current purposes. The central argument of the chapter is to show that while the 'arrangement of given facts into relations and qualities may be necessary in practice … it is theoretically unintelligible' (Bradley 1893, 25). To restate the point made in the Introduction regarding Kant's observation that most of Hume's critics had misunderstood Hume's point, Bradley is likewise not contesting the relevance of relations and qualities, he simply argues that they are not ultimately justified in reality.

More precisely, Bradley argues that the notion of qualities without relations is unintelligible, and so too is the notion of qualities with relations. If we take any quality, A for instance, and accept that it is different from another quality, B, then the question is where the difference between A and B comes from. If the difference comes from outside A or B, or from that which is not A or not B, then 'we have relation at once', Bradley argues, for we have the relationship between A and that which is outside A, and hence a relation that accounts for the difference between A and B. If the difference between A and B is internal to A, 'then inside A', Bradley argues, 'we must distinguish its own quality and its otherness' (29); that is, we must accept a relation within A itself that accounts for its difference from B, or for the fact about A that can explain its difference from non-A, or B in this case. A distinctive quality, therefore, cannot be conceived without a relationship to an-other that accounts for the distinctiveness of the quality itself. We also cannot, Bradley argues, escape relations by affirming a single quality, a single uniform feeling that would short-circuit the need for any relations or differences at all, since there are no other qualities with which to enter into relation. This approach is self-defeating, Bradley claims, for 'a universe confined to one feeling would not only not be qualities, but it would fail to be even one quality, as different from others and distinct from relations' (28–9). As Bradley has already argued, what makes a quality distinctive is precisely that which differentiates it from other qualities, and hence differences and relations cannot be eliminated without also eliminating the distinctive qualities that presuppose them. The notion of a quality without differences or relations is thus, Bradley concludes, unintelligible.

But why not simply embrace relations and accept that qualities inevitably come with differences and relations? This will not work either, Bradley claims, for we have both the problem of relations and Bradley's added claim that there can be no difference without distinctions. If there is a difference, then there must be something distinctive on which this difference is based; difference for Bradley entails the irreducibility of one distinct element, A, to another distinct element, B. If there is no distinction, or there are no distinct elements, then there can be no difference. Similarly, for Bradley, there is no distinction without difference; a quality is distinct precisely because it differs from other qualities, as we saw, and as a distinctive quality it can enter into, and be constitutive of, various different relations. It is for this reason that Bradley argues that any given quality will necessarily have a 'double character' (1893, 31), wherein the quality both *constitutes* and is *constituted by* its relations. In a given quality A, for instance, there is A as *constituted* by its differences, differences that enable us to see A as distinctive, which Bradley labels as the α character of A. For Bradley, then, every quality entails a dependence on other qualities, and thus a nature that always brings it beyond itself. As he summarises this point, quality A as *a* 'is the difference on which distinction is based, while as α ... [it] is the distinctness that results from connection. A is really both somehow together as A (*a* – α)' (31). In a Hegelian move, therefore, Bradley is arguing that for A to be the unique, distinctive quality that it is, its nature must be constituted by its relation to other different qualities, and it is because of this dependency on other qualities that constitute (through a process of sublation as Hegel might put it) the distinctive quality that it is, that a quality is then constitutive of the relations of which it becomes a term. These are the 'diverse aspects' of any distinctive quality, or the sense in which quality A (e.g., a shade of red) *is made by its relations* to others, i.e., by the differences from other qualities, other shades of red and other colours; at the same time A *is not made by its relations* in that it is a distinct quality able to enter into varying relations, for we would not have relations at all, Bradley argues, if there were not distinct terms to enter into them. But, and this is key, if 'A is really both somehow together as A (*a* – α)', then this presupposes, Bradley claims, 'an internal relation [where] ... A at first becomes *a* in relation with α'; but with this move 'A's unity disappears, and its contents are dissipated in an endless process of distinction' (31). In other words, we have within A a fundamental difference, *a* – α, but we cannot have a difference without distinction, for Bradley, and hence we have within A a distinct quality, a quality that is in turn what it is by virtue of another internal difference, what Bradley calls $a^1 - α^1$, a difference with its own distinctive qualities, and from here we have a process Bradley admits can go on 'without limit' (31) (for Deleuze's understanding of this process, see Deleuze 1994, 222; see also below §8.3–4). The result of this regress, Bradley claims, is that the notion of a quality in relation is unintelligible, since it requires thinking an infinite series of qualities and relations that never gets us to the independent, self-explanatory reality that will finally account for the quality and the relation. Bradley thus concludes that 'qualities in a relation have turned out as unintelligible as were qualities without one' (31–2).

3. Bradley's Regress and the TMA

With Bradley's regress argument in hand we can now return to the TMA. The nature of the Forms, on the *Parmenides* reading that gives rise to the regress, are such that they have precisely the 'diverse aspects' that generated Bradley's version of the regress. For instance, the beautiful itself, as Form, is beautiful, as is that which partakes of this Form. But the Form as Form is different from that which partakes in it (by NI), and it is this difference that accounts for why the Form is distinct from that which partakes of it. The Forms are thus constituted by their differences, or they exemplify the characteristic *a* (to use Bradley's distinction). As so constituted, the differences that are inseparable from the constitution of the Forms themselves also entail their own distinctive qualities (no differences without distinctions) that are capable of being seen in relation to other Forms, particulars and even to the Form itself (by SP), or the Forms illustrate the characteristic α, to use Bradley's distinction again. It was precisely this that generated the TMA regress when another Form is called upon to account for the quality the first Form and the many particulars share. Stating the regress in Bradley's slightly different terms, the Form implies a difference that makes it the quality it is, distinct from other Forms and qualities, including especially the things that have this quality and partake in the Form, including the Form itself when this Form is seen as having the quality (e.g., 'absolute beauty' is itself beautiful [by SP]); and it is this distinct quality that is also different from other qualities, a difference that requires distinct qualities, qualities that likewise involve their own differences from other qualities, differences requiring their own distinct qualities, and so on *ad infinitum*.

4. The Imperfection Argument and Bradley's Regress

Can we avoid Bradley's regress if we take Fine's Imperfection Argument approach rather than the argument of the *Parmenides*? Unfortunately, we cannot. As we saw earlier (§5.3), the Imperfection Argument avoids the TMA regress because the Form is understood, on Fine's interpretation of this argument, to be the single, perfect embodiment of the Form, whereas the many things that partake in this Form do so by imperfectly resembling it. We thus do not have a quality held to be in common with a collection of the many things, including the Form itself, a quality we would then need another Form in order to account for their shared nature, and so on. The reason for this was because there is, Fine argued, a fundamental difference: the Form is the only One that is perfect, and the Form is perfect by virtue of itself (it is self-explanatory); the things that are imperfectly the Form are what they are by virtue of their imperfect resemblance to this perfect Form. We thus did not need to move beyond the collection to something else, to another Form, to account for that which they have in common. Despite this move, however, we still have a relation between the quality of the perfect Form and the many things that imperfectly resemble it, and this relation is sufficient to get the Bradley regress going. The Form Beauty, even if it is absolute and self-explanatory, is nonetheless a quality different from other qualities, both from other perfect Forms and from the imperfect manifestations of its own nature. Once we allow for this difference, Bradley argues, we then open within the Form itself a relation between the differences from other qualities and the distinct qualities these differences presuppose (again, no differences without distinctions), distinct qualities that in turn have their own internal differences, and so on *ad infinitum*. In the end, if Bradley's arguments from the 'Relation and Quality' chapter of *Appearance and Reality* are sound (and they are not without their critics [see §7]), then Plato's effort to understand the relationship between fundamental qualities (Forms) and those things that have these qualities is doomed to failure because the 'arrangement of given facts into relations and qualities … is theoretically unintelligible' (Bradley 1893, 25).

5. Relative and Absolute Relations (Again)

Where does Bradley believe this leaves us? In short, we are left with the Absolute. The minute we attempt to account for reality in terms of a plurality of distinct realities such as Forms, Bradley believes we open up the regress of relations (of distinctions with differences) that keeps us from ever arriving at the true, independent reality. Bradley's solution, therefore, is to claim that pluralism and diversity are in the end merely appearances of reality rather than real in themselves, and what is fundamentally real for Bradley is simply the one absolute reality. Bradley is quite forthright in arguing that a plurality of independent beings is self-contradictory because the very differences that constitute the plurality also undermine the independence of these beings and open onto the regress. Thus, Bradley concludes, 'to be different, and yet not essentially relative, is to be a self-contradiction. And so we conclude that the Reality must be a single whole' (Bradley 1893, 143).

We can now begin to plug in Bradley's arguments to our earlier distinction between relative and absolute relations (§5.8). Plato implicitly calls upon a distinction, I argued, between a relative relation between the One and the Infinite – between, for instance, the One distinct and determinable Form of Beauty and the infinitely determinate musical sounds that may partake of this Form – and, by contrast, the absolute relation between the One and Becoming, between Being, or 'is', and Becoming, 'is'–'is-not', which in this case is a relation without determinate terms, such as the distinct Form of Beauty and the many determinate things that are beautiful. Whereas Plato will argue that the One is distinct and determinable, and Bradley will claim that all distinctive qualities and differences are appearances, Becoming is not distinct and determinable, but is a relation that is without limits (*apeiron*) and forever eludes becoming distinct and determinate – it has 'no fixedness whatsoever' (*Philebus* 59b). We called this relation an absolute relation, and turned to Bradley to motivate the need for such a relation. We can now see that for Bradley every relation, if taken to be a relation among independent, distinct realities, including a distinct and determinate One or Absolute, is ultimately self-contradictory and hence such relations are not real but are relative in that they are simply appearances of the Absolute 'Reality [that] must be a single whole'. Bradley would thus reject the reality of relations between independent, distinct realities, but what about the absolute relation between the One and Becoming, where both Being (One) and Becoming (Many) are understood to be absolutely infinite and forever elude distinct identity? Taking Becoming first, Bradley will not deny the reality of Becoming, or the diversity of relations we see in everyday experience, but he will argue that they are appearances that belong to the one Absolute reality. 'Whatever is rejected as appearance', Bradley argues, is 'no mere nonentity. It cannot bodily be shelved and merely got rid of ... it must belong to reality' (Bradley 1893, 135). With respect to Being, if the 'one Absolute reality' is not determinate or distinct, as Bradley argues, and if Becoming eludes distinct identity, then how can there be a relation of any type between Being and Becoming? To push Bradley, and to anticipate arguments I will make using Plato's method of mixture, I will argue that reality itself is nothing less than tendencies to an Absolute One on the one hand (Bradley's and Spinoza's position, among others), and to a plurality of Many substances on the other (Leibniz's, Russell's and many others' position). This is the nature of problematic Ideas; it is, paradoxically, an absolute relation without determinate or distinct terms. To set the stage for this move to problematic Ideas, let us first address (in §7) some of the influential criticisms of Bradley, criticisms that paved the way in large measure for the rise of analytic philosophy in the twentieth century. We will also discuss Michael Della Rocca's more recent reworking of Bradley's arguments in order to lay the groundwork for our account of problematic Ideas as an absolute relation.

§7 Moore, Russell and the Birth of Analytic Philosophy

1. Birth of Analytic Philosophy

The most notable and influential criticisms of Bradley were those of Bertrand Russell and G.E. Moore, criticisms that are often seen as critical to the advent of analytic philosophy (see Candlish 2007 and Della Rocca 2013 [discussed below]). As a sociological and descriptive fact, the history of twentieth-century philosophy in the English-speaking world is marked by a shift away from Idealism and Pragmatism towards an approach that models itself on the use of scientific methods, which in philosophy is best seen in the application of the formal analytic tools of logic and set theory. Although the task of identifying the precise point that marks the beginning of this shift is fraught with difficulties, turning to Moore and Russell is far from an arbitrary choice. The primary reason for this is that this is the narrative Russell himself tells. As Russell recalls, 'It was towards the end of 1898 that Moore and I rebelled against both Kant and Hegel. Moore led the way, but I followed closely in his footsteps' (Russell 1959, 54). Bradley was grouped in the Idealist crowd with Hegel, and thus their rebellion against Hegel is exemplified in their critique of Bradley (on the errors of Russell grouping Bradley with Hegel, see Candlish 2007, 29–30). Whether the break with Idealism (and by extension the break with Pragmatism and continental philosophy) is truly a clean and definitive break has been hotly contested of late (see Bell et. al. 2015, Gordon 2012). For our purposes, we will think through the details of this 'break' by looking at the role the Third Man Argument plays in both Moore's and Russell's arguments. By looking at both Bradley's and Moore's/Russell's arguments as arguments that develop in an effort to respond to the TMA, the implications and consequences of their debate for twentieth-century philosophy will become much clearer, and along the way we will further motivate my argument supporting problematic Ideas.

2. Moore on Bradley

When Russell looks to the 'end of 1898' as the beginning of the rebellion against Kant and Hegel, he is referring to Moore's now famous essay 'The Nature of Judgment' (Moore 1899). Although the essay was published in 1899, Moore first presented it on 9 December 1898 at a meeting of the Aristotelian Society (which Russell likely attended), and Moore and Russell had corresponded about the essay a few months before. In this essay Moore immediately states the point over which he claims he and Bradley disagree, namely the assumption that, as Moore cites Bradley, '"Truth and falsehood … depend on the relation of our ideas to reality"' (Moore 1899, 176; citing Bradley 1893, 2). In detailing the difficulties he finds with Bradley's understanding of the relation of 'ideas to reality', Moore points to Bradley's efforts to show how ideas 'must not be confused either with their existence in the mind or with their particular character as so existent, which may be called their content' (1899, 176). In other words, Bradley is attempting, as do Moore and Russell, to avoid the psychologism of equating ideas with mental phenomena on the one hand, and with the objective content of the idea on the other, this content being that which the idea is taken to be true of. The latter approach fails to account for the fact that a true judgment is true of something, and if one reduces the idea to the objective content itself then the difference between the idea and this content is erased and so too is the possibility of the 'relation of our ideas to reality', to the something our judgments are judgments of. Bradley's path through this Scylla and Charybdis is, as Moore again cites him, to argue that '"all ideas are signs"' (176; Bradley 1893, 5), and '"A sign is any fact that has a meaning"', while '"meaning consists of a part of the content (original or acquired) cut off, fixed by the mind, and considered apart from the existence of the sign"' (176; Bradley 1893, 4).

It is at this point where Moore begins to see problems with Bradley's account. More precisely, as Moore sees it, Bradley succumbs, perhaps despite his best efforts to the contrary, to the vicious regress of the TMA. The regress arises, Moore argues, when we attempt to determine how we can 'cut off a part of the character of our ideas, and attribute that part to *something else*' (1899, 178, emphasis added). If the meaning of an idea, with the idea taken as a sign for something else, 'consists of a part of the content cut off, fixed by the mind', then the question for Moore is how the mind can fix this cut off part of the content unless it already has another idea of the content from which the mind will cut off a part. If this new idea, however, is similarly related to the content, content that is to be 'considered apart from the existence of the sign', then it too will need to be thought of as a meaning that is neither a mental phenomenon nor the content itself, but as a meaning 'cut off from a content to be considered as something else, which will in turn need yet another idea of the content from which this new part is to be cut, and so on. As Moore summarises these difficulties, he explicitly evokes the TMA: 'These difficulties, which are of the same nature as the famous τρίτος ἄνθρωπος [Third Man] urged against the hypostatized Platonic ideas, inevitably proceed from trying to explain the concept in terms of some existent fact' (178), and a fact taken to be some reality external to the idea. Moore's proposed way around the vicious regress he finds Bradley falling into is to urge that 'truth and falsehood are not dependent on the relation of our ideas to reality' (177).

The rest of the 'Nature of Judgment' consists of Moore laying out his alternative explanation of judgment, one that avoids understanding truth as a relation of 'ideas to reality', and hence one that avoids the consequences of the TMA. The path Moore charts between the Scylla and Charybdis of psychologism and objectivism is to argue that all judgment proceeds by concepts. All explanations that rely on facts, 'whether mental or of any other nature', Moore claims, 'presuppose the nature of the concept', and a concept, he adds, 'is not a mental fact, nor any part of a mental fact' (1899, 178–9). Concepts are themselves irreducible for Moore: they 'are possible objects of thought; but that is not a definition of them [and] ... It is indifferent to their [a concept's] nature whether anybody thinks them or not ... and the relation into which they enter with the knowing subject implies no action or reaction' (179). Moore even goes so far as to argue that, in order to avoid a TMA-styled regress, 'It seems necessary, then, to regard the world as formed of concepts' (182). In one fell swoop, therefore, Moore's approach allows for a complete rethinking of the nature of judgment, and one that avoids both 'Kant's reference to experience', in particular the transcendental unity of apperception, and 'Mr. Bradley's reference to reality' (192). In short, Moore avoids Idealism on the one hand, including Kant's transcendental idealism, and he avoids any view which holds that the truth of a judgment depends 'on the relation of our ideas to reality'. For Moore there are nothing but concepts, and concepts are in themselves neither true nor false; they become true or false when they become part of a proposition, and it is propositions that are the proper subject of true or false judgments.

3. Moorean Brute Facts and End to Regress

Moore is quite clear regarding the nature of propositions – 'A proposition is composed not of words, nor yet of thoughts, but of concepts ... A proposition is a synthesis of concepts' (1899, 179). For instance, Moore argues that when one says 'This rose is red' (to use his example, 179), one is not 'attributing part of the content of my idea to the rose', that is to the something other from which the meaning of rose is 'cut off', in a process which initiates, as we saw, a vicious regress; 'nor yet', Moore continues, is one 'attributing parts of the content of my ideas of rose and red together with some third subject', a third subject or thought that accounts for the relationship between the first two ideas, a thought or idea whose relationship to each of the original two ideas also needs to be accounted for, so that at this point we are off on yet another vicious regress. What we are doing instead when we say 'This rose is red' is asserting 'a specific connexion of certain concepts forming the total concept "rose" with the concepts "this" and "now" and "red"; and the judgment is true if such a connexion is existent' (179). Moore's claim that the judgment is true if 'such a connexion (of concepts) is existent' does not entail a return to the traditional view of relating our ideas to reality, but is rather simply to gesture to something that cannot be explained. Moore is quite upfront on this point when he states that 'what kind of relation makes a proposition true, what false, cannot be further defined, but must be immediately recognized' (180). And again, in discussing the proposition, 'This paper exists', Moore says that 'if it is true, it means only that the concepts, which are combined in specific relations in the concept of this paper, are also combined in a specific manner with the concept of existence. This specific manner is something immediately known, like red or two' (180–1). To avoid the regress, therefore, Moore short-circuits the differences that generate it, calling instead for brute facts, for facts that do not need something different to account for them but are immediately, intuitively obvious. Such facts will later become the core of Moore's common sense realism and they are often referred to today as Moorean facts. Such facts, Moore argues, cannot be argued for by means of propositions and arguments; rather, such arguments and propositions presuppose a truth that is immediately known. This is, in fact, Moore's conclusion to his essay 'Nature of Judgment': 'For our conclusion is that truth is itself a simple concept; that it is logically prior to any proposition' (182).

4. Russell on Bradley

As we will now see, Russell was indeed right to say that Moore led the way, and more precisely led the way in showing how one can avoid the TMA regresses. We find Russell, for example, grappling with the regress arguments Bradley set forth in *Appearance and Reality*, regresses that led Bradley to deny that relations are real but are mere appearances. Russell himself will later admit that arguing for the reality of relations was one of the concerns that most preoccupied him. In fact, Russell says that a difference between him and Moore was his concern with 'certain purely logical matters. The most important of these, and the one which has dominated all my subsequent philosophy, was what I called the "doctrine of external relations"' (Russell 1959, 11–12). What Russell understands the doctrine of external relations to mean is that there are relations that do not affect the nature of the terms that enter into these relations. Bradley, according to Russell, asserts the opposite opinion, which he takes to be the view that if 'an object x has a certain relation R to an object y [then] this implies complexity in x and y, i.e., it implies something in the "natures" of x and y in virtue of which they are related by the relation R' (Russell 1910, 373). We saw earlier (§6.2) that, for Bradley, to say x is in relation to y does indeed entail an internal difference to x, or complexity for Russell (i.e., the $a - \alpha$ or difference-distinction difference), and it is this internal difference that accounts for both why x constitutes (as distinct) and is constituted by (as different from y) the relation; and yet this internal difference entails further distinct qualities (there is no difference without distinction), qualities with their own internal differences, and so on. For Russell, however, if we do not resist Bradley's conclusions, and hence do not affirm the doctrine of external relations, then mathematics becomes 'inexplicable' (Russell 1959, 12). From Russell's perspective, this makes perfect sense. If we take the mathematical relation $\geq$, for instance, then to do mathematics with this relation one needs to understand it such that one can indefinitely substitute various quantities for x or y without affecting these quantities and make the mathematical statement x $\geq$ y true or false. This entails, according to Russell, accepting the doctrine of external relations, which Bradley, and unfortunately so from Russell's perspective, does not.

We find Russell's most sustained critique of Bradley in a series of exchanges between the two in the journal *Mind* during 1910 and 1911. Russell first aired his criticisms of Bradley in his *Principles of Mathematics* (1903), which is unsurprising given Russell's concern with defending external relations in order to make mathematics explicable. Here Russell argues that a mathematical relation such as x $\geq$ y can be understood both as a whole and as a whole that can nonetheless be analysed into its constituent parts. Bradley, by contrast, 'is driven to the view that the only true whole, the Absolute, has no parts' (Russell 1903, 226), a view Russell will argue is ultimately self-contradictory given, following Moore's analysis, Bradley's call for understanding judgment in terms of meanings that are parts cut off from a reality that is something other. To his 'On Appearance, Error and Contradiction' (1910), Bradley will add a supplementary note defending his views against Russell's criticisms. In particular, Bradley argues that Russell's whole approach relies upon two contradictory notions: on the one hand, as Bradley puts it, 'he [Russell] defends a strict pluralism, for which nothing is admissible beyond simple terms and external relations ... [and yet] throughout stands upon unities which are complex and which cannot be analyzed into terms and relations' (Bradley 1910, 179). In Russell's reply to this objection he argues that 'everything here turns upon the sense in which such unities cannot be analysed. I do not admit that, in any strict sense, unities are incapable of analysis ... What I admit is that no enumeration of their constituents will reconstitute them, since enumeration gives us a plurality, not a unity' (Russell 1910, 373). Such unities, Russell argues, maintain an 'identity in difference', as he puts it, without which 'the apparent multiplicity of the real world is otherwise inexplicable' (Russell 1907, 43). In tasting a cup of coffee, for instance, a coffee taster may note the different flavours and characteristics, and through analysis list them. The taste, however, maintains, for Russell, an identity and unity that persists and remains whole despite the different properties one tastes. Bradley is unmoved, countering Russell's claim with a query: 'Is there anything, I ask, in a unity beside its "constituents", i.e., terms and the relation, and, if there is anything more, in what does this "more" consist?' (Bradley 1911, 74). In his 'Analysis' chapter from his later book, *An Inquiry into Meaning and Truth*, Russell will continue to hold to his 'identity in difference' principle, arguing that 'we can experience a whole W without knowing what its parts are, but that, by attention or noticing [such as when a coffee taster engages in what Russell calls analysis], we can gradually discover more and more of its parts ... But it is assumed that the whole W can preserve its identity throughout the process of analysis' (Russell 1940, 315). Bradley's likely response would again be to ask about this whole, this something more than the parts. What is this?

With respect to the disagreements between Bradley and Russell, Russell may well have homed in on the crux of their continuing differences when he claims that Bradley's understanding of relations 'seems to rest upon some law of sufficient reason' (Russell 1910, 373), which Russell defines as follows: 'the law of sufficient reason, according to which nothing can be just a brute fact, but must have some reason for being thus and not otherwise' (Russell 1907, 40). As Russell sees it, Bradley's 'search for a "sufficient reason" is mistaken' (1910, 374). This point is critical: it does indeed highlight the key difference between Russell and Bradley, and it also shows how Russell himself is following the lead of Moore. If the law of sufficient reason is mistaken, as Russell claims, then one can accept brute, inexplicable facts. This is precisely what Russell does, and with this move he is also able to bring regresses to an end at these brute facts. Russell deploys this tactic, for instance, in 'Nature of Truth', where he offers the example of the relation 'greater than' and argues that if we attempt to use adjectives associated with each of the terms of the relation, then we cannot avoid an 'endless regress' (Russell 1907, 42). If I say this cup of coffee, x, is hotter (greater) than your cup of coffee, y, for example, then I am not saying anything about the nature of either x or y other than that x is hotter (greater) than y. If we look, in accordance with the law of sufficient reason, for why x is hotter (greater) than y, we may then appeal to adjectives that capture the distinctive qualities of x and y, or to the predicates that tell us something about the nature of x and y. We may say that my cup of coffee, x, is 100 degrees centigrade whereas your cup of coffee, y, is 90 degrees centigrade. But now we need to account for the relation between 100 degrees centigrade and 90 degrees centigrade, or know something about the nature of 'being 100 degrees centigrade' in order to understand why it is greater than 'being 90 degrees centigrade'; and this in turn, Russell argues, leaves us with two new 'adjectives [that] must still have a relation corresponding to "greater than", and so on' (42) – namely, a new adjective about their respective natures, e.g., kinetic energy, etc. Russell is thus led to the following Moorean conclusion: 'Hence we cannot, without an endless regress, refuse to admit that sooner or later we come to a relation not reducible to adjectives of the related terms' (42). At some point we simply come to complex facts and relations, to wholes or unities, that are brute facts and cannot be accounted for or explained by way of the nature of the terms of the relation, even though the constituents of a relation may well be discerned through the process of analysis (Russell 1910, 374: 'whenever we have two terms x and y related by a relation R, we also have a complex, which we may call 'xRy', consisting of the two terms so related').

Russell's philosophy will continue to work from the largely Moorean basis we have just sketched. Although Russell will modify and rework his thought throughout his career, as has been widely noted and discussed (for a good overview and history of Russell's thought, see Hylton 1993), his commitment to brute facts in order to forestall a TMA-styled regress remains a consistent thread. Russell concludes his essay 'On the Nature of Truth', for example, by saying that we can safely speak of 'a world of many things, with relations which are not to be deduced from a supposed "nature" or scholastic essence of the related thing. In this world, whatever is complex is composed of related simple things, and analysis is no longer confronted at every step by an endless regress' (Russell 1907, 44). In 'The Philosophy of Logical Atomism' (1918) Russell sets forth his famous distinction between knowledge by acquaintance and knowledge by description; in the case of the former our knowledge is of particulars, of which we 'have a full, adequate, and complete understanding of the name, and no further information is required' (Russell 1970, 202). Russell will stress that these particulars stand 'entirely alone and [are] completely self-subsistent … that sort of self-subsistence that used to belong to substance' (202). These brute particulars are what enter into complexes, or what Russell calls atomic facts, facts which 'contain, besides the relation, the terms of the relation'; these 'terms which come into atomic facts I define as "particulars"' (199). And finally, in his *Inquiry into Meaning and Truth*, Russell will continue to speak of those brute, self-dependent particulars which serve as 'my momentary epistemological premises', premises that are the only true premises, Russell argues, whereas 'the rest must be inferred' (1940, 127).

5. Moore/Russell and Brute Facts

For both Moore and Russell, therefore, core features of their philosophies can be understood to be the results of an effort to avoid the type of regress arguments one finds in the TMA and Bradley. In his own defence, Russell would argue that his approach not only puts an end to needless regress arguments, but it is also more compatible with modern science. 'In favour of the premises from which I start', Russell argues in the concluding paragraph to his reply to Bradley, there is 'a kind of inductive argument: they allow much more truth to science and common sense than is allowed by the opposite premises [i.e., Bradley's]' (Russell 1910, 377). For his part, Bradley broaches a theme that will be discussed at much greater length below (see §15, §16). In particular, he admits that Russell's argument is one he is 'very far from undervaluing', and that he holds the doctrine that he does 'largely because it seems to me to remain, more than others, in harmony with life as a whole' (Bradley 1911, 76). In contrast to Russell, for Bradley 'the things which matter most in life are not to be resolved into terms with relations between them … The question is in a word as to experiences which, to a greater or less extent, are non-relational' (76). Bradley admits he does not know whether Russell allows for non-relational facts or not. Russell may argue that Bradley has missed his point, however – namely, that science, on his view, requires the basic data upon which its findings are built, or logically constructed as Russell will put it, and his approach provides us with the particulars that suit that purpose.

6. Defending Bradley

In Bradley's defence, his point was not to deny the reality of relations but to understand the nature of reality, and he remains sceptical that the particulars Russell highlights are indeed the 'self-subsistent' realities or substances he claims they are. For Bradley, if our effort to understand the nature of something requires us to go beyond that which is before us, then what is before us is not ultimately real but rather an appearance of reality. Bradley thus argues that 'You have an appearance wherever, and so far as, the content of anything falls outside of its existence, its "what" goes beyond its "that". You have reality on the other hand so far as these two aspects are inseparable' (Bradley 1910, 157). Bradley's regress argument, therefore, does not justify the appeal to brute facts, for these are not explanations but rather bring all explanations to an end – they are self-explanatory and 'no further information is required' (Russell 1970, 202). To the contrary, Bradley's arguments highlight the fact that all our explanations are always only finite and partial explanations, and as such they rely upon a reality, content, or a 'what' that goes beyond them. Bradley is forthright on this point: 'Now in every finite centre (on our view) the Whole, immanent there, fails to be included in that centre. The content of the [finite] centre therefore is beyond itself' (Bradley 1910, 157). This point is often overlooked, Bradley admits, and in large part this is precisely because of the needs of practical life, needs that the sciences themselves follow unquestioningly as well. Bradley thus argues that '[i]n the realm of the special sciences and of practical life, and in short everywhere, unless we except philosophy, we are compelled to take partial truths as being utterly true' (163; see also §10, §13 for more on this theme). Now Moore could come in at this point and argue that Bradley is himself susceptible to succumbing to his own regress argument. Just as Moore found problems with Bradley's attempts to understand the nature of a true judgment in terms of the relation of an idea to reality, he would likely find the same difficulties with relating the partial truth of the specialised sciences to the Absolute Reality from which the partial truths are 'cut off'. This is an important point and we will return to it (see §10).

We can also defend Bradley's commitment to the principle of sufficient reason, rejecting Russell's claim that 'the search for a "sufficient reason" is mistaken' (Russell 1910, 374). Is there a point where seeking explanations reaches an end, an end finite reasoners such as ourselves can attain, a point where, as Wittgenstein puts it in the *Philosophical Investigations*, 'I have exhausted the justifications [and] I have reached bedrock, and my spade is turned' (Wittgenstein 2009, §217, 202)? We will discuss this further in the next section, but for the moment what is important to note is that a primary motivation for upholding the principle of sufficient reason – namely, the principle that there is no difference without a distinction, or something distinct without differences – is that by ignoring this principle and relying upon brute facts one risks making arbitrary distinctions, distinctions that ignore relevant differences that are inseparable from brute facts. The political implications of this point will be the focus of *Towards a Critical Existentialism* (*TCE*), but for the moment the implications are clear, for it is common across a broad swath of political thought, from classical republicanism to contemporary versions of liberalism, to find fault with any of a number of forms of arbitrary power. In his *Second Treatise*, for instance, Locke's chief criticism of monarchy, and his subsequent call for political power to be based upon the will of the people, is that monarchical power is arbitrary: 'Despotical power is an absolute, arbitrary power one man has over another, to take away his life whenever he pleases; and this is a power which neither Nature gives, for it has made no such distinction between one man and another' (Locke 1988, 382). In other words, the unquestioned assumption of many of Locke's day, such as Robert Filmer, the subject of much of Locke's criticism in the *First Treatise*, is that monarchical power is common sense, or the bedrock foundation upon which society is and ought to be based. This common sense assumption, however, reflects instead, for Locke, an overlooked distinction and difference between those with power and those subject to it, a difference that is not itself accounted for or justified. In contrast to arbitrary power, Locke seeks instead a power based upon reasons, a power exercised by those capable of making rational decisions. Locke's arguments are also found in the late twentieth-century debates between Robert Nozick and John Rawls. In his *Theory of Justice*, Rawls sets out to argue for principles whereby the basic structure of society will be perceived to be just (see Rawls 1971). What Rawls means by this is that those who do not know anything about their worldly condition (their gender, ethnicity, wealth, etc.) will consider the structure of society to be fair if it does not arbitrarily benefit one group at the expense of another. Nozick counters Rawls' arguments by questioning how it is that we know what is truly arbitrary or not, and who is to say that the current distribution is unfair (see Nozick 1998). As long as the processes that lead to the current distribution of wealth do not violate the rights of others, Nozick argues, then the resulting distribution ought to be considered fair. Now more can be said about this, of course, and it will become a focus of *TCE*, but it should be clear for the moment that there are political implications, and significant ones as well, tied to accepting brute, unexplained facts, and the tendency such facts have to bring arbitrary differences in their wake. To clarify this point, and return to its philosophical and metaphysical implications, we can turn to Michael Della Rocca's work. In a series of essays, Della Rocca defends Bradley's 'no difference without distinction principle', and shows how the Moorean/Russellian attempt to avoid the regress by relying upon brute facts brings along with it a problematic reliance on arbitrary distinctions, an arbitrariness that undermines the arguments the brute facts were used to support. It is thus to Della Rocca's work that we now turn.

7. Michael Della Rocca on the Method of Intuition

Della Rocca's Bradley/Spinoza-inspired critique of the methodology and assumptions of contemporary analytic philosophy can be found in his essay 'Taming Philosophy' (Della Rocca 2013). The central argument of this essay is that much of twentieth-century philosophy, especially analytic philosophy, has been reliant upon what Della Rocca calls the method of intuition (MI). The influence of Moore upon Russell is integral to Della Rocca's narrative, especially Moore's move which averts a TMA regress by resorting to intuitively obvious, self-evident truths. As a result of this move, Moore ends any potential regress upon a bedrock whereby the 'kind of relation [that] makes a proposition true, what false, cannot be further defined, but must be immediately recognized' (Moore 1899, 180). As Della Rocca defines the MI, it involves a method of theorising on the basis of one's 'immediately recognised' intuitions, and from there aims 'to arrive at an overarching theory that somehow accommodates these intuitive responses as well as possible' (Della Rocca 2013, 179). As generally understood within the literature, Della Rocca claims that these intuitions are often 'regarded as ordinary beliefs or as expressions of common sense (whatever that is) ... [and/or] ordinary language ... [and for others, such as Bealer 1998a, as a] privileged kind of seeing or insight' (180). What philosophical theorising attempts to construct, therefore, is a theory that accommodates our philosophical principles with our intuitions, in what John Rawls (1971) and later Nelson Goodman (1983) will call the method of reflective equilibrium, whereby 'rules and accepted inferences' (Della Rocca 2013, 182) are brought into harmony with each other. Della Rocca's criticism of MI, in short, is that relying on common sense intuitions entails a 'privileging of ordinary beliefs [that] is arbitrary and unjustified' (188). The proper response to the TMA regress is not, therefore, as it was for Moore and Russell, to end them with a brute, self-evident fact, for then the cure is worse than the disease. The proper response, Della Rocca argues, is the Spinozist response.

8. Della Rocca's Spinozist Solution to the Problem of Relations

In delving into the more detailed criticisms of the method of intuition (MI), Della Rocca begins, perhaps surprisingly, with Quine. Quine, Della Rocca argues, draws upon the charge of arbitrariness in his famous criticism of the analytic-synthetic distinction (Quine 1980, 20–46). Quine's criticism, in short, is that wherever one draws the line between analytic statements (statements that are true by definition, or true 'come what may' as Quine puts it) and synthetic statements (statements that are true by virtue of empirical evidence), one could, with sufficient reworking of the related judgments, or the web of belief as Quine will call it, arbitrarily draw the line somewhere else: 'Any statement can be held true come what may, if we make drastic enough statements elsewhere in the system ... Revision even of the logical law of the excluded middle has been proposed as a means of simplifying quantum analysis' (43). Quine's conclusion is that 'for all its *a priori* reasonableness, a boundary between analytic and synthetic statements simply has not been drawn' (37). Quine is thus adopting, as Della Rocca reads him, a Bradley-style argument by rejecting arbitrary distinctions that have no reason to be drawn in one place rather than another, and are thus ungrounded distinctions (distinctions without a difference), or are not really distinctions at all, as Bradley argues. Della Rocca will push this Bradley-style regress argument and generalise it to offer a critique of much of contemporary philosophical practice. He offers three primary criticisms of MI, for instance, each of which, in the end, 'turn on the unpleasant fact that each version of the MI relies on arbitrary and inexplicable relations' (Della Rocca 2013, 198). First, Della Rocca claims that with MI 'the relation between claims that are accepted and claims that are not is arbitrary and inexplicable' (198). Ordinary, common sense beliefs are accepted and privileged to the exclusion of others, and with no reason or justification. Why can we not think that strange, out of the ordinary beliefs are precisely the beliefs we need, or that today's heresies are tomorrow's orthodoxies, among other options? Secondly, the relation between claims that are valuable and those that are not is likewise arbitrary, and thus intuitions are taken to be more valuable than facts about the world, but again with no reason or justification. Third and finally, it is arbitrary which beliefs one revises in the face of recalcitrant intuitions, for, as Quine pointed out and as alluded to above, we could revise any and every belief with sufficient effort. Once we begin to explain these inexplicable relations, however, unpacking the arbitrary implications they bring with them, then we open the door to Bradley's regress, which Della Rocca summarises as follows:

> Consider a relation, R between relata *a* and *b*. Given the demand for grounding [or an explanation] that Bradley accepts, this relation must be grounded in some thing or things. But in what things? R cannot be grounded in *a* alone (to the exclusion of *b*) because that would be arbitrary: *b* is equally eligible to be a ground for R. Similarly, R cannot be grounded in *b* alone. So what, then, is R grounded in? It's natural to say that R is grounded in *a* and *b* not separately, but in *a* and *b* together, i.e., in the fact that *a* and *b* co-exist, i.e., in the fact that *a* and *b* are related somehow. But this is to ground R in another relation, which simply raises the question of the ground of a relation again, and we are off on Bradley's regress. (201)

It is the effort to avoid this regress argument, Della Rocca claims, that accounts for the success of the MI over the past century, for in answering his own question as to why the MI has acquired nearly hegemonic status, Della Rocca argues that it is because 'the rejection of Bradleyan monism required the acceptance of inexplicable relations that paved the way for the adoption of the MI' (206). To avoid the regress, and as we have seen Moore and Russell argue above, it becomes necessary to accept certain inexplicable facts, brute facts that have the 'sort of self-subsistence that used to belong to substance' as Russell put it (1970, 202).

In a later essay on Hume, Della Rocca (2017) applies this argument to Hume, arguing that Hume came quite close to Spinoza but could not quite bite the bullet and accept the monism that both Spinoza and Bradley do. In his embrace of diversity, an embrace Russell will self-consciously follow (see Russell 1940, 311), Hume famously claims that 'what is distinguishable is separable' (T, 1.2.2.3; SB 30[2]), and, 'every thing, that is different, is distinguishable; and every thing that is distinguishable, may be separated' (T, 1.2.3.10; SB 36). In accepting what is known as the separability principle, Hume thus accepts a version of Bradley's principle that there can be no difference without distinction. Hume also calls upon another important distinction, Della Rocca argues, in his argument against causality, when he argues that what is causally distinct in a causal relation is not really distinct but only rationally distinct, or a consequence of an action and contemplation of the mind. As Della Rocca follows the implications of these two key assumptions of Hume's arguments, he argues that they do not ultimately justify the reality of diversity. The reason for this is that at some point – following Spinoza (and anticipating Bradley) – we need to differentiate between those distinctions that are merely rationally distinct and ultimately depend upon another reality or content (e.g., the whiteness and sphericity of the cue ball that depends on the reality of the cue ball itself) and those distinctions that are really separate and distinct, such as the A and B in the causal relation between A and B. It was as a consequence of his embrace of the separability principle that Hume was led to argue against the idea of necessary connection, or the thought that one entity necessarily and conceptually entails another. If the rationalist accepts Hume's argument, Della Rocca argues, then they cannot simultaneously accept *both* the claim that causal relations are merely rationally distinct *and* the separability principle that asserts they are really distinct, for the acceptance of the latter entails the rejection of the former. To accept the former, the rationalist will also have to accept that all causal distinctions

---

2. This is the standard reference for Hume's *Treatise*, with numbers corresponding to book, part, section and paragraph. SB refers to the commonly used Selby-Bigge edition.

are merely rational distinctions, or appearances dependent on the nature of one single reality (à *la* Spinoza and Bradley). This is precisely what Hume pushes the rationalists to do, Della Rocca concludes, when he argues that from Hume's perspective 'the only consistent form of rationalism is one that accepts a form of monism and denies any multiplicity of distinct objects' (Della Rocca 2017, 479). Leibniz does not bite this bullet, and goes to great lengths, as we will see below (§8), to set forth a metaphysics that embraces a 'multiplicity of distinct objects' – namely, the monads. For Spinoza, by contrast, and later Bradley (and Della Rocca), it will be monism full stop and the attendant denial of a plurality of distinct objects. It is for this reason that Della Rocca believes that Hume subjects Spinoza to 'especially harsh invective near the end of book I of the *Treatise*', for despite delivering his 'best shot against rationalism', in the end 'Spinoza doesn't or wouldn't flinch' (479), and ultimately Spinoza simply accepts the conclusion that denies a multiplicity of distinct objects.

9. Method of Intuition and Analytic Philosophy of Time

Returning to the method of intuition (MI) as forged by Moore and Russell in response to Bradley's regress arguments (and to the TMA more generally), Della Rocca (2011) shows just how dominant the habits of the philosophical tradition have been over the past few generations. To take just one example, Della Rocca takes on an important topic in contemporary analytic philosophy of time, the debate between 3d'ism and 4d'ism with respect to the nature of persistence through time. By virtue of what, the question is raised, does an object persist through time? According to the 3d'ist, the persistence of an object is explained, Della Rocca argues, 'in terms of the persistence of the object itself. Thus persistence of the object is not really explained at all; it is primitive' (2011, 596). It is the persistence of A itself that explains the nature of persistence through time. The 4d'ist, by contrast, does not account for persistence by basing it on the persistence of one and the same object but rather by virtue of the causal and qualitative continuity between 'the relevant states of two objects' (596).

Della Rocca's reasons for rejecting 3d'ism are by now familiar. In particular, he rejects any acceptance of brute, primitive facts that bring in their wake the necessity of arbitrary distinctions. To set up the arguments that follow, Della Rocca puts forth what he calls Parfit's Plausible Principle (PPP), building on Derek Parfit's 1984 book *Reasons and Persons*. In a hypothetical, Parfit has us assume that a person, A, has his brain divided in half and each half is placed in a separate and distinct body, B and C. The question is which body continues, if any or either, to be A? To claim that either B or C would be the persistence and continuation of A would be arbitrary in that it excludes one without reason or justification. Thus to identify A with either B or C would be ungrounded, and hence in violation of PPP. Interestingly, Leibniz offers a similar example in a letter to Arnauld (Leibniz 2016, 189) when he discusses the planarian worm, a worm that can be cut in half and the newly severed half will continue on and live just like the other half. In response to the question regarding whether the soul of the original worm continues on into the two halves, Leibniz says no, that it only continues in one of the two, though this, Della Rocca would no doubt argue, is itself a similar violation of PPP.

Della Rocca will continue along similar lines for the rest of the essay, moving from branching cases of continued identity, as in Parfit's example, to non-branching cases, and in each he shows the prevalence among the protagonists of these debates of an adherence to primitive persistence, or to an ungrounded identity that is in violation of the spirit of PPP. In the end, Della Rocca argues, what is needed is a view of persistence that is identity-free: 'To demand that persistence not be primitive is to insist on identity-free explanations of persistence; that is, it is to insist that in a case of persistence, A persists in virtue of some fact beyond the very persistence of A itself' (2011, 610). 3d'ism clearly falls afoul of this demand for an identity-free explanation, but so too, Della Rocca argues, do the 4d'ist accounts of Theodore Sider and David Lewis. The difficulty that each of these accounts runs into is to determine how an object can be understood to persist through diverse and distinct times. If there is difference, how can we be sure it is the same object, and if there is no difference, how can we be sure there was persistence through distinct, different times? Each of the attempts Della Rocca analyses ultimately violates PPP, or what we might also call, following Bradley, the Della Rocca Indiscernibility Principle (DRIP), a variation of Leibniz's Principle of the Identity of Indiscernibles (PII). For Leibniz, PII states that if there are no discernible differences between two entities, then we do not have distinct entities but one entity, and if we have two distinct entities then there must be discernible differences between them (see Leibniz 1973, section 9). In Della Rocca's version of this principle, if there is no discernible, non-arbitrary reason to account for the relation of two or more objects, then the relation is arbitrary and ungrounded. Ungrounded and arbitrary relations, moreover, are in violation of the principle of sufficient reason, which asserts that for every fact or relation there is a reason or explanation for why it is the way it is rather than another way, or why it is not different or other than the way it is. By applying these principles (e.g., DRIP) to the arguments regarding persistence through time, as well as to the arguments regarding the founding moves of analytic philosophy (i.e., MI), Della Rocca, like Bradley and Spinoza before him, bites the bullet and accepts the consequence that his arguments lead 'to the rejection of a multiplicity of objects' (Della Rocca 2011, 615).

10. Monism or Pluralism?

We have thus seen two prominent responses to the TMA regress. On the one hand, there is the monistic response of philosophers like Spinoza, Bradley and Della Rocca. The regress gets started when the nature of distinct objects is to be accounted for by appealing to a content that is outside these objects, such as a Form, Idea, or simply another distinct object, and this is an assumption that leads to failure, as the TMA and Bradley regress arguments highlight. For the monists, the solution is simply to reject the reality of distinct objects, reject pluralism – there is just one absolute reality, and a reality that is not a numerically distinct object for what we take to be a distinct object is merely an appearance of this one reality. On the other hand, there is the pluralist response, the response found most commonly within the analytic tradition, and a response that is often supported with the aid of what Della Rocca calls the method of intuition. Here the regress is halted by simply asserting that certain facts are immediately, intuitively obvious and in need of no further explanation. There is no need, it is argued, to go beyond what is given, and hence no possibility for the regress to get started. Earlier, however, we suggested (see §5.7 and §6.5) that in the *Philebus* Plato offers an example of a method of mixture, a mixture of the One and the Infinite (Becoming), a mixture I will call problematic Ideas, that could be further developed to address the TMA. In light of the arguments we have discussed to this point, we are now well placed to see just what this might entail.

§8 Russell and Deleuze on Leibniz

1. Russell on the Task of Analysis (and the Taste of Coffee)

To set the stage for the Platonic arguments to follow, let us first imagine that Russell has taken up a temporary position as a coffee taster, identifying the various attributes of a wide array of coffees as they come into London. After a few weeks of training, Russell shows up to the coffee warehouse and takes his seat next to another, more experienced taster. With the first coffee he tastes, Russell identifies it as a light body coffee with fruity notes and sweet aromatics. The more experienced taster agrees, though he adds that the fruity notes are actually raspberry in character. Russell tastes the coffee again and excitedly agrees, 'That's it, exactly!' he says. The experienced taster also identifies a hint of molasses. Russell tastes the coffee again; this time he is not as sure he tastes the molasses his more experienced colleague tastes, but he trusts the latter's abilities and reputation enough to assume that the molasses notes are likely there.

Back in his Bloomsbury flat, Russell reflects upon how the day's experience typifies his more general understanding of analysis. In his 1940 lectures, Russell argues that all judgments of perception are 'of the form "P is part of W"', and thus when we say of 'this' coffee that it has raspberry notes we are making the perceptual judgment that P (raspberry notes) is a part of W, the coffee being tasted, and 'what we naturally call "this", is a complex which the judgment of perception partially analyses' (Russell 1940, 315). Moreover, Russell recognises that 'we can experience a whole W without knowing what its parts are, but through attention or noticing we can gradually discover more and more of its parts' (315). Russell did indeed experience the whole of the coffee's taste, and through focused attention, and with a little help from his experienced colleague, he was able to discover more parts of the coffee's taste. Throughout the process of analysing and picking apart the various attributes that are part of the coffee's flavour profile, 'it is assumed', Russell argues, 'that the whole W can preserve its identity throughout the process of analysis' (315). Moreover, Russell admits to the inadequacy of words to completely describe the perceptual experience associated with 'the whole W', in this case the taste of the coffee. For Russell, the 'words we use never exhaust all that we could say about sensible experience. What we say is more abstract than what we see' (52).

2. Russell on Leibniz

The groundwork for Russell's understanding of analysis had been long in the making, beginning most notably in his early book on Leibniz (Russell 1900). Leibniz is especially relevant here for Russell because of a key distinction between sensibilia and sensation that emerges in Russell's work in the early 1900s. As part of his effort to replace Bradley's idealism with realism, Russell argues that 'the actual data in sensation, the immediate objects of sight or touch or hearing, are extra-mental, purely physical, and among the ultimate constituents of matter' (Russell 1915, 402). Russell will use the term 'sensibilia' to refer to these physical constituents of matter, the data of sensation, and he will use the term 'sensation' for the sensibilia that have become the object of acquaintance; or, as Russell puts it, 'sensibilia ... have the same metaphysical status as sense-data [or sensations], without necessarily being data to any mind' (Russell 1917a, 148). Russell finds a similar distinction at work in Leibniz, and he is quick to stress its importance. As Russell reads Leibniz, 'We are never without perceptions, he says, but often without apperceptions, namely when we have no distinct perceptions' (Russell 1900, 155). In short, Russell is drawing attention to the distinction Leibniz draws between unconscious and conscious perceptions, whereby 'unconscious perception is a state of consciousness, but is unconscious in the sense that we are not aware of it' (156). Unconscious perceptions are thus like sensibilia in that they are not present to a mind that is aware of them, though they are still, for Leibniz, before a consciousness, which may seem to be at odds with Russell's claim that sensibilia are there whether or not anyone is aware of them. It should be noted, however, that for Leibniz monads are the fundamental substances, and each monad has a perspective, limited and confused though it may be, on the entire universe, and thus unconscious perceptions do include those that may never become subject to conscious awareness.

It is at this point that the contrast between clear and confused perceptions becomes important, both for Russell and for Leibniz. As Russell explains the contrast: 'A confused perception, we may say, is such that we are not separately conscious of all its parts. Knowledge is confused, in Leibniz's phraseology, when I cannot enumerate the marks required to distinguish the thing known from other things' (Russell 1900, 157). In our example of Russell's efforts at coffee tasting, for instance, he had a confused knowledge of the coffee when he described it as fruity, for at that time he was unable to 'enumerate the marks' that distinguish a raspberry fruity note in coffee from raisin, prune, cherry, etc. Once told the fruity note was actually a raspberry note, he acquired a conscious awareness of this part of the taste and thus his knowledge of this particular coffee became less confused. As for the taste of molasses which he did not clearly distinguish, on the reading of Leibniz offered by Russell the element or sensibilia that is already there 'must reach a certain magnitude before we become aware of it, and thus sufficiently minute perceptions are necessarily unconscious' (158). Echoing Hume's essay 'Of the Standard of Taste', especially his example of the wine tasters, Russell admits that through experience and education one may attain the threshold necessary to detect what others cannot, as did the more experienced coffee taster who was able to discern the molasses while Russell could not.

Up to this point, Russell's reading of Leibniz appears to be in perfect accord with what Leibniz says. In his *New Essays on Human Understanding*, for instance, Leibniz offers his famous example of the 'roaring noise of the sea' (Leibniz 1996, 54) to clarify the relationship between minute perceptions and confused perceptions. To hear the roaring noise of the sea as we do, 'we must hear the parts which make up this whole, that is the noise of each wave, although each of these little noises makes itself known only when combined confusedly with all the others, and would not be noticed if the wave which made it were by itself' (54). As with the molasses notes in the coffee, the minute perceptions were too minute for Russell to detect them, and yet they were there, as perceptions or sensibilia that had not yet become a sensation to Russell. Similarly for Leibniz, we are exposed to minute perceptions, even if we are unable to detect them, for if they were truly nothing, truly indiscernible, then we would hear nothing, since, as Leibniz argues, 'a hundred thousand nothings cannot make something' (54). The conclusion Leibniz comes to, then, is that 'noticeable perceptions arise by degrees from ones which are too minute to be noticed. To think otherwise is to be ignorant of the immeasurable fineness of things, which always and everywhere involves an actual infinity' (56–7).

We will turn to the actual infinity of things in a moment, but first it should be noted that, despite the similarity between Russell and Leibniz just sketched, Russell himself concludes that Leibniz has misunderstood the implications of his own distinctions. More precisely, Leibniz's arguments progress as if 'minute and unconscious perceptions are, after all, very nearly synonymous, and that confused perceptions are such as contain parts which are minute or unconscious' (Russell 1900, 158–9). The problem with this, however, is that it renders problematic Leibniz's account of innate truths which are unconscious, for such innate truths are taken by Leibniz to be already distinct, and their coming to consciousness is not a matter of degrees, a matter of their reaching a certain threshold; rather, the innate unconscious truth simply becomes a truth one is consciously aware of, and in a process that has not added parts or minute perceptions to the truth itself. As Russell summarises his critique, he argues that Leibniz 'does not seem to have perceived that confused perception, if it gives any true knowledge, must be partly distinct' (159). In other words, if confused perception can lead to determinate, distinct knowledge, then that which is confused must be at least partly distinct. Where Leibniz's argument appears to have gone off the rails, at least according to Russell, is in his attempt to assert that physical, extended reality, the world of things, entails an actual infinity – an infinity of infinitely divisible things, of worlds within worlds, etc. – while at the same time arguing for simple, indivisible substances, the monads, which are indestructible, incorporeal substances. As Russell sees it, Leibniz's claim that there are certain innate truths that are unconscious is a failed attempt to bridge the infinite divisibility of the world of perceptible things with the world of incorporeal, indestructible monads.

Leibniz does indeed push the distinction that Russell finds problematic. As Leibniz argues in the *New Essays*, the world of physical things, in all its infinite divisibility, is a result of an aggregation of indivisible monads, incorporeal substances that, when combined, give rise to the effects of physical things with their own distinct identity. As Leibniz puts it, 'the only perfect unity that these "entities by aggregation" have is a mental one, and consequently their very being is always in a way mental, or phenomenal, like that of the rainbow' (Leibniz 1996, 146). Russell abandons the attempt to ground his metaphysics in indivisible, immaterial substances that are different in kind from the physical things we perceive, and grounds it instead in the very physical nature of perception itself, in perceptions or particulars (brute facts) that are 'among the ultimate constituents of matter' (Russell 1915, 402). Recall Russell's claim, cited earlier [§7.4], that particulars stand 'entirely alone and [are] completely self-subsistent ... that sort of self-subsistence that used to belong to substance' (Russell 1970, 201–2). According to Russell, Leibniz should have maintained that the conditions for knowledge are of a piece with the knowledge that is conditioned, but instead he relied upon a difference in kind between indivisible monads, the conditions, and the world of infinitely divisible physical things, the conditioned.

3. Deleuze on Leibniz

In his reading of Leibniz, Deleuze argues that Leibniz was correct to call for a difference in kind between the conditions and conditioned. In fact, according to Deleuze, Leibniz offers a profound critique of the representational model of knowledge, by which he means a knowledge which re-presents that which was already given, already present to a consciousness that then comes to recognise it and then re-present it in the form of a judgment. On Russell's reading of where he thinks Leibniz was on the right track, this is precisely what Leibniz does. The confused perceptions are simply minute perceptions whose differentiating marks are present but have yet to be recognised and made conscious. Once the threshold is reached, or once experience, education and technological advances give us a more refined discernment of what is already there, then our knowledge becomes less confused and more accurately represents reality. With more experience and exposure to the different tastes of coffee, Russell may come to discern the molasses notes, notes that are already there as sensibilia on Russell's account. As it is, however, Russell believes that Leibniz did not consistently follow through on this effort, and his call for a metaphysics of indivisible, incorporeal monads ultimately undermines his efforts. For Deleuze, by contrast, it is precisely the difference in kind between monads and the physical world, or between conditions and conditioned, that enables Leibniz to offer a critique of this representational model. For Deleuze, this becomes most evident in Leibniz's attempts to rethink Descartes' understanding of clear and distinct ideas.

The challenge confronting Leibniz, among many, is his effort to uphold Descartes' representational model of thought, or what Deleuze calls the common sense/good sense image of thought and its guiding principle, namely Descartes' 'principle of the "clear and distinct"': 'It is in effect with Descartes that the principle of representation as good sense or common sense appears in its highest form' (Deleuze 1994, 213). As common sense, 'clarity-distinctness constitutes', Deleuze argues, 'the light which renders thought possible in the common exercise of all the faculties' (213). A common coordinating power is necessary, on the representational model of thought, in order to keep the distinct faculties such as sight, smell, etc., all on the same page addressing the same things. In the case of Kant, for Deleuze, this common sense power is 'the identity of the Self in the "I think" which grounds the harmony of all the faculties and their agreement on the form of a supposed Same object' (133). For Descartes, common sense is assured by the *cogito*, and it is at work in Descartes' famous example of the beeswax (see Descartes 1996, Second Meditation), where one identifies the melted wax as being the same wax that had previously been solid, cool to the touch, coloured, etc. It is the common sense operations of the *cogito* that enable the various faculties of touch, sight, hearing, etc. to work harmoniously together to identify the wax as the same, self-identical wax. Good sense is the appropriateness and ability of the faculties to identify what is there to be identified; that is, the faculties, when functioning well (i.e., with good sense), contribute to our knowledge the givenness of what is already present and there to be re-presented (recall again Hume's example of the wine tasters, tasters with exemplary good sense). Russell's work, as we have seen, also presupposes the Cartesian principle of the 'clear and distinct'. By working together, with common sense, in good order and with good sense, the faculties can successfully come to identify what is there. For instance, by drawing on the faculties of sight, smell and taste, Russell was able to discern the raspberry note within the cup of coffee, a taste that was already there, as was also the case with the molasses notes identified by his more experienced partner. The question, then, is how successfully Leibniz upholds the principle of clarity and distinctness.

On a first reading, it appears that Leibniz has complicated and perhaps undone the principle of the clear and distinct. Russell criticises Leibniz for failing to see that confused perceptions must be partially distinct, or that what comes to be consciously distinct must also be distinct at the unconscious level, and distinct in the same way but just to a lesser degree. Leibniz's own texts can be used to support this reading, though Deleuze will offer an alternative reading. When Leibniz claims that 'a hundred thousand nothings cannot make something' (Leibniz 1996, 56), the implication is that the minute perceptions are something in the same way as conscious perceptions are something, for otherwise they could never account for how they make conscious perceptions possible. On the alternative reading, and the reading that leads Russell to criticise Leibniz, Deleuze finds an ally in Leibniz. In particular, what Deleuze claims is most crucial to Leibniz's understanding of clear and distinct ideas is the role differentials play. As Deleuze puts it, 'No one has been better able to immerse thought in the element of difference and provide it with a differential unconscious ... all in order to save and reconstitute the homogeneity of a natural light *à la* Descartes' (Deleuze 1994, 213). With this differential unconscious in mind, Deleuze then proposes two readings of the roaring noise of the sea example:

> Consider Leibniz's famous passages on the murmuring of the sea. Here too, two interpretations are possible. Either we say that the apperception of the whole noise is clear but confused (not distinct) because the component little perceptions are themselves not clear but obscure; or we say that the little perceptions are themselves distinct and obscure (not clear): distinct because they grasp differential relations and singularities; obscure because they are not yet 'distinguished', not yet differenciated. (Deleuze 1994, 213)

On the first of the two interpretations, we have the traditional Cartesian-Russellian understanding of clear and distinct. The murmuring of the sea, as with the taste of the coffee, is perceived clearly, as a whole (W), but the microperceptions that are part of this whole are confused because they are not yet clearly distinguished from one another. In themselves, however, the microperceptions are clearly distinct and determinate, and Russell simply did not, for instance, distinguish the raspberry or molasses notes of the coffee (W), despite the fact that they were already determinately present. On the second interpretation, and the one Deleuze will stress, the minute perceptions are not already clearly distinguished and merely awaiting a thought to recognise them; rather, they are 'distinct and obscure (not clear)'. In elaborating why minute perceptions are distinct and obscure, Deleuze adds that they are distinct because they 'grasp differential relations', meaning that the differential relations themselves are distinct but they are not yet clear for the terms of the relations have not been determined. The differential relations are obscure until they come to be distinguished, which occurs when the relations are differenciated (to use Deleuze's term, borrowed from differential calculus).

To clarify Deleuze's emphasis upon differentials in Leibniz, and most notably the differential unconscious, we can turn to Leibniz's own 'Justification of the Infinitesimal Calculus by That of Ordinary Algebra' (in Leibniz 1956). In our earlier discussion of relations (see §6.2), we have seen how Bradley argues, as does Della Rocca, that an attempt to account for a relationship between terms generates a regress. If in accounting for the relation xRy we do so on the basis of x, then, following Della Rocca's account (or DRIP), the account would be arbitrary for we could just as well base the explanation on y. If we attempt to account for R by basing it upon a special relationship between x and y, say xy, then we have another relation that needs to be accounted for and we are off on the regress. The Spinozist solution to the regress, we saw, was to ground relations in a single, absolute reality. Diversity and plurality are to be understood, on this approach, as appearances of this one reality. Leibniz, by contrast, sets out to defend pluralism – an infinite pluralism – and he does this in his 'Justification of the Infinitesimal Calculus', and in other places as well, by making an infinite, differential series constitutive of identity.

Leibniz begins with ordinary algebra, for here we have relations between variables rather than determinate, already known and identified terms. As Dan Smith has shown in his discussion of the importance of differential relations for Deleuze, in an algebraic relation, such as $x^2 + y^2 - R^2 = 0$, 'a determinate value no longer needs to be assigned to the terms; the terms of the relation are variables ... [but] the variables must none the less have a determinable value' (Smith 2012, 245). With differential relations, by contrast, Smith points out that 'the terms between which the relation is established are neither determined nor even determinable ... The only thing that is determined is the reciprocal relation between the terms' (246). In his 'Justification

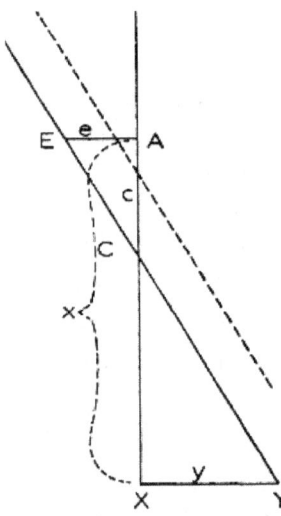

of the Infinitesimal Calculus', Leibniz offers the example of a hypotenuse of a triangle. As the line of the hypotenuse (EY on the accompanying diagram[3]) approaches the opposite point of the right triangle (point A), the two other sides of the triangle (e and c) get progressively smaller. As the hypotenuse EY reaches point A, the lines c and e become zero, or 0/0 as this was often written in the seventeenth and eighteenth centuries. For Leibniz, however, the relation between the two sides subsists even after the determinate values for c/e become 0/0, or, as Leibniz puts it, 'c and e still have an algebraic relation to each other. And so they are treated as infinitesimals' (Leibniz 1956, 886). What we have, then, for Leibniz, is a process where the infinitesimals give us, at the limit, a new third term, such as the tangent on a curve for instance. The differentials, as elements in this process of 'becoming zero', give us, at the limit of differentiation, a differenciated difference or term that is irreducible to the differentials themselves. As Smith puts it, 'The terms [of a differential relation] are reduced to vanishing terms, to vanishing quantities (or virtualities), yet the relation between these vanishing quantities is not equal to zero, but refers to a third term that has a finite value: $dx/dy = z$ ... We can say that z is the limit of the differential relation, or that the differential relation tends toward a limit' (Smith 2012, 246). As Leibniz will make very clear, this process of differentials tending towards a limit does not mean that the limit is the same as the series of differentials. As Leibniz states it:

> Although it is not at all rigorously true that rest is a kind of motion, or that equality is a kind of inequality, any more than it is true that a circle is a kind of regular polygon, it can be said, nevertheless, that rest, equality, and the circle terminate the motions, the inequalities, and the regular polygons which arrive at them by a continuous change and vanish in them. And although these terminations are excluded, that is, are not included in any rigorous sense in the variables which they limit, they nevertheless have the same properties as if they were included in the series, in accordance with the language of infinities and infinitesimals, which takes the circle, for example, as a regular polygon with an infinite number of sides. (Leibniz 1956, 887)

---

3. 'Leibniz and calculus' image is figure 16 from Leibniz, *Mathematische Schriften*, Bd. IV, edited by C.I. Gerhardt (Halle, 1859), reproduced as 'Justification of the Infinitesimal Calculus by That of Ordinary Algebra, 1701', in Leibniz, *Philosophical Papers and Letters*, edited by Leroy E. Loemker (Dordrecht: Kluwer Academic Publishers, 1969), 545, and reproduced in Gilles Deleuze, *The Fold* (London: Athlone Press, 1993), 18.

For Leibniz, therefore, infinitesimals (differentials) are vanishing points that are virtual yet real. They are virtual for they are real vanishing points, realities 'on the point of becoming zero', or becoming the differential relation 0/0, and yet the differential relation is a real, reciprocal relation that subsists even as the values become zero. Moreover, a result of the values becoming vanishingly small, or effectively becoming zero by losing quantitative determinacy, the reciprocal relation of the differential becomes freed from any determinate and determinable value, and it is at the limit of this process whereby the differentials, or the differential unconscious, conditions the emergence of the determinate – e.g., the circle as the limit of a polygon, equality as the limit of inequalities, etc. – and these limits are thus the determinate, actual identities made possible by the infinite series of differentials that 'vanish in them [the identifiable limits]'. What Leibniz gives us therefore with this notion of differentials is an understanding of relations that are external in a way that is more fundamental than that which Russell argues for. As we saw earlier (see §7.4), one of the primary concerns throughout Russell's career was the doctrine of external relations, relations he felt were necessary to make mathematics explicable. The mathematical relation $\geq$, for instance, needs to be understood as a relation external to the determinate quantities or variables that may be put into this relation, such as 10 or 7, x or y, without their nature being affected, the result being a mathematical statement, e.g., $x \geq y$ ($10 \geq 7$), that is either true or false. For Russell, therefore, relations are external precisely because they can be brought to bear on independent terms and quantities without affecting the nature of these terms and quantities. With Leibniz's understanding of differentials, by contrast, we have a reciprocal relation that is not to be confused with any actualised, determinate term or quantity, but is rather that which makes possible the identity of such terms and quantities. This is the reading of Leibniz that Deleuze will stress, the reading that finds in Leibniz a 'differential unconscious' that is not of the same kind as that which it makes possible – the infinite series of polygons is not to be confused with the circle this series vanishes into – and hence we have a reading that undermines the representational model of thought Russell had hoped to find in Leibniz. Deleuze, to the contrary, is happy to find an ally in Leibniz to critique the representational model of thought, and for this reason we frequently find Deleuze echoing Leibniz's arguments.

The influence of Leibniz in Deleuze's philosophy is evident, for instance, as he begins Chapter V of *Difference and Repetition*, where he argues that 'Difference is not diversity. Diversity is given, but difference is that by which the given is given, that by which the given is given as diverse' (Deleuze 1994, 222). Rather than following the common sense/good sense model of representational thought whereby the given is already there to be thought, and it is thought when the faculties work together (common sense) in an upright, well-honed manner (good sense), Deleuze argues that the given itself is made possible by difference. In clarifying how this is so, Deleuze becomes Leibnizian. 'Every phenomenon', he argues, 'refers to an inequality by which it is conditioned', an 'intensity [that] is differential', and thus 'Every intensity is E − E', where E itself refers to an e − e', and e to $\varepsilon - \varepsilon$' etc. ... We call this state of infinitely doubled difference which resonates to infinity *disparity*. Disparity ... is the sufficient reason of all phenomena, the condition of that which appears' (222). That which is given, in other words, is to be seen as the limit of an infinitely doubled difference, or *disparity*; or it is difference in itself, as Deleuze will put it, for rather than a difference between determinate terms, a determinate E and *E* for instance, it is a difference without determinate terms, the difference or disparity that makes the given and determinate possible. The consciousness of the raspberry notes in the cup of coffee that Russell was able to detect once prompted by his partner entail, for example, an infinitely doubled difference, a differential relation of two series that are composed of heterogeneous terms, and thus raspberry notes, R, on this reading are conditioned by the differential of two minute perceptions, r − r', that remain unconscious, just as the consciousness of fruity Russell initially detected was itself conditioned by a differential of, let us say, raspberry and blueberry, r − b, and each of these elements, in turn, is conditioned by another differential, and so on. The determinate, as given, presupposes this infinitely doubled series, and at the limit, at difference in itself, we have the transformation that accounts for the given as given. This is why Deleuze will refer to this infinitely doubled difference, or disparity, as 'the sufficient reason of all phenomena, the condition of that which appears' (222).

Twenty years after the publication of *Difference and Repetition*, Deleuze will continue to argue along these Leibnizian lines in, unsurprisingly, his book on Leibniz (Deleuze 1993). Here the example Deleuze offers is the perception of green, where 'yellow and blue can surely be perceived, but if their perception vanishes by dint of progressive diminution, they enter into a differential relation db/dy' (Deleuze 1993, 88). In other words, as blue and yellow become vanishingly small they ultimately become a differential and, at the limit, at difference in itself, a third identifiable term, or green in this case, becomes possible. The same is the case for the perception of the 'sound of the sea', 'hunger' and for all conscious phenomena where, as with the waves example, 'at least two waves must be minutely perceived as nascent and heterogenous enough to become part of a relation that can allow the perception of a third, one that "excels" over the others and comes to consciousness' (88). For each of these minutely perceived waves, there is a differential series that vanishes into them, just as the differential series blue/yellow vanishes into green. This last point is important, for as Deleuze argues, *à la* Leibniz, 'nothing impedes either yellow or blue, each on its own account, from being determined by the differential relation of two colors that we cannot detect' (88), and so on and so forth; thus we have an infinite differential series that, far from being problematic, is precisely, for Deleuze (following Leibniz), the condition for the determinate individuation of phenomena. Every phenomenon thus opens the door, Deleuze argues, to an infinitely doubled difference, or *disparity*, that conditions each of the conscious phenomena, and this disparity is not to be confused with the given, with that which is conscious and determinate, much as an infinite series of polygons is not to be confused with a circle. It is this disparity that Deleuze has in mind when he speaks of the moves Leibniz made in the direction of affirming a 'differential unconscious' (Deleuze 1994, 213).

4. Clear and Distinct/Confused and Obscure; or, on Differential Unconscious

We can now return to Descartes' principle of clarity and distinctness and reinterpret it in light of Deleuze's reading of Leibniz. What is most important for Deleuze about Leibniz's theory of minute perceptions is that it has the potential to undermine Descartes' representational theory of thought. From Deleuze's perspective, the 'weakness of the theory of representation, from the point of view of the logic of knowledge, was to have established a direct proportion between the clear and the distinct' (Deleuze 1994, 253). In other words, the more distinct that which is known, the more clearly it is known; hence, for Russell the task of analysis is to bring from confusion those elements that are already distinct but confusedly grasped and bring them out into the (natural) light of day and thereby bring about clear knowledge. The raspberry notes to the coffee were confused, but already given and distinct, and as the distinctness of the notes became conscious to Russell so too did his knowledge of the coffee itself become clearer. The problem with this approach, according to Deleuze, is that it already presupposes what it is to know or to think that which is given, what Deleuze calls the dogmatic image of thought, rather than accounting for how the given comes to be given in thinking and knowledge. As Bradley might put it, thought is simply taken, as a brute fact, to be already given. What Leibniz offers instead, and where Deleuze follows suit, is an account that explains how the given comes to be given and thereby taken up in a thought or representation, and the focus of this account, for Deleuze, as we saw, is 'disparity ... the sufficient reason of all phenomena, the condition of that which appears' (222).

What in particular emerges in Leibniz's account is, as we have seen, the role differentials play in the genesis of that which is given to be known. As Deleuze summarises Leibniz's approach, 'Only Leibniz approached the conditions of a logic of thought, inspired by his theory of individuation and expression' (Deleuze 1994, 253). What this means for Deleuze is that expression is integral to individuation, to the process of becoming an identifiable, determinate, individuated substance of which one can say that it is, that it is given. What is expressed in this process is 'the continuum of differential relations or the unconscious virtual Idea' (253); that is, the expressed is precisely the continuum of differential relations that vanishes into the limit, the polygons into the circle, the differential unconscious, or the problematic Idea as I will refer to this below. This continuum is unconscious and virtual precisely because it is not actualised or given as a determinate, identifiable phenomenon (which is why Deleuze uses the term Idea, with intended Platonic allusions, as was discussed earlier in the Introduction and will be returned to shortly). Deleuze reiterates this point in the conclusion to *Difference and Repetition* when he states that 'something which exists only in the Idea may be completely determined (differentiated) and yet lack those determinations which constitute actual existence (it is undifferenciated, not yet even individuated)' (280). The differential series of polygons, or the progressively diminishing blue and yellow, may be completely determined and differentiated, but they are not to be confused with the actuality they make possible – the polygons are not to be confused with a circle, nor blue and yellow with green. Now this 'continuum of differential relations' comes to be given as it is expressed, and thus it is by way of expressions that the expressed comes to be given. On his reading of Leibniz, it is intensity that expresses the differential relations, the intensity E, as we saw earlier, expresses $e - e'$, and so on, and thus Deleuze argues that 'all the intensities are implicated in one another, each in turn both enveloped and enveloping, such that each continues to express the changing totality of Ideas … However, each intensity expresses only certain relations … Those that it expresses clearly are precisely those on which it is focused when it has the enveloping role. In its role as the enveloped, it still expresses all relations and all degrees, but confusedly' (252). In the case of hearing the waves of the sea, or tasting the distinct notes of a cup of coffee, 'our perception', Deleuze argues, 'confusedly includes the whole and clearly expresses only certain relations or certain points by virtue of our bodies and a threshold of consciousness which they determine' (253). The differential unconscious becomes conscious and individuated only as it comes to be expressed, but the expressions within which it is expressed are clear only by virtue of a threshold which marks the transformation from unconscious, pre-individual and virtual to conscious, individuated and actual. This transformation is yet another reason for rejecting 'the rule of proportionality between the clear and the distinct', for Ideas are and remain, according to Deleuze, 'distinct–obscure' (280); that is, they may be differentiated and as such distinct, but they are only clear once taken up in an expression, and this occurs only at the threshold point where differential relations become actual and given to clear perception and thought. This transformation that occurs at the threshold, moreover, is properly to be understood as an incorporeal transformation. As the differential continuum approaches the limit and, to recall Leibniz, 'arrive[s] at them [the limits] by a continuous change and vanish[es] in them' (Leibniz 1956, 887), this continuum or differential unconscious is not to be confused with the limits it vanishes into, and yet this transformation from non–actual to actual, from polygon to circle, is a transformation that is continuous with its expressions. In short, the unconscious virtual Idea is continuously expressed in that which is conscious, determinate and actual, and thus this expression involves an incorporeal transformation, for that which is expressed is not to be confused with the corporeal and bodily that clearly expresses the Idea, and yet the corporeal would not be given if it were not for the Idea that is expressed; therefore, the givenness of the corporeal and actual is made possible by an incorporeal transformation that remains inseparable from it.

We can begin to add some details to Deleuze's Leibnizian understanding of the process of individuation, or the process whereby the given is given by virtue of difference, if we turn to the reasons behind his use of the Platonic term Idea. As we saw earlier, if a Platonic Idea is understood to be a perfect, self-predicated essence, then it is susceptible to the Third Man Argument (TMA), and we are as a result never able to explain why something, for example, is beautiful. If a painting is beautiful because it shares or participates in the Idea of beauty, and if the Idea of beauty is itself beautiful, then we will need another Idea to enable us to account for why both the Idea of beauty and the painting are beautiful, an Idea that is also beautiful, and in need of yet another Idea to account for why it is beautiful, and so on as the regress is off and running. The result of this regress is that we never end up with an account that does not itself need to be accounted for, and thus we never satisfactorily explain why anything is beautiful. The key to this regress getting started, however, is that the Idea is understood to be a pure, self-predicated essence, and the self-same essence that everything which participates in it also has. This is not how Deleuze understands Plato's Ideas. For Deleuze, 'If we think of the Plato from the later dialectic [e.g., *Philebus*], where the Ideas are something like multiplicities that must be traversed by questions such as *how? how much? in which case?*, then yes, everything I've said has something Platonic about it' (Deleuze 2004, 116). On first blush, it is clear how Deleuze's Leibnizian reading of differential relations leaves us with a condition for actualities that is certainly not to be confused with that which is actual, and with relevance questions that are not to be confused with truth questions, to recall our earlier discussion (in the Introduction). If an Idea is understood to be given in the same sense as that which participates in it, then the regress gets started, but this is not how Deleuze understands Plato's theory of Ideas (nor did Fine for that matter). Deleuze also adds that if we take Ideas to be 'something like multiplicities', multiplicities traversed by 'how?', 'how much?' and 'in which case?' questions (i.e., relevance questions), then yes what he is doing is very Platonic. The key to understanding this claim is to recall that an intensity expresses a differential, a differential that is itself composed of a differential relation between two intensities – e.g., green as expressing a differential of blue and yellow (db/dy), and blue itself expressing a differential of unseen intensities, and so on. These intensities thus envelop and are enveloped by other intensities, as multiplicities, with no predetermined end to the infinite regress they bring in their wake – which was why Deleuze embraces the regress, the infinitely doubled difference he calls disparity. Some of these intensities are taken up in a clear perception. This clear perception results when there is an incorporeal transformation from the differential unconscious, the series vanishing to zero, and the actualisation that occurs at the limit which transforms the differentials to that which is clearly given. This transformation, however, requires a mediator, something determinate, such as a body, which expresses the Idea, but only in line with the thresholds and limits that individuate this particular body (or mediator). Ideas are thus not separate from determinate, existent actualities, in a realm all their own, but rather they subsist within the determinate actualities as their conditions of relevance, meaning the conditions that provide the problems to which the determinate and actual provides the solution. A body (or mediator), therefore, is individuated by what it can do, by what is clearly given to it, and this in turn is made possible by the differential unconscious, or by the intensities the body (mediator) is capable of expressing as a result of a filtering of differential relations from the Idea, the differential unconscious. This filtering of the differential unconscious is no less than the Idea as problem, or problematic Idea; 'problem' is the appropriate term here since the selection of differential relations remains an unresolved and unactualised condition that is inseparable from the intensities that are actualised and given to the body (mediator). Since the differential relations are extracted from an infinite series, or *disparity*, there forever remains the question or problem of returning to the Idea as differential unconscious to draw forth ever new selections and thresholds, and with that ever new and different intensities. The conditions for this return to the Idea as multiplicity and problem are best expressed precisely as the how, how much, and in which case questions that seek to differentiate the differential relations that may well result, through an incorporeal transformation, in something new being actualised to the body (mediator). Deleuze will stress this very point in his book on Leibniz, where he will argue that Leibniz's arguments 'appeal to both obscurity and clarity … because for Leibniz clarity comes of obscurity and endlessly is plunging back into it' (Deleuze 1993, 89). By plunging back into the obscurity of the Idea as problem and multiplicity, something new may come to be given, something new that is irreducible to anything that is already given or actualised.

On this last point regarding an Idea as problem and multiplicity, or problematic Idea, Deleuze draws from a number of sources in addition to Leibniz, and perhaps most important among them is the work of Albert Lautman and Jean Cavaillès in the philosophy of mathematics. Due to their untimely deaths while fighting on behalf of the resistance against the Nazi occupation of France during the Second World War, Lautman's and Cavaillès' careers were cut short, and this leaves one to wonder how the trajectory of French philosophy after the war might have differed had they survived. This is not to say that their influence ended with their deaths. Far from it, and Deleuze, in particular, can be seen to be continuing the efforts of both Lautman and Cavaillès, though Lautman especially.[4] Lautman stressed a point that becomes key to Deleuze's understanding of problems – namely, that problems are not exhausted by their solutions. As Lautman puts it, 'it is possible to conceive what we will call the exigency of a logical problem, without the consciousness of this exigency implying in any way an attempt at a solution' (Lautman 2011, 188). In other words, the exigency of a logical problem is not to be confused with the determinate solutions that respond to the problem, nor does it predetermine the manner in which solutions are attempted. It is for this reason that Lautman will also refer to problems as Ideas, or the 'Idea of a dialectical problem of the relations between the Whole and part as knowing if global properties can be inscribed in local properties' (221). As the exigency of a dialectical problem is addressed, new global properties and relations may come to be discerned in local properties, and yet these determinations, or the solutions that come to be attempted, do not eliminate or exhaust the reality of the dialectical problem or Idea. Like Lautman, moreover, Deleuze stakes out a Platonic position: '[n]owhere better than in the admirable work of Albert Lautman', Deleuze claims, 'has it been shown how problems are first Platonic Ideas…' (Deleuze 1994, 163). It is to begin to clarify this claim that problems, or problematic Ideas, are 'first Platonic Ideas', and the implications of this claim, that we now turn.

---

4. For the influence of Lautman on Deleuze's thought, see Duffy 2006; and for the influence of Cavaillès on Deleuze's generation of philosophers, see Peden 2014.

§9 On Problematic Fields

1. Plato, Leibniz and Problematic Fields

Earlier (§5.2) we saw that on Wilfrid Sellars' reading of Plato it was not until the later dialogues (the *Sophist* in particular) that Plato was successfully (depending on who you ask!) able to deal with the problem of non-being, and hence adequately address the nature of Becoming whereby things are continuously becoming something they are not (Sellars 1955, 430). Sellars points to the *Republic* (478d), for instance, and notes that Becoming is placed 'between' the unchanging reality or Being of the Forms and the nonexistent, though 'he could have viewed Becoming as somehow a mixture of Being (the Forms) and a Not-Being conceived as an ontological principle or, better, stuff' (430). As Socrates puts it in the passage from the *Republic* Sellars cites, 'if anything should turn up such that it both is and is not, that sort of thing would lie between that which purely and absolutely is and that which wholly is not' (478d). Becoming is thus a mixture of what is and is not, and this understanding of becoming as mixture, as we have argued, becomes a central theme in the *Philebus*. As discussed earlier, Plato is quite forthright in his call for a method of mixture. As Socrates puts it, 'the wise men of the present day make the one and the many too quickly or too slowly, in haphazard fashion ... they disregard all that lies between them' (17a). In other words, in light of the fact that 'God revealed in the universe two elements, the infinite and the finite', most rush off either to embrace the One (Being) or the Infinite (Becoming) without looking to 'a third, made by combining these two' (16c). Plato offers the examples of grammar and musical composition to explain the nature of this combined mixture, which in (§5.7) we called a relative relation. With the arguments we have developed to this point, we can now expand upon Plato's conception of a mixture between the One and Infinite, or an absolute relation as I called it earlier, and bring in the notion of a problematic Idea in light of the Leibnizian arguments discussed in the previous section.

Plato's caution regarding the rush to the One or the Infinite is particularly apt at this point, especially in light of Deleuze's Leibnizian arguments. Crucial to these arguments was the distinction between an infinite series of differential relations, the differential unconscious, and the actualised, determinate entities and givens of which we can become conscious and represent in thought, discourse, etc. This distinction mirrors Plato's point about God revealing 'in the universe two elements, the infinite and the finite', and it was precisely these two elements that the 'wise men of the present day' rush to while disregarding 'all that lies between them'. The same is likewise true with respect to the Leibnizian arguments we have set forth. We must not rush to the assumption that the relationship between the unconscious and the conscious, between the infinite differential series (what Deleuze will frequently refer to as the virtual) and the actualised, given as given, is sufficient to account for the nature of reality. That it is not so is the enduring lesson of the Third Man Argument, as well as Bradley's regress, and it is a lesson Plato himself learned. If we are to do as Plato recommends, therefore, and look to 'a third, made by combining these two [one and infinite, actual and virtual]', then what will this entail? The short answer to this question is that the third that is between the actual and the virtual, between determinate, identifiable entities on the one hand, and the unconscious, infinite series of differentials (disparity) on the other, is a problematic Idea.

To be even more precise, we could say that problematic Ideas, as multiplicities, can also be thought of as problematic fields, fields that express the problematic Ideas that are inseparable from them. A problematic field, as a mixture, thus consists both of the tendency towards the actual, determinate and numerically distinct, *and* of the tendency to the infinite series of differentials, to the unconscious dimension of the virtual. In other words, problematic fields express the dual tendencies of differentiation, the move towards the determinate and distinct, and dedifferentiation, the move towards the differential unconscious that is not to be confused with anything determinate and distinct (hence its confused and obscure nature [recall §8.5]). These tendencies are reciprocally involved in the reality of a problematic field, and the problematic Ideas these fields express, and hence it is the third that 'lies between them', the third which avoids, as we will see below, the Third Man arguments that got us started.

2. Problematic Fields and Field Theory

To begin to unpack the nature of problematic fields, let us start with the term 'field'. We are drawing from two distinct traditions. The first is the use of field in field theory, as found in physics, most notably quantum field theory, and the second is the understanding of fields as found in sociology, most especially the work of Pierre Bourdieu. As for the use of field theory in physics, it was first employed by mathematical physicists in the eighteenth century to overcome the difficulties of calculating the gravitational interactions of multiple bodies. Whereas Newton's equations are straightforwardly applied to two massive bodies, when multiple bodies are each interacting with one another, such as in a solar system, then it quickly becomes increasingly difficult to calculate the gravitational effects upon any one body at any particular point. A gravitational field simplifies this process by replacing the action of one body on another with, as Steven Weinberg puts it, 'a numerical quantity (strictly speaking, a vector) which is defined at every point in space, which determines the gravitational force acting on any particle at that point, and which receives contributions from all the material particles at every other point' (Weinberg 1977, 18). Understood in this way, a field is still a heuristic device to aid in calculations of gravitational effects among bodies, with the bodies taken to be primary. With Michael Faraday and later James Clerk Maxwell's work on electromagnetic fields, fields began to be understood as independent realities capable of producing their own effects. It was not until quantum field theory emerged, however, in large part on the shoulders of Einstein's work, that fields come into their own as being thought of as the true nature of reality, with particles being merely effects of fields. Weinberg summarises this perspective quite succinctly: 'They [Heisenberg and Pauli] showed that material particles could be understood as the quanta of various fields, in just the same way that the photon is the quantum of the electromagnetic field ... Thus, the inhabitants of the universe were conceived to be a set of fields ... and particles were reduced in status to mere epiphenomena. In its essentials, this point of view has survived to the present day' (23). These fields, however, are quite real, and with measurable effects upon material particles. As Oppenheimer discovered, when one calculates the effects of the infinite number of potential relations between virtual particles (i.e., a field, but not actualised) and their material counterparts, the result of the equations is an infinity that prompted physicists to devise numerous techniques (most notably, the method of renormalisation) in order to rein in the infinities that were the result of the equations. As Weinberg puts it, 'it goes against the grain to suppose that a quantity like the bare mass [i.e., the mass of an elementary particle at the limit, that is as the scale of distance approaches zero and the energy of particle collisions approaches infinity] which appears in our fundamental field equations could be infinite; but after all, we can never turn off the electron's virtual photon cloud to measure the bare mass, so no paradox arises' (27). Without delving too far into the nuances of quantum theory, our understanding of fields as problematic fields is similar. Just as the particles that were once thought to constitute the eternal, fundamental stuff of nature are now thought to be merely epiphenomenal effects of fields, similarly, determinate, identifiable entities, the very entities that can be conceptualised in representational thought, are also to be understood as merely the epiphenomenal effects of problematic fields. The effort of physicists to address the infinities that result from calculating the relations between the 'virtual photon cloud', for instance, and a given electron, are accomplished by limiting the equations to 'a small number of physical parameters' (33); likewise, the tendency of the problematic field towards the infinite series of differential relations is avoided by virtue of the fact that a problematic field, as will be argued further below, is structured in such a way that it is reducible neither to an infinite series nor to the solutions and actualities the problematic fields make possible. This is one sense, then, in which we are following Plato and looking towards a third that is between the One (the actual, determinate and distinct) and the Infinite (the virtual, indeterminate and infinite series of differential relations).

3. Bourdieu on Fields

Turning now to Pierre Bourdieu's work, it is first to be noted that his use of the concept of field is similar to but importantly different from the understanding of fields among physicists (unsurprisingly!). The comparison does seem to be quite straightforward. Just as Weinberg argued that the consensus view among physicists, up to his present day (1977), was that '[material] particles [such as photons] were reduced in status to mere epiphenomena [of, for example, electromagnetic fields]' (23), so too, in sociology, is the agency of individuals to be understood as a 'mere epiphenomenon' of various social fields, such as kinship structures, etc. This is the structuralist understanding of agency. Bourdieu, however, pushes back against this theory. For Bourdieu, his project is to be viewed as one where he 'wanted, so to speak, to reintroduce the agents that Lévi-Strauss and the structuralists, among others Althusser, tended to abolish, making them into simple epiphenomena of structures'. As he goes on to add, 'Social agents, in archaic societies as well as in ours, are not automata regulated like clocks, in accordance with laws [or structures] which they do not understand' (Bourdieu 1990, 9). It is for this reason that Bourdieu adds the concept of habitus to the concept of field, in order to avoid falling back into a structuralist determinism on the one hand, and a form of conscious voluntarism or phenomenology on the other. The various intellectual alternatives one is supposed to choose between, whether they be empiricism, structuralism or phenomenology, are 'completely fictitious and at the same time dangerous' (34), according to Bourdieu, and it is these 'very alternatives', he argues, 'that the notion of habitus is meant to exclude, those of consciousness and the unconscious, of explanation by determining causes or by final causes' (10). In other words, Bourdieu can be seen to be paying heed to Plato's dictum: do not rush into either the One or the Infinite, to one of two alternatives, and look instead to a third.

For Bourdieu, his theory of habitus in its relationship to a social field is this third. In particular, Bourdieu believes that his account 'of the relation between habitus and field supplies us with the only rigorous way of reintroducing agents and their individual actions without falling back into the amorphous anecdotes of factual history' (Bourdieu 1990, 460). In other words, the habitus of an individual is neither an epiphenomenon of social structures nor is it reducible to being a phenomenological aspect of subjective experience; rather, it is what Bourdieu describes as a 'feel for the game', whereby an agent's actions are 'immediately adjusted to the immanent demands of the game' (11), and thus their behaviour can be seen as being 'directed towards certain ends without being consciously directed to these ends, or determined by them' (9–10). The 'notion of habitus was invented', Bourdieu claims, 'in order to account for this paradox' (10). Habitus, in other words, is what accounts for an agent whose 'feel for the game' results in actions that are irreducible both to the social field in which they occur, and hence to the structural rules and laws that might be used in an attempt to model such behaviours (which is a point Bourdieu stresses repeatedly [see 1990, 21]), but also to the agent's conscious awareness of why they are doing what they're doing when acting, and hence to a phenomenological account.

We can now return to our concept of problematic fields and provide a fuller account of how we are using this concept. As with the understanding of fields in the case of physics, a problematic field is understood here to be the real, genetic condition for the possibility of the determinate, individuated entities that are the manifestations or epiphenomena of their fields. Bourdieu will also adopt this understanding of field and echo the physicists when he claims that 'the individual, like the electron, is an *Ausgeburt des Felds*: he or she is an emanation of the field' (Bourdieu and Wacquant 1992, 107). In particular, for Bourdieu, what a field makes possible is 'a species of capital', such as 'the knowledge of Greek or of integral calculus' (98). In relation to a particular field, the knowledge of Greek, for instance, may place one in an advantageous social position vis-à-vis others who lack this knowledge, and the same will be true of various other species of capital whose existence depends upon fields. A field is thus, as Bourdieu defines it, 'a network, or a configuration, of objective relations between positions' (97), such as the relations between those who do and do not have specific forms of capital. This is where the difference emerges between Bourdieu's understanding of field and that found in physics – for Bourdieu the 'objective relations between positions' are themselves contested by the various social agents who bear the various species of capital made possible by fields. Fields thus have a history, a history of contestations whereby 'the regularities and the rules constitutive of this space of play [i.e., field]' (102) will themselves undergo transformation. In a certain 'pathological state of fields', such as 'Total institutions – asylums, prisons, concentration camps – or dictatorial states', one finds 'attempts to institute an end to history' (102), and hence an attempt to create fields that are completely determinative of the individuals they make possible. Problematic fields resist such pathological 'end of history' states and are rather the basis for the emergence of entities that are the solutions to their problematic conditions and are themselves subject to transformation. Stated differently, fields are a set of relations that are external to, and constitutive of, the terms they themselves make possible, but these terms and relations are in turn subject to transformation, to becoming other fields.

4. Russell on the Externality of Relations to Terms

With this last point we have returned to an earlier theme that was central to Russell's concerns – the externality of relations to their terms. As was discussed earlier (§7.4), for Russell we cannot begin to explain the possibility of mathematics unless we accept that there are relations that are external to their terms, meaning that the relations do not affect or modify the terms when they enter into the relation. For instance, we can place terms into the relation 'greater than or equal to', $\geq$, and infinitely substitute for these terms, without altering either the terms themselves or the relation, and the result is a mathematical proposition that is either true or false. Thus, with $x \geq y$, we can substitute 6 for x, 5 for y, and the resulting mathematical proposition, $6 \geq 5$ is true, and we can continue this process of substitution without end and without altering the terms or the relation. For Russell, both terms and relations are real, in contrast to Bradley who, as we saw, argued that the idea of relations between terms was incoherent unless they are understood to be merely appearances of the one absolute reality. For Bourdieu, by contrast, and for our understanding of problematic fields as well, a field is a set of relations that is constitutive of the elements or terms that are the epiphenomena of this field, and constitutive in a way that avoids a return of the TMA (as we will see below). For Bourdieu, therefore, what is real are the relations rather than the terms, if terms are taken as substantial entities, or as the particulars Russell himself described as having 'that sort of self-subsistence that used to belong to substance' (Russell 1907, 44). Bourdieu will thus offer a twist on Hegel's famous claim that the real is rational and argue instead 'that the real is relational' (Bourdieu and Wacquant 1992, 97). In fact, a primary motivation for Bourdieu's theory of fields was to 'move beyond the Aristotelian substantialism that spontaneously impregnates social thinking' (97). But how, precisely, do fields constitute the terms that are their epiphenomena?

5. Problematic Fields and Bourdieu's Fields Contrasted

It is at this point that our understanding of problematic fields differs from Bourdieu's use of the concept of field. Bourdieu understands fields to be 'a network, or a configuration, of objective relations between positions' (Bourdieu and Wacquant 1992, 97), with this being understood as a network or configuration of actual positions (e.g., whether one has studied Greek or not); it is the efficacity of these positions that both produces the species of capital that is the epiphenomena of the field and defines the limit of the field itself – in short, the field ends 'where the effects of the field cease' (100), and thus where the species of capital ceases to have force. A problematic field, by contrast, is not a network or configuration of actual positions but a network or configuration of becomings, or incorporeal transformations. The difference here is subtle but significant. As the Platonic third between the One and the Infinite, incorporeal transformations are, as we saw earlier, both tendencies towards the infinite, towards the Leibnizian differential unconscious that vanishes into the limit, and they are tendencies towards the One, towards the determinate, individuated givens into which the infinite series (disparity) vanishes. An incorporeal transformation is neither the differential unconscious, nor determinate, individuated entities; rather, an incorporeal transformation is precisely what a problematic field makes possible. Instead of the infinite series, a problematic field is a field or network relative and relevant to a determinate entity (or One). There are no problematic fields independent of the solutions they make possible; problems are only discernible relative to their solutions. At the same time, the solutions are not autonomous entities that can exist independently of the problematic fields that make them possible, and these solutions can themselves become transformed since the problematic field is not reducible to its solutions and further solutions remain possible. Returning to the example of music from the *Philebus*, a grasp of the relevant intervals, etc., between the infinite possibilities of sound-making and the one form of Beauty enables the musician to have a taste for the relevant in music and thereby create beautiful music. The grasp of the relevant in music, or the third between the One and Infinite, is not independent of the actual music-making abilities of the musician – this ability presupposes this taste for mixture, for the relevant (i.e., problematic field) – and the music they make (i.e., solutions) also presupposes the third that may well lead them to make yet other music. The problematic field is also subject to transformation as the conditions of relevance change, as elements enter and leave the scene and transform the nature of the problem.

A problematic field also entails incorporeal transformations, or a multiplicity of such transformations, for it is irreducible to any corporeal entities – corporeal entities are epiphenomena of problematic fields, or emanations of fields as Bourdieu argued – and thus as the conditions of relevance for the emergence and transformation of determinate, individuated entities, corporeal or otherwise, problematic fields entail incorporeal transformations. It is here where the difference with Bourdieu lies, for a problematic field is not to be understood as a configuration or network of 'objective relations between positions', with these positions taken to be *determinate, individuated* positions that are actual positions within a given field. On this point, our understanding of fields is closer to the view found in physics, where fields are what make actual, material particles such as electrons possible. Although these fields are real and inseparable from the actual material particles that emanate from them, they are not composed of actual particles, nor are they to be confused with actual particles, but instead they consist of virtual particles (e.g., virtual photons). We can see here as well why Deleuze will use the term virtual when discussing that which accounts for the emergence of determinate, actual entities. As Deleuze will say on a number of occasions, the virtual is real but not actual (see, for example, Deleuze 1994, 211: 'the virtual is not opposed to the real; it possesses a full reality by itself'). For us as well, a problematic field is a network or configuration of incorporeal transformations, a virtual field that is real and not to be confused with a set of actual positions, nor with the 'objective relations between [actual] positions' that form the basis of Bourdieu's understanding of fields.

6. Austin and Performatives

Let us turn to some examples to clarify further the nature of problematic fields, and most especially their nature as a network or configuration of incorporeal transformations. We can, perhaps surprisingly, turn to the work of J.L. Austin for an example of an incorporeal transformation, an example both Foucault and then Deleuze and Guattari will each cite in their own work. In his work on performatives (Austin 1962), Austin offers a subcategory of the performative, the verdictive, whereby what is done with words is to make something the case. Austin offers the examples of 'official acts', such as 'a judge's ruling makes law; a jury's finding makes a convicted felon; an umpire's giving the batsman out, or calling a fault or a no-ball, makes the batsman out, the service a fault, or the ball a no ball. It is done in virtue of an official position' (153). By simply issuing various verdicts by way of words, an accused is transformed into a convicted felon, a batsman into an out, etc. Now not just anyone can utter the words and effectuate such a transformation; the words must come from someone who occupies 'an official position', such as a jury foreman, an umpire, etc. As Austin summarises the conditions necessary for a successful performative, two rules must be followed if 'the act we purport to perform [is to avoid being] a misfire': first, there must be a convention which is being invoked and this convention 'must exist and be accepted'; 'the second rule, also a very obvious one, is that the circumstances in which we purport to invoke this procedure must be appropriate for its invocation' (224). If these two rules are satisfied, then the mere utterance of the word 'guilty' can transform an accused into a convict and bring with this transformation all that it entails (e.g., being led off in handcuffs, etc.). Although the consequences of the transformation are very real and have physical effects (e.g., being handcuffed, put in a jail cell, etc.), the actual transformation by way of the performative is itself incorporeal. The word itself did not physically cause the accused to become a convict, the batter to become an out, but the utterance, given the appropriate circumstances (conditions of relevance), was able to effectuate what can appropriately be called an incorporeal transformation. It is precisely this aspect of Austin's theory that Deleuze and Guattari stress.

After earlier crediting Austin for broadening our understanding of language, in particular for showing that language is neither a code nor a vehicle for transmitting information (see Deleuze and Guattari 1987, 77), Deleuze and Guattari borrow from him the example of a guilty verdict and argue that while the transformation is one that affects bodies – 'the body of the convict, the body of the prison' – 'the transformation of the accused into a convict' is nevertheless 'a pure instantaneous act or incorporeal attribute that is the expressed of the judge's sentence' (80–1). In other words, what we have here is a distinct point, a singular event (or singularity), whereby what is expressed in the word 'guilty', when it is expressed in the appropriate circumstances, is precisely the incorporeal transformation that marks the transformation from accused into convict. This is thus a distinctive point in the same way in which the point of the tangent is distinctive, or each of the four corner points of a square are distinctive. Each of the points on the four sides of the square is a regular point, but the corner is a distinctive point for it is to be identified as a point neither of one side of the square nor of the adjoining side, and yet it is by virtue of the four distinctive points that we have a square. Similarly, the guilty verdict is a distinctive point, a singularity that marks one of the (incorporeally) transformative events of the now convicted person's life.

7. Weimar Republic and 20 November 1923

In our next example we turn to Deleuze and Guattari's discussion of the Weimar Republic's response to hyperinflation in Germany in the early 1920s. The dated subtitle to the 'Postulates of Linguistics' chapter from *A Thousand Plateaus* is 20 November 1923, which is the date that the Rentenbank established the new exchange rate for the new currency (the Rentenmark) that replaced the hyperinflating Papiermark. With this example we can begin to clarify the relationship between the singular event – the distinctive point or incorporeal transformation that occurred on 20 November 1923 – and the appropriate circumstances that made this incorporeal transformation possible (for a more thorough discussion, see Bell 2018a). The nature of these circumstances seems straightforward enough, and it is in line with Austin's two rules. First, there was an established set of conventions, conventions that allowed for a series of singular events in addition to the event that established the exchange rate of the Rentenmark and effectively ended the hyperinflation. Among the various events in 1923, there was the ascension of banking-reform advocate Gustav Stresemann to the Chancellorship on 12 August; the establishment of the Rentenbank on 17 October; then legislation by the Reichstag that enabled the Rentenbank to issue a new currency, which it began to do, in limited quantities, on 15 November. Each of these events entailed incorporeal transformations of legal/political decrees, orders, laws, etc., that were made possible by an established, accepted convention (Austin's first rule) – typically an accepted legal and/or political convention – and these conventions were invoked appropriately (Austin's second rule), the result being the various transformative events that in turn made the 20 November event possible. In other words, the circumstances that made the 20 November decree possible appear to be nothing more than the historical context that is presupposed by each and every event – or at least that is what is presupposed if one accepts the claim that nothing happens in a historical vacuum.

Deleuze and Guattari, however, are interested in more than just the historical context of an event. They acknowledge that there is indeed a 'real history' of the Weimar economy and the events surrounding the decree of 20 November 1923, but insist that there are also 'pure acts intercalated into that development', into that history (Deleuze and Guattari 1987, 81). A 'pure act' is precisely the 'pure instantaneous act', an incorporeal transformation, such as the guilty verdict expressed by a jury foreman in the appropriate circumstance. Moreover, what effectuates this pure act is not simply the historical circumstances, or the social field in Bourdieu's sense, but the problematic field that is inseparable from these circumstances. Deleuze and Guattari point us in this direction when they explicitly argue that the conditions that allow the pure acts to effectuate their incorporeal transformations are not simply external, historical circumstances (we 'should not leave the impression that it is a question *only* of external circumstances' [82]). In addition to the historical circumstances, what is also necessary is what Deleuze and Guattari call a 'collective assemblage of enunciation', and it is this 'collective assemblage' that is expressed by a particular act and the transformations this act effectuates. As Deleuze and Guattari put it, the transformative effects of language are made possible because language itself is coextensive with a collective assemblage of enunciation; language also 'expresses the set of incorporeal transformations that effectuate the condition of possibility of language' (85). In other words, every historical act which effectuates an incorporeal transformation through language presupposes a 'set of incorporeal transformations', or a network or configuration of such transformations. It is this network or configuration that we have called a problematic field.

8. Problematic Fields and External Circumstances

With these two examples, however, the impression may still be that a problematic field is yet another way of referring to the structure of given circumstances, with the structure needing to be such that the incorporeal transformations associated with certain conventions become possible. Without the proper set of circumstances surrounding a courtroom, trial, etc., the read verdict of the appointed jury foreman would have no effect, and similarly for the set of circumstances that led to declaring the exchange rate of the newly issued Rentenmark. In other words, despite Deleuze and Guattari's claim that the collective assemblage of enunciation, or problematic field, is a 'set of incorporeal transformations' that is not to be confused with being a matter '*only* of external circumstances', it might seem from our two examples to be nothing more than the set of external circumstances that accounts for the incorporeal transformations that interested Deleuze and Guattari (following Austin). If we recall, however, *both* our earlier point that a problematic field, following Leibniz (see §8.3), is a differential unconscious that is not to be identified with that which it makes possible – for instance, the infinite series of polygons is not to be confused with the circle the infinite series vanishes into – *and* our understanding of the problematic field as that which can account for the emergence of the new, then we can more fully clarify the manner in which incorporeal transformations are not reducible to being *only* effects of external circumstances. To restate this point using the conception of fields from physics: the set of incorporeal transformations that constitutes a problematic field is a set of virtual elements – distinctive points, singular events – that are not to be confused with the actual positions (*à la* Bourdieu) the transformations make possible. Problematic fields, as the condition for the determinate positions and transformations that become identifiable, do not themselves consist of determinate, identifiable conditions, and it is for this reason that problematic fields can account for the new without reducing it to that which already is. If B, for instance, emerges out of context A, with B being something new, then the problem of the new is to account for the manner in which A becomes B without reducing B to being merely an extension or modification of A. In *What is Philosophy?*, Deleuze and Guattari argue that in the becoming of B from A 'There is an area *ab* that belongs to both *a* and *b*, where *a* and *b* "become" indiscernible' (Deleuze and Guattari 1994, 19–20). This 'area *ab*' is what we have been calling a problematic field, and it belongs to *a* and *b* to the extent that it is the condition inseparable from the conditioned, or the problem to which both *a* and *b*, as determinate actualities, are a solution. To state this in yet another way, and pave the way for our next examples, the 'area *ab*' is the condition that makes learning possible, the condition that consists of a set of distinctive points – singular events – being brought together into a network or configuration, a problematic field, that allows for the possibility of something new coming into being – i.e., that which is learned.

9. On Learning

The concept of learning is arguably one of the more important concepts running throughout Deleuze's corpus, and it plays a pivotal role in works from *Difference and Repetition* (1968) to the late work with Guattari, *What is Philosophy?* (1991).[5] In *Difference and Repetition*, for example, Deleuze argues that 'Learning is the appropriate name for the subjective acts carried out when one is confronted with the objecticity [*objectité*] of a problem (Idea), whereas knowledge designates only the generality of concepts or the calm possession of a rule enabling solutions' (Deleuze 1994, 164). Deleuze immediately follows this claim with an example of learning: the 'well-known test in psychology [that] involves a monkey who is supposed to find food in boxes of one particular colour' (164). Deleuze is likely referring to the experiments Harry Harlow conducted while developing his 'learning set' theory (see Harlow 1959). As Deleuze summarises the experiment, the monkey initially picks up boxes at random, discovers food under a box and

---

5. For more on the concept of learning in Deleuze and Guattari, see Bell 2016, and also *TCE*, especially the Introduction, §1.3.c and §2.1.c.

continues searching for food; eventually, 'there comes a paradoxical period during which the number of "errors" diminishes even though the monkey does not yet possess the "knowledge" or "truth" of a solution in each case' (Deleuze 1994, 164). This paradoxical period is precisely the 'area *ab* that belongs to both *a* and *b*, where *a* and *b* "become" indiscernible' (Deleuze and Guattari 1994, 19–20), and thus it belongs both to the random searches of the monkey on the one hand, and to the knowledge or truth that the food is under the boxes of one particular colour. This paradoxical 'area ab' is the 'objecticity [*objectité*] of a problem (Idea)', the problematic field, that is essential to the process of learning.

Just a few lines after citing these well-known experiments – used to illustrate the point about learning being the 'appropriate name for the subjective acts carried out when one is confronted with the objecticity of a problem (Idea)' – Deleuze continues the theme by returning to the example of learning to swim, which he claims involves being able 'to conjugate the distinctive points of our bodies with the singular points of the objective Idea in order to form a problematic field' (Deleuze 1994, 165). In other words, in order to learn to swim one must be able to bring together the relevant elements – distinctive points of our bodies and singular points of the objective Idea, such as the distinctive elements of the water, its buoyancy, currents, etc. – in a way that allows for the possibility of something new to emerge, which in this case would be the new skill of being able to swim. For Deleuze, moreover, this will become more than a pedagogical point about the nature of learning, and will be extended to a metaphysics of encounters with and among the world of elements that need to be conjugated into a problematic field, or problematic Ideas. Deleuze will thus come to understand the emergence of the given itself, the determinate realities that can then come to be the subjects of representational thinking, in terms of a metaphysical extension Leibniz's argument (discussed earlier, see §8.4) that the 'idea of the sea ... is a system of liaisons or differential relations between particulars and singularities corresponding to the degrees of variation among these relations – the totality of the system being incarnated in the real movement of the waves' (165). Just as the real sound of the waves, the sounds heard clearly, presupposes and incarnates, as a solution, the con-fusion of many minute waves, the incarnation of which becomes the clearly heard roar of the sea once it reaches a transformative threshold point, so too for any determinate, identifiable phenomenon as given there is presupposed the differential relations that remain obscure to the solutions that presuppose them until they too have been con-fused into a problematic field, that paradoxical 'area *ab*', that then vanishes into the solutions that actualise (incarnate) the conditions of the problematic field, the conditions of relevance. It is at this point that Deleuze fully asserts his

Leibnizian metaphysics: 'problematic Ideas are precisely the ultimate elements of nature and the subliminal objects of little perceptions' (165).

10. Problematic Fields and Platonic Ideas

Let us pause here in order to clarify the admittedly abstract Leibnizian moves Deleuze is making. The key to the Deleuzean metaphysics of problematic fields – and to the theory being developed in the current work – is the use of the term Idea, with a capital 'I', and in full recognition of the Platonic tradition the term brings with it (recall the Introduction). We can thus begin to understand problematic fields more clearly if we first think of them as Ideas in the conventional manner in which Plato's theory of Ideas is often interpreted. Understood in this way, an Idea is the unconditioned basis upon which one can account for that which is conditioned by the Idea. As discussed earlier, the reason a painting or anything else is beautiful is because, on the standard Platonic account, its reality as something that is beautiful is conditioned by the nature or Idea of beauty itself. There is thus in the beautiful thing, a painting for instance, a share of the reality that is in the Idea itself, and it was here that the Third Man regress got started (see §5.2). The key to the regress, as we saw, is that the Idea is not to be confused with the particulars that share in this idea (by NI), and yet there is a shared nature that both the Idea and the particulars have – e.g., beautiful things each share in the nature of beauty – and it was here that the regress found its legs. In Deleuze's Leibnizian metaphysics of Ideas as problematic fields, an Idea is also not to be confused with the determinate actualities it makes possible, or the solutions that express the nature of the Idea as problem. For this reason, Deleuze argues that 'A problem is determined at the same time as it is solved, but its determination is not the same as its solution: the two elements differ in kind, the determination amounting to the genesis of the concomitant solution' (Deleuze 1994, 163). If we take the decree of 20 November 1923 as an incorporeal transformation that determines the problem at the same time that it solves it, then the point for Deleuze is that the determination of the problem as Idea is indeed 'not the same as its solution': the particular, singular event of 20 November 1923 expresses the problematic field or Idea in its very solution, but this solution is not to be confused with the Idea. Understood as problematic fields, therefore, Ideas are not simple essences that remain the same throughout their manifold instantiations. As a problematic field, an Idea serves as the totality of conditions for the possibility of the particular events and incorporeal transformations that express this Idea. This totality, however, is not a totality defined in terms of a simple, self-same essence; rather, it is precisely the conjugation, network and set of incorporeal transformations and distinctive points that constitute the very becoming of the incorporeal transformation that expresses this totality. It is at this point that Deleuze echoes Plato, but not the conventional Plato. As we cited earlier (§8.3), Deleuze sees his work as Platonic 'If we think of the Plato from the later dialectic [e.g., *Philebus*], where the Ideas are something like multiplicities that must be traversed by questions such as *how? how much? in which case?*, then yes, everything I've said has something Platonic about it' (Deleuze 2004, 116). By multiplicities, Deleuze has in mind the set of incorporeal transformations that constitutes the problematic Ideas that are the 'ultimate elements of nature' (Deleuze 1994, 165), and these multiplicities are nothing less than the conjugation and network of incorporeal transformations, the set of becomings that is incarnated in a singular event, or what was discussed earlier as a collective assemblage of enunciation (§9.6) that makes possible the incorporeal transformation of the accused into the convicted felon when the jury foreman reads the word 'guilty'. As incarnated in the singular events and distinctive points that express them (e.g., the singular event associated with the date 20 November 1923), problematic fields subsist as an immanent retinue of further problems and directions – the how? how much? in which case? questions – which ensure the further becoming of the events that express them. This is the nature of multiplicities, the nature of problematic Ideas, the 'ultimate elements of nature'. Deleuze will reiterate this point later in *Difference and Repetition* when he argues that '"Multiplicity", which replaces the one no less than the multiple, is the true substantive, substance itself' (182). As a set of becomings, problematic Ideas are also the unconditioned immanent to the conditioned, 'the unconditioned in the product' (297), as Deleuze puts it when speaking of Nietzsche's theory of eternal return. In this context this can be understood as the return of that which cannot be determinately known and identified, the return of the timeless, eternal, unconditioned problematic Ideas. And these problematic Ideas are expressed in the very becoming of incorporeal transformations, in the becoming that is irreducible to that which becomes, to that which comes to be identified as being the case, including that which comes to be identified as new. We can thus see how problematic fields as Ideas can account for the new without being reduced to anything that comes to be identified as new. With this reading of Ideas we can also explain Deleuze and Guattari's interpretation of the creative genius of J.M.W. Turner, whose work they claimed was 'sometimes termed "incomplete"', the reason for this being that, 'from the moment there is genius, there is something that belongs to no school, no period, something that achieves a breakthrough – art as a process without goal, but that attains completion as such' (Deleuze and Guattari 1977, 370). Problematic Ideas are precisely these processes without a goal, the unconditioned in the product that attains completion as such as the Idea is expressed in the incorporeal transformation of a singular event.

Many questions remain. The nature of problematic Ideas (or fields) might remain far from clear – perhaps, since they are obscure and confused, this is necessarily so – but we can re-enter the subject from another perspective, namely, by way of Kant. By clarifying the manner in which Kant appropriates and uses Plato's term Ideas for his own philosophical purposes, we can gain further insight into how problematic Ideas are put to the purpose of accounting for the new. Let us then turn to Kant.

§10 Kant and Problematic Ideas

1. Kant and Plato

Kant uses the term Ideas at the moment in his most important work when he takes up the theme that gives that work its title – the critique of pure reason. Although Kant recognises that a 'thinker often finds himself at a loss for the expression which exactly fits his concept', and he was no doubt stretching the use of concepts beyond what others might recognise as legitimate, he nonetheless concludes that 'To coin new words is to advance a claim to legislation in language that seldom succeeds' (Kant 1965, 309, A312/B368). Kant thus opts to borrow Plato's term Ideas. The choice of term is appropriate, however, for as Kant argues, 'Plato made use of the expression "idea" in such a way as quite evidently to have meant by it something which not only can never be borrowed from the senses but far surpasses even the concepts of understanding ... inasmuch as in experience nothing is ever to be met with that is coincident with it' (310, A313/B370). And the term Idea is appropriate as well for clarifying the role reason plays in human life, since, as Plato and Kant will both argue, 'our reason naturally exalts itself to modes of knowledge which so far transcend the bounds of experience that no given empirical concept can ever coincide with them' (310, A314/B371). We can thus see that when Deleuze uses the term Ideas in referring to problematic fields, he is also following Plato and Kant in arguing for something that is not to be confused with that which can be given in experience.

In drawing the term Idea from Plato and using it both to capture the sense of that which can never be given in experience and to characterise the tendency of reason to move towards Ideas, that is, towards that which transcends 'the bounds of experience', Kant is thus setting up an important contrast between Ideas and that which can be given within 'the bounds of experience'. To clarify the latter, Kant uses the term 'concepts of understanding', which are 'thought *a priori* antecedently to experience and for the sake of experience' (Kant 1965, 308, A310/B367). The understanding, as Kant had argued in the transcendental analytic sections of the *Critique*, is what provides for the *a priori* unity of experience by way of certain rules – namely, the concepts of understanding, or the categories. Kant will use the term Ideas, or transcendental ideas, to refer to the 'concepts of reason', which, he claims, 'contain the unconditioned, they are concerned with something to which all experience is subordinate, but which is never itself an object of experience' (308, A310/B367). In the move towards Ideas, however, or the move towards attempting to think the unconditioned basis 'to which all experience is subordinate', one encounters the infinite. This is perhaps the defining characteristic of human reason for Kant, and in his essay, 'Speculative Beginning of Human History', he charts a possible path from the limits of actual experience to the infinity opened up by reason. Initially, Kant opines, humanity simply lived in accordance with instinct, and 'was well-served by it' (Kant 1983, 50). 'But reason soon began to stir', he argues, and when it did it 'sought, by means of comparing foods with what some sense other than those to which the instinct was tied – the sense of sight, perhaps – presented to it as similar to those foods, so as to extend his knowledge of the sources of nourishment beyond the limits of instinct' (50–1). With this move, Kant speculates that 'man became conscious of reason as an ability to go beyond those limits that bind all animals'; but with this ability comes a *problem*, for 'besides the particular objects of desire on which instinct had until then made him dependent, there opened up to him an infinitude of them, among which he could not choose, for he had no knowledge whatsoever to base choice on' (51). As Kant will state this point in the *Critique of Pure Reason*, with the advent of reason we push towards the unconditioned, to the absolute whole and totality that includes the infinity of all possible choices, but this 'absolute whole of all appearances', Kant argues, 'is only an idea; since we can never represent it in image, it remains a problem to which there is no solution' (Kant 1965, 319, A328/B384). The task of Kant's critique, therefore, is to address the implications of this problem with no solution, or the tendency for reason to open onto an infinity without a basis for filtering or limiting this infinity.

2. Infinity and Antinomies

To restate the problem, reason confronts us with an infinity that leaves us with an inability to choose, since we lack the conditioned, experiential basis for making a choice among the infinite possibilities. With the advent of reason and the opening of an infinitude that moves rational beings beyond 'those limits that bind all animals', the problem now is one of establishing a basis for judgment in the face of the infinite – e.g., is this plant, of the many possibilities now before me, edible or not? Reason thus sets us off on a search for reasons, for conditions that can then justify a choice, provide reasons for a judgment, but this search for conditions leads us to look for the conditions of the conditions we find, and so on *ad infinitum*. Kant's well-known antinomies are the result of the regresses opened up by reason's move beyond the limits of actual experience. In the first antinomy, for instance, the question is whether or not the world has a beginning in time and whether it is limited as regards to space. If we assume that there is no beginning, then any given moment in time will presuppose an infinite series of previous times, an infinite series that 'can never be completed' but that must be completed if the given moment is to occur as that which is conditioned by previous moments; consequently, Kant concludes that it 'thus follows that it is impossible for an infinite world-series to have passed away'. The same is true for the view that the world is not limited as regards space, which would mean that 'the world is an infinite given whole of co-existing things' (Kant 1965, 397, A427/B455). If such a world is to be thought, then this will likewise entail a synthesis of infinite parts, a synthesis that will take 'an infinite time … [and is thus] impossible' (398, A428/B456). If we assume that there is beginning of the world in time and limits to it in space, we come upon related difficulties. If the world has a beginning in time, then 'there must have been a preceding time in which the world was not, i.e. an empty time', but nothing can come to be from an empty time, Kant argues, for 'no part of such a time possesses, as compared with any other, a distinguishing condition of existence rather than of non-existence', and thus Kant concludes that there can be no beginning to the world and it must therefore be 'infinite in respect of past time' (398, A428/B456), which brings us back to our earlier problems. Kant comes to a similar conclusion from assuming the world is limited in space – if this were true, then there would be a relation between the world and that which is outside the world, that which limits it, but this would then undermine Kant's assumption that 'the world is an absolute whole beyond which there is no object of intuition' (398, A428/B456). Anything that can be an object of intuition will be an object of the world itself. The conclusion, therefore, is that the world cannot be limited in space and is 'infinite in respect of extension', which again brings us back to the earlier problems. The result of the first antinomy – and the same will be true for the other three Kant discusses – is that there is no basis upon which we can choose between the two options. For Kant, it is thus impossible for us to know whether the world does or does not have a beginning in time, or whether it is or is not limited in spatial extent. We seem to have a problem with no solution.

A solution is to be had, however, if we turn to the conditions necessary for the possibility of experience. Rather than take experience, as Hume argued, to be the basis upon which all knowledge is derived, Kant argued that experience itself presupposes certain *a priori* connections. This argument emerges in response to Hume's famous claim that cause and effect relations are known only as a result of experience. Kant argues, to the contrary, that experience itself presupposes an *a priori* synthesis of cause and effect. Kant's project develops this general insight; as he puts it in his *Prolegomena*: he 'soon found out that the concept of the connection of cause and effect is far from being the only concept through which the understanding thinks connections of things *a priori* … I proceeded to the deduction of these concepts, from which I henceforth became assured that they were not, as Hume had feared, derived from experience, but had arisen from the pure understanding' (Kant 2004, 10). The deduction Kant is referring to is his famous transcendental deduction of the categories, the categories being the concepts of the pure understanding, a deduction Kant himself admits is exceedingly difficult ('this deduction, I say, was the most difficult thing that could ever be undertaken on behalf of metaphysics' [10]), so much so that he reworked and rewrote the deduction for the second edition of the *Critique of Pure Reason*.

3. Returning to Kant and Hume

Kant's reference to Hume, and especially to Hume's argument that causal relations are only known through experience, is particularly relevant because for Hume, as we saw in the Introduction, causation is the only association of ideas that moves us beyond the given. As Hume puts it, if we are to reach any 'conclusion beyond the impressions of our senses [this] can be founded only on the connexion of cause and effect' (T, 1.3.2.2; SB 74). As we come to acquire beliefs in the necessary connection and power of causation, we come upon a means to speculate about that which is not given and yet which is necessarily connected to what is given. This necessity, however, is not a rational necessity (i.e., it is not *a priori*) but is rather a strongly held belief such as believing that when smoke is seen (given) there must be fire, a belief that has its strength and vivacity as a result of actual experiences that have over time reinforced the strength of this connection. It is thus a consequence of habit and learned experience that human beings, with the psychological machinery they have by nature, come to think of the many things that are not actually given to experience. Some of these beliefs, however, may come about through hearsay, or through being repeatedly told that there are necessary connections among certain phenomena. Hume gives the example of believing that '[a]n Irishman cannot have wit, and a Frenchman cannot have solidity', and believing this despite the fact that what one may actually be experiencing is a 'visibly very agreeable' conversation with an Irishman and a 'very judicious' conversation with a Frenchman. Hume admits that 'Human nature is very subject to errors of this kind; and perhaps this nation as much as any other' (T, 1.3.13.7; SB 146–7). In further clarifying the reasons for such prejudices, Hume argues that they 'proceed from those very principles, on which all judgments concerning causes and effects depend. Our judgments concerning cause and effect are deriv'd from habit and experience' (T, 1.3.13.8; SB 147). Given an upbringing where one's experience was suffused with the expression of beliefs that Frenchmen have no solidity and Irishmen no wit, one will, on encountering one or the other, naturally and habitually infer that they too will have the character trait the prejudice says they should have, even if that belief is 'contrary to present observation and experience' (T, 1.3.13.8; SB 147 [more on this in *TCE*]). One of the critical tasks of philosophy for Hume is thus to evaluate our beliefs relative to what experience actually gives us, or to engage in an experimental testing of hypotheses, with our beliefs understood to be much like hypotheses that are simply the set of expectations that largely determine our behaviours and beliefs. For Hume, therefore, experience is both what accounts for our ability to move beyond what is actually given in experience and the final arbiter as to which moves beyond the given are proper and appropriate.

For Kant, by contrast, experience will not be adequate to the task of accounting for and policing our moves beyond what is given to and in experience. The simple reason for this is that one cannot actually experience the infinite, and yet it is precisely the infinite that is opened up as humans use reason to 'move beyond the limits of instinct' (Kant 1983, 52), a move that also leads us to the antinomies and Ideas that are problems with no solutions. Since the infinite that is opened up cannot be experienced, Hume's efforts to account for and limit our moves beyond what is actually experienced will not be available to Kant. Kant will thus seek to establish the proper limits to our moves beyond experience on the basis of that which is not reducible to experience itself. This is otherwise known for Kant as the effort to determine whether synthetic *a priori* judgments are possible, judgments that are not reducible to experience. The transcendental deduction is key to this effort, for if there are categories that are necessary for the possibility of experience, categories that are not accounted for in terms of experience but instead are what account for experience itself, then any judgments involving these categories will be synthetic *a priori* judgments – synthetic because as judgments they combine a subject and a predicate (e.g., x is caused by y), and *a priori* since the categories, and hence the judgments which include them, are not based on experience, as *a posteriori* judgments are. For Kant, therefore, since the relation of cause and effect is one of the categories he deduces, a judgment that includes this category, such as the judgment that every event has a cause, is a valid synthetic *a priori* judgment. This thus clarifies Kant's claim that 'though all our knowledge begins with experience, it does not follow that it all arises out of experience' (Kant 1965: 41, A1/B1). Although knowledge of the specific causal relations among things is indeed something we can only gain from experience, the knowledge that every event has a cause is not something we can derive from experience, for we cannot experience the infinite instances that would be necessary to know this judgment to be true. We do not need to know this judgment to be true from experience, however, precisely because it is a synthetic *a priori* judgment that Kant has shown to be necessary for the possibility of experience. The transcendental deduction thus emerges as a crucial step in Kant's response to Hume, and also lays the basis for his effort to provide a criterion for legitimating our moves beyond the given.

4. Unity of Consciousness

To understand Kant's efforts on this latter front, it is important to note his founding distinction between sensibility and understanding. As Kant states this distinction at the start of his *Critique of Pure Reason*, 'Objects are given to us by means of *sensibility*, and it alone yields us *intuitions*; they are thought through the *understanding*, and from the understanding arise *concepts*' (Kant 1965, 65, A19/B33). What is given, Kant argues, is a manifold of representations (for reasons to be detailed below), and although these representations may be given to sensibility through an intuition, 'the form of this intuition', Kant argues, 'can lie *a priori* in our faculty of representation', a faculty Kant claims 'must be entitled understanding' in order 'to distinguish it from sensibility' (151, B130). What the understanding does is combine the representations, or perform a synthesis of the manifold, and this synthesis is made possible by virtue of the fact that every representation is a representation for one and the same consciousness, one and the same 'I think'. As Kant puts it, 'Only in so far, therefore, as I can unite a manifold of given representations in *one consciousness*, is it possible for me to represent to myself *the identity of the consciousness in* [i.e., throughout] *these representations*' (153, B133). For example, I see some ducks crossing the road, and I hear their quacking as they slowly waddle along. Each of these representations are given in one consciousness, mine, and it is the identity of this consciousness that provides the basis for the faculty of understanding's capacity to synthesise the representations as representations of one object; that is to say, I claim to know that it is one and the same object quacking and waddling across the road, or, as discussed earlier (§8.3), it is the common sense operations of the unity of consciousness, the 'I think', that brings the various faculties together to give me one object. Kant is clear on this point: 'Now all unification of representations demands unity of consciousness in the synthesis of them. Consequently, it is the unity of consciousness that alone constitutes the relation of representations to an object, and therefore their objective validity and the fact that they are modes of knowledge' (156, B137).

5. Kant, Russell and the Otherness of the Given

This leads us to a similarity between Kant and Russell that it would be helpful to address at this point. In particular, both Kant and Russell accept the notion that there is something there for consciousness, even if it is not an object of consciousness. For Russell this is expressed in terms of the distinction between sensibilia and sensations. As we saw earlier (§7.4), sensibilia are 'those objects which have the same metaphysical status as sense-data, without necessarily being data to any mind [i.e., sensations]' (Russell 1917b, 148). For Kant as well there are representations that are not present before a mind. In laying out the 'serial arrangement' of the kinds of representations, Kant begins by claiming that the 'genus is *representation* in general', and '[s]ubordinate to it stands representation with consciousness (*perceptio*)' (Kant 1965, 314, A320/B376). Kant thus clearly identifies representations that are and are not representations we are conscious of, but he does not stop here, for he goes on to catalogue other types of representations, such as the perceptions that relate 'solely to the subject as the modification of its state', which he calls sensation, and then there are the objective perceptions Kant associates with knowledge. Of the latter type, there are objective perceptions that relate 'immediately to the object and [are] single', which Kant calls intuition, as well as those that relate to the object 'mediately by means of a feature which several things may have in common', which Kant calls conceptual knowing. Of conceptual knowing, there is empirical and pure; the former involves sensibility and the latter 'has its origin in the understanding alone', which Kant calls a notion. And finally, a 'concept formed from notions and transcending the possibility of experience is an idea or concept of reason'. Kant's conclusion, at this point, is that once one understands the different kinds of representations, one 'must find it intolerable to hear the representation of the colour, red, called an idea' (314, A320/B376).

Kant's serial arrangement of the types of representations now brings us to a key difference with Russell's approach. Russell sought to avoid the types of regresses Bradley claimed infected any account that accepted the reality of relations. Russell's solution, as we saw, was to end the regresses at brute facts, facts that do not need to be explained and that hence prevent the regress from ever getting started. These brute facts are precisely the sensibilia that form the foundation for the inferences and logical constructions we are able to (or ought to) make based upon them, or they are the particulars we become conscious of (or know by acquaintance to use Russell's term). Russell thus calls upon a foundation whereby infinite regresses will be halted in their tracks, a bedrock at which point our spade is turned and nothing more need or can be said. As we have seen, in 'The Philosophy of Logical Atomism' (1918), Russell states his point that the particulars we know by acquaintance stand 'entirely alone and [are] completely self-subsistent ... that sort of self-subsistence that used to belong to substance' (Russell 1970, 202); and again in his *Inquiry into Meaning and Truth* (1940), he will refer to these brute, self-dependent particulars as being 'my momentary epistemological premises', the only true premises, he argues, whereas 'the rest must be inferred' (Russell 1940, 127). Kant, by contrast, is not setting out to end the infinite regress but rather to limit it by establishing the rules whereby we can gain a foothold in the infinite and proceed with the syntheses that come to constitute our knowledge of the things of the world. This follows for Kant from the very manner in which the given is given, namely in the form of space and time. As Kant argues in the Transcendental Aesthetic section of his first *Critique*, every representation that is given presupposes its being given in space and time, but this immediately opens onto an infinite series in that what is given in the present presupposes a relationship to a previous moment, and that moment to yet another moment, and so on *ad infinitum*; similarly for what is given in the form of space, since Kant argues that space is presupposed when one establishes the limits of that which is given in extensity, limits that can be decreased or increased by yet further limits, and so on. It was just these regresses that gave rise to the antinomies.

One advantage Kant's approach has over Russell's is that Kant is better able to account for how the given is given from elsewhere. In fact, Kant's arguments in the Transcendental Aesthetic can be seen as a reworking of Descartes' own efforts to answer the question of how we can know whether that which is given to consciousness is given from elsewhere or is simply a product of our own mind. Whereas Descartes concludes from the fact that we cannot be the source of the idea of an infinite being (God) of which we are clearly and distinctly aware, that therefore this idea must be given to us from elsewhere (namely, from God), Kant argues that the very manner in which the given is given in space and time presupposes an infinite series that we cannot synthesise or know directly, and hence all we have are representations of that which is given from elsewhere rather than knowledge of the thing as it is in itself. Kant is quite forthright on this point, arguing in the B Deduction that if we were 'to think an understanding which is itself intuitive (as, for example, a divine understanding which should not represent to itself given objects but through whose representation the objects should themselves be given or produced), the categories would have no meaning whatsoever in respect of such a mode of knowledge' (Kant 1965, 161, B145). What an infinite intellect such as God's would be able to do, in other words, is to intuit and synthesise the actuality of an object and the infinite synthesis of space and time this entails. God is thus not limited to representations of things as they are in themselves, and hence for God the categories have no meaning; God has no need for rules with respect to how the syntheses of representations should proceed, but simply intuits (produces) the things themselves. Representations are thus not for Kant, as they were for Russell, the self-subsistent particulars that short circuit the possibility of an infinite regress; to the contrary, representations presuppose an object that is given from elsewhere precisely because it entails the possibility of an infinite regress. Russell's self-subsistent particulars, since they do not entail the regresses and antinomies that Kant's representations do, are thus not well equipped to resolve the Cartesian question regarding whether the given is given from elsewhere or from the mind. Russell would likely be nonplussed and unbothered by these arguments, for, as he admits, it would give him 'the greatest satisfaction' to dispense with analogical arguments in favour of the sense-data of other people, of thoughts and things from elsewhere, or the sense-data we do not know by acquaintance, and he would therefore be perfectly happy to 'establish physics upon a solipsistic basis. And yet most people are psychologically predisposed,' Russell recognises, to 'not shar[ing] in my [Russell's] desire to render solipsism scientifically satisfactory' (Russell 1917b, 158).

6. Kant, Infinite Regresses and Infinite Tasks

We can begin to see at this point how the possibility of infinite regresses provides a basis for Kant's efforts to show how the faculty of sensibility is related to the faculty of the understanding. The duality of sensibility/ understanding will become one of the most contentious aspects of Kant's philosophy and will be both asserted and rejected by a host of post-Kantian philosophers. As Frederick Beiser has shown, a major fault line in the post-Kantian tradition concerns precisely whether or not the dualism between sensibility and understanding, among the other dualisms such as form and content, appearance (phenomena) and thing in itself (noumena), is embraced or rejected – the neo-Kantian tradition stemming from Fries, Herbart and Beneke embraced these dualisms, while the post-Kantian rationalist-speculative tradition of Reinhold, Fichte, Schelling and Hegel rejected them (see Beiser 2014, 12–13). Wherever one lands on this debate (and more will be said below), a place where both traditions intersect is in addressing the nature of infinite regresses. This follows since the infinite regresses result from the manner in which the given is given to experience in space and time, and the infinite that is opened up to rational creatures such as human beings who can entertain ideas for which there is no counterpart given in experience. What accounts for the infinite series the givens bring in their wake, both to sensibility and understanding, is, I shall argue, the problematic Idea. For Kant, however, the problematic Idea retains a precise meaning, and one which keeps him committed to a limited and limiting understanding of the relationship between sensibility and understanding.

To state Kant's approach succinctly, he sets out to account for the relationship between sensibility and understanding in terms of a synthesis of representations – that is, a rule-based limitation of the infinite – that does its work on the model of an extensive corralling of elements, with the representations being these elements. The most basic element for Kant is the givenness of the present moment to consciousness, to the 'I think', and it is this self-identical present, along with the identity of the self-same consciousness throughout the indefinite series of moments in which something can be given, that forms the basis for the possibility of anything being given at all, the possibility that a synthesis of representations is my synthesis, or what Kant calls the 'synthesis of apprehension' (Kant 1965, 131, A99). Kant thus stresses in the A Deduction that while '[e]very intuition contains in itself a manifold which can be represented as a manifold' – in other words, the manifold as given presupposes the form of time and space in which the manifold is given and thus the infinite series of times and spaces this brings with it – this intuition of a manifold can be represented, or given, 'only in so far as the mind distinguishes the time in the sequence of one impression upon another, for each representation, in so far as it is contained in a single moment, can never be anything but absolute unity' (131, A99). Each moment, therefore, is a bounded, absolute unity, and it is this unity that is intuited and given in a representation; the unity of apperception, the self-same identity of the 'I think', is what makes possible the synthesis of absolute unities throughout a sequence of other times and spaces. As Kant restates this point in the B Deduction, he argues that 'A manifold, contained in an intuition which I call mine, is represented, by means of the synthesis of the understanding, as belonging to the necessary unity of self-consciousness; and this is effected by means of the category' (160, B144). Since we are not God, we are unable to carry out an infinite synthesis of representations, or completely synthesise the manifold as such, and thus our thoughts are syntheses of representations of a given that is not itself thought or represented, a given that is outside of thought and possible experience (the infinite manifold). It is at this point that the categories, as the presupposed rules of synthesis, come in to effectuate the syntheses of the understanding and deliver an object for thought, and for a thought of the manifold 'contained in an intuition which I call mine'. As mentioned earlier, a divine understanding would have no need for the categories since it would be capable of delivering the object for thought as it is in itself. A divine understanding contains the entirety of an infinite series; in other words, it involves the absolute totality and condition for the infinite series of conditioned things that are given in time and space. The categories, however, presuppose the necessity of limits, or the fact that our finite faculties are incapable of performing an infinite synthesis, and thus the totalities they give us are always necessarily limited in range and scope. The task of Kant's *Critique* is to establish these limits, and the arbiter of whether or not reason has properly operated within the scope of these limits is whether the totalities that emerge can become objects of possible experience.

This is the essential moral and conclusion that Kant draws from his *Critique of Pure Reason*. By virtue of having reason, we are opened to an infinite task, to a world where infinite regresses forever await our speculative thought, but if we hew to that which can become an object of possible experience then our thoughts will not veer into speculative metaphysics, and may, with luck, contribute to our knowledge of the things of the world, and so give to philosophy the 'universal and lasting acclaim' (Kant 2014, 5) it had heretofore lacked. The antinomies, for example, would violate the restriction of falling within the range of possible experience, for they presuppose, as we saw, an absolute totality or unconditioned that can never be an object of possible experience. The key problem for Kant at this point, however, is to show how the pure concepts of the understanding (i.e., the categories), which have 'their origin in the understanding alone' (Kant 1965, 314, B377 [from the 'serial arrangement' of representations discussed above]), are nonetheless able to connect with that which is given in intuitions by way of the sensibility. The pivot upon which the relationship between understanding and sensibility turns is knowledge, and as Kant makes clear, the pure concepts of the understanding yield knowledge 'only through their possible application to empirical intuition': 'they serve only for the possibility of empirical knowledge, and such knowledge is what we entitle experience' (314, B377). Our experience of what is the case, if it is an experience made possible by the categories, is therefore a case of knowledge, and the categories are only legitimately exercised when they yield objects of possible experience. This is precisely Kant's conclusion: that 'the categories, as yielding knowledge of *things*, have no kind of application, save only in regard to things which may be objects of possible experience' (162, B147–8).

7. Possible Experience to Real Experience

It is at this point that cracks begin to surface in Kant's account, as has been widely recognised and which has been the source of many of the variations one finds among post-Kantian philosophers. In particular, Kant argues for a distinction between the objective and subjective validity of knowledge. As just noted, the categories provide the means whereby the representations of an empirical intuition become the knowledge Kant entitles experience. What is objectively valid, for Kant, is the 'necessary relation of the manifold of the intuition to the one "I think", and so through the pure synthesis of understanding which is the *a priori* underlying ground of empirical synthesis' (Kant 1965, 158, B140). In other words, it is the categories in their role as 'necessarily and universally valid' rules of synthesis – as exemplified in such universal judgments such as 'every event has a cause' – that yield knowledge which is objectively valid. By contrast, for Kant the fact that 'a certain word suggests one thing [to one man], to another some other thing' (158, B140) is a unity that may be empirical but is not 'necessarily and universally valid' – it is not necessarily the case that the same word suggests the same thing to different people. But how do we account for this difference between a synthesis of representations that is 'necessarily and universally valid' and a synthesis that is only subjectively valid? In both cases it would appear that there is a synthesis of the manifold, a synthesis of the potentially infinite series of time and space, especially since each 'representation, in so far as it is contained in a single moment, can never be anything but [an] absolute unity' (131, A99). The further syntheses of representations that presuppose each of these absolute unities, and the self-same identity of the 'I think' that remains the same throughout the synthesising process, are what yields, by way of the categories, the knowledge of things Kant calls experience. But if I hear someone say Pliny the Elder and this suggests to me the excellent beer from the Russian Red River Brewing Company, this would seem to be just as much my experience as would be the experience of someone else for whom Pliny the Elder suggests the Roman author and naturalist. My experience of thinking of a beer when I hear the name 'Pliny the Elder' reflects the trajectory of my life, a life that has entailed a pursuit of fine beer, while someone else who has lived a different life will no doubt have a different experience. Kant is indeed on the trail of an important difference when he highlights the difference between subjective and objective validity. In short, there is a difference between the ordinary and the universal that Kant identifies with objectively valid experiences – i.e., those that are 'necessarily and universally valid' – and the singular and particular which he identifies with subjectively valid experiences. To state this differently, and as Deleuze himself will understand what is going on here, Kant is working with a difference between the conditions of possible experience and the conditions of real experience. The former experiences, possible experiences, are objectively valid, while the latter, real experiences, may be subjectively valid but are not necessarily objectively valid. If, however, we assume that for Kant all experiences are conditioned in the same way, then the distinction between objectively and subjectively valid experiences becomes problematic. Henry Allison, for instance, has argued that Kant 'conflates the empirical unity of apperception with the subjective unity of consciousness' (Allison 1983, 157). In particular, Allison argues that there is a difference between the empirical unity of our experiences over time, such as the number of times I have drunk Pliny the Elder, and the association of ideas that comes with this on the one hand, *and* our consciousness of this unity on the other. With respect to the former we may be unconscious of the unity, or in the manner of Hume it may be the result of principles of association that lead me to think of beer when I hear Pliny the Elder; but when we are conscious of the unity of this experience then we bring to bear the objective unity of the categories. Since Kant did not make this distinction clearly in the context of distinguishing between objectively and subjectively valid experience, Allison argues that the distinction itself becomes problematic. If what Kant is concerned with, however, is not the nature of real experience, but the nature of possible experience, the experience that can give us knowledge of things, then the objective/subjective distinction plays an important role in Kant's project. Kant does not put the distinction in this way, however, and he no doubt relegates subjective knowledge to a lower status because he feels that the objectively valid knowledge of possible experience is more real than what we are calling real experience. It is here that the limited and limiting aspects of Kant's project become prominent. To see how this is so, and to clarify the distinction between real and possible experience, we can turn to discuss the 'inner differences' Kant focuses on in his example of the left hand seen in the mirror, an example which shows how experience (real experience) can involve a 'difference between similar and equal but nonetheless incongruent things' (Kant 2004, 38).

8. Kant's Left-Hand Paradox

In his now famous example, Kant says of the left hand seen in the mirror, 'I cannot put such a hand as seen in the mirror in the place of its original' (Kant 2004, 37). Whereas my left hand fits in a left-handed glove, the mirror image of my left hand, although appearing in the mirror to be a right hand, would fit neither in a left-handed nor right-handed glove. From this example, Kant recognises that there are inner differences between the left hand and its mirror image that cannot be accounted for in terms of the extensive properties and qualities of that which is given – 'Now there are no inner differences here that any understanding could merely think; and yet the differences are inner as far as the senses teach, for the left hand cannot, after all, be enclosed within the same boundaries as the right (they cannot be made congruent), despite all reciprocal equality and similarity; one hand's glove cannot be used on the other' (38–9). As Kant explains what is going on with this example, he argues that the difference between the left hand and its mirror image shows that what we have here 'are surely not representations of things as they are in themselves, and as the pure understanding would cognize them, rather, they are sensory intuitions, i.e., appearances, whose possibility rests on the relation of certain things, unknown in themselves, to something else, namely our sensibility' (38). In other words, since the representations of the hand in the mirror are incongruent with the hand being reflected, 'despite all reciprocal equality and similarity', this incongruity is evidence, for Kant, of an incongruity between the reality, an unknown 'something else', and the manner in which this reality is related to our sensibility. In particular, we have an incongruity between, on the one hand, an understanding that synthesises the unities of experience by way of the pure concepts of the understanding, and does so on the basis of parts, namely representations as absolute unities, and on the other hand the appearances that are given through sensibility in the form of space and time where determination proceeds from the whole of space to the part given in intuition. As Kant puts this point, 'the inner determination of any space is possible only through the determination of the outer relation to the whole space of which the space is a part ... that is, the part is possible only through the whole' (38), and this is to be contrasted with how the understanding operates, where it is not the case that the 'part is possible only through the whole' but, to the contrary, it is the whole, the unities synthesised by the understanding, that is possible only through the parts, the representations. The representations of possible experience, therefore, or the experiences with objective validity, are those with a necessary connection to a whole or totality that is not itself given but serves as an ideal for the understanding in its task of synthesising representations. The appearances given through sensibility, by contrast, and hence our experiences that have only subjective validity, are those where the part, the appearances, are 'possible only through the whole', and yet these appearances are given as diverse and with no necessary connection between them, other than connections established through association (*à la* Hume). It is the task of the understanding, therefore, to transform that which is given in appearances and with subjective validity into that which can become objective knowledge, or possible experience as Kant understands it. As Kant put it in the A Deduction, 'The appearances might, indeed, constitute intuition without thought, but not knowledge; and consequently would be for us as good as nothing' (Kant 1965, 138, A111), for the understanding is unable, as Kant now argues in the B Deduction, to yield by way of the categories a 'knowledge of things', things which are good for something, the 'things which may be objects of possible experience' (162, B148).

9. Kant, Plato and Frege

We can now return to the theme with which we began this section – the nature of problematic Ideas – and in particular to the Platonic response to the Third Man Argument we find in the *Philebus* and as we have been developing throughout this work. As we have seen, for Socrates in Plato's *Philebus*, 'the wise men of the present day make the one and the many too quickly or too slowly, in haphazard fashion ... they disregard all that lies between them' (17a). The problematic Idea, I have been arguing, is precisely the mixture, or that which lies between the one and the many. We turned to Kant to begin to elucidate the nature of problematic Ideas, and we can now see that Kant both rushed too quickly to the one and the many but also, and more significantly, pointed the way to an understanding of problematic Ideas that is irreducible to the one or the many. Kant rushes to the one and the many by understanding representations as discrete, determinate unities that are synthesised by way of the categories so as to yield the knowledge of things 'which may be objects of possible experience'. These discrete unities are the parts that are taken up in the process of the understanding's effort to create the totalities that account for the nature of things. It was this process that gave rise to the antinomies, for in seeking the totalities that account for the nature of things we are led, by reason, to seek the absolute totality, the unconditioned, that is the ultimate condition for the knowledge we have of things. The absolute totality, the unconditioned, cannot itself become an object of possible experience, and thus for Kant the problematic Idea – the Idea that is a problem for which no solution is possible – is in the end a totality that can never be thought, for we can never, since we are not God, synthesise an infinite number of parts into an extensive totality. Rather than accept the reality of problematic Ideas, as I have been arguing for, following through on Deleuze's Leibnizian metaphysics, for Kant these Ideas serve as regulative ideals, as rules for thinking; in short, we are to proceed in our pursuit of knowledge *as if* the absolute totality were real and that which guides our enquiry and supports the relative conditions for the knowledge of things that may and do become objects of possible experience.

Despite offering a metaphysics that rushes to the one and many, Kant does gesture towards the type of mixture Plato called for. In particular, with his example of the left hand in the mirror Kant recognises, as we saw, the role inner differences play with respect to spatial appearances, with these appearances being understood to involve inner differences and determinations that presuppose a whole, and thus for these appearances 'the part is possible only through the whole'. We will generalise from this case, following Deleuze, and argue that where the part is possible only through the whole, then the whole is the condition of real experience rather than possible experience.[6] Kant does not make this distinction between the conditions of possible and real experience, for in the end he understands the real to be an extensive totality; consequently, those experiences that cannot be accounted for in terms of the extensive categories and their ultimate relationship to an ideal totality become relegated to being merely second-class experiences – namely, subjectively valid experiences. Rather than attempting to account for the things that are known in terms of extensive totalities, and thus ultimately in terms of a relationship between parts and a whole, I am arguing for a totality that is an intensive totality. This is what we take to be the nature of problematic Ideas. As intensive totalities, problematic Ideas cannot be thought. On this point, Kant was indeed right, but the reason problematic Ideas cannot be thought is not because we are not divine and hence unable to synthesise an infinite number of elements into an extensive totality; rather, problematic Ideas cannot be thought because they cannot be thought in terms of extensive totalities. Problematic Ideas are thus not concepts in Frege's sense of the term, for whom 'it must be determinate for every object whether it falls under a concept or not; a concept word which does not meet this requirement

---

6. At this point one can see how Hegel picks up where Kant leaves off. Hegel could well argue that he has embraced the Absolute that Kant does not embrace. Whereas Kant simply posits an absolute totality as a regulative ideal, an ideal that assists and guides the process of transforming appearances into the objects of possible experience, Hegel argues for an absolute that is the condition of real experience rather than possible experience (I want to thank Nathan Widder for raising this point). A discussion of Hegel, however, would take us too far afield of the concerns of this book. Stated simply, the reason for focusing on Kant here is precisely in order to highlight the key distinction between the conditions and the conditioned, or the Leibnizian difference between a differential unconscious and the determinate, extensive realities this unconscious makes possible. As Henry Somers-Hall (2022) has shown, Hegel's embrace of the absolute continues to adhere to the model of judgment that presupposes a relation between a subject and an object, whereas the Kantian model of problematic Ideas, as I am developing it, accounts for the possibility of judgment itself.

on its *Bedeutung* [reference] is *bedeutungslos* [meaningless]' (Frege 1997, 178). Frege's claim that concepts need to have sharp boundaries if they are going to be significant has been the subject of much discussion, especially among those who defend various forms of vagueness (see, for example, Williamson 1996, 37–46). What is presupposed throughout this debate is precisely Kant's assumption that what is important to thought is the role concepts play as extensive totalities which involve a relationship between a whole and the parts that fall under this whole. With theories of vagueness, likewise, the general strategy is to work within the parameters of concepts as extensive totalities. Kant, however, as suggested above, gestures towards an alternative understanding of thought as a process whereby the whole is an intensive totality, and this totality cannot be thought if thought is taken to be thought in terms of Fregean concepts. To state this point differently, what Kant gestures towards, although he does not venture down this path, is an understanding of thought as a dynamic relationship without parts, a process that is inseparable from the elements it makes possible but is nonetheless irreducible to them and is not to be confused with the thoughts it makes possible.

10. Kant and Problematic Ideas

To return to an earlier example (§9.10), problematic Ideas are what is at work in Turner's paintings, where, 'from the moment there is genius, there is something that belongs to no school, no period, something that achieves a breakthrough – art as a process without goal, but that attains completion as such' (Deleuze and Guattari 1977, 370). As 'a process without goal' a problematic Idea 'attains completion' only insofar as it is an intensive completion without extensive, determinate parts. It is in this way that problematic Ideas are the third or mixture Plato looks towards in order to avoid rushing off into either the one or the many. To restate this point yet again, but in the Leibnizian terms developed earlier, problematic Ideas are the differential unconscious, the intensive reality that is not to be confused with the determinate elements and extensive totalities that it conditions; in other words, the problematic Idea is the reality that is expressed in determinate, actual experiences, in what Kant calls possible experience, including the Fregean concepts and extensive totalities that come with this experience, but problematic Ideas remain irreducible to these experiences. In fact, whereas the distinctive parts (representations) are what is real for Kant, and the extensive totality of the whole is an ideal we are to think of *as if* it were real, problematic Ideas, as argued for here, are the intensive, processual reality that is expressed in determinate elements and totalities, including the moments, the absolute unities, that were Kant's starting point. By making these determinate elements the realities (many/plurality/infinite) upon which totalities (One) depend, Kant has indeed rushed to the one and the many, bypassing the method of mixture, and he has also in effect committed, *avant la lettre*, what Whitehead identified as the fallacy of misplaced concreteness. Rather than accounting for the determinate and extensive – that is, the conditioned – in terms of an intensive, processual totality that is the condition it presupposes, Kant accounts for totality itself as that which is conditioned by the determinate, extensive parts that are synthesised by means of the pure concepts of the understanding. To put it in Kant's own terms, he has succumbed to a version of his transcendental illusion, which he claims is what happens when we 'take the subjective necessity of a connection of our concepts, which is to the advantage of the understanding, for an objective necessity in the determination of things in themselves' (Kant 1965, 288, A297/B353). In other words, the categories, as pure concepts of the understanding, are the conditions necessary for the possibility of objectively valid experience, but what is necessary for an objectively valid experience is not to be confused with the nature of objective reality in itself, or the things as they are in themselves. Since we lack a divine understanding, we simply cannot know what the nature of things in themselves might be. The same is the case with respect to the relationship between problematic Ideas as dynamic, intensive realities and the determinate elements and extensive totalities problematic Ideas makes possible; we are not to confuse what is necessary for the possibility of determinate, extensive totalities with determinate, extensive totalities themselves.

A version of the propensity to succumb to this version of Kant's transcendental illusion will become a dominant theme in *TCE*, where we will discuss the political and social implications of succumbing to what we will call the illusion of solutions without problems. For now, however, let us return to Plato's *Philebus* and explain further our conception of problematic Ideas in light of more recent work in analytic philosophy on universals and mereology (that is, the relationship of parts to wholes), as found in the work of D.M. Armstrong and David Lewis. This will allow us both to show how problematic Ideas help us to address the problem of one and many (from §4) and to detail how problematic Ideas are intensive and inseparable parts, but not extensive, determinate and thus separable parts of the extensive and determinate realities they make possible.

§11 Armstrong and Lewis on the Problem of One and Many

1. Kant's Transcendental Illusion

In the previous section we began with Kant's use of the term Idea. As he himself admitted, he borrowed the term from Plato because an Idea for Kant, as for Plato, is not to be confused with any concrete, determinate particulars, with anything given in experience. As Kant further elaborated upon this point, an Idea comes to be understood as a problem without a solution. This became most clear in Kant's efforts to address the antinomies.

It was in our discussion of the antinomies that our focus shifted to the problematic nature of the Idea, or what we have called the problematic Idea. In short, Kant was concerned with the conditions of possible experience, which meant, as we saw, that possible experiences are identified with already actualised experiences, and hence with the determinate and extensive nature of an actualised, objective experience. With the shift of focus to problematic Ideas, by contrast, we were concerned, following Deleuze, with the conditions of real experience, by which was meant the intensive, differential (following Leibniz) conditions for an experience that does not resemble that which conditions it. Stating this point differently and in reference to Kant's transcendental illusion, which consisted of confusing the conditioned with the conditions, we must not succumb to the illusion of assuming that the conditions for experience resemble conditioned experience. This discussion of Kant's transcendental illusion led us, finally, to contrasting understandings of totality. For Kant, totality is an ideal, an infinite synthesis that only a divine understanding could perform, and as a result we are to understand experience and the pursuit of knowledge *as if* the absolute totality were real and that which guides and conditions our enquiry. From the perspective of problematic Ideas, by contrast, the totality is an intensive, processual whole, a differential unconscious (to use our Leibnizian terminology), that is, as Deleuze and Guattari put it, 'a process without goal, but that attains completion as such' (1977, 370). From this perspective, it is the determinate, extensive totalities and unities that are conditioned by this processual completion and whole that then come to be understood *as if* they were unconditioned realities.

At this point a critic may, with good reason, accuse us of falling into a version of the transcendental illusion we have just charged Kant with. In particular, are we not understanding the relationship between the processual whole, the problematic Idea and the differential elements that come to constitute this whole – the Leibnizian differential unconscious – in a manner equivalent to Kant's understanding of the relationship between an extensive totality – the Absolute, infinite totality – and its parts, whereby the parts come to form or constitute the whole? It was Kant's argument for the synthesis of totalities from the determinate, extensive moments (the absolute unities as Kant put it) that led us to charge him with succumbing to the transcendental illusion. Problematic Ideas, I have also argued, are inseparable from the extensive, determinate elements they make possible, even though they are not to be confused with them, and it was precisely for this reason that Deleuze, following both Kant and Plato, will also use the term Idea for the nature of problems. But what is the relationship between these determinate, extensive elements and problematic Ideas, the differential unconscious, and how are we to avoid the charge of succumbing to the transcendental illusion?

2. Frege and the Third Man Argument

To begin we can return to where we started – with the TMA. We have now added Frege's understanding of concepts to the mix. For Frege, we saw, it must be clearly determinate whether something does or does not fall under a concept word, otherwise the concept word is *bedeutungslos*. A concept word for Frege thus serves a function, a propositional function as it will come to be called, in that it takes a particular, determinate object as an argument to be substituted for a variable – such as in the function 'x is a problem', where x is the variable and 'is a problem' the concept word, or unsaturated predicate as Frege will understand it; a concept word that is not *bedeutungslos* will result in a proposition that is either true or false depending on the object that is substituted for the variable. If the argument (object) substituted for the variable is indeed a problem, then the proposition is true, if not it is false. But how do we know whether an object falls under the predicate or concept word, or whether that which we encounter in an experience is properly captured by a predicate? If an Idea (or Form) is used to answer this question, then there is the potential, as we saw, to unleash the infinite regress of the TMA, and with this regress we fail to account for whether or not a predicate is applied properly. For instance, if in an art gallery I claim that a particular painting is beautiful, while the one next to it is not, then on Frege's account I am claiming that the one painting falls under the concept beauty while the other does not. Frege recognises that we may be mistaken in our concepts, or mistakenly include an object under a concept that it does not belong to. Ideally, however, as science progresses, Frege believes we will become increasingly more accurate in our ability to place things under concepts. But how do we do this, whether we are mistaken or not? If it involves a comparison between an attribute of the concept or Idea (Form) and an attribute of the particular, then we bring in the possibility that there is a third Idea that enables us to see both the concept and the particular object as sharing the same attribute, a third Idea that must also share this same attribute, and with this move we have opened up the Third Man regress.

3. Armstrong on Universals

One way to avoid the consequences of the TMA, and a common strategy among contemporary analytic metaphysicians, is to understand predicates (Fregean concepts) as immanent universals that are non-spatiotemporal parts of the particulars that instantiate them. D.M. Armstrong's approach is the most influential of these attempts to understand predicates as immanent universals. For Armstrong, universals account for why many different particulars are all seen as being of the same type, with this sameness of type being, as David Lewis summarises Armstrong's position, a basic 'Moorean fact: one of the many facts which even philosophers should not deny, whatever philosophical account or analysis they give of such facts' (Lewis 1983, 351). By arguing that universals constitute a non-spatiotemporal part of the particulars that instantiate them, Armstrong avoids the Third Man regress for there is no relationship between the universal and the particular; rather, the universal simply constitutes part of the brute, Moorean fact that a particular is a particular of a certain type. On the debate between nominalists and realists, therefore, Armstrong sides with the realists, but his realism, as Lewis points out, 'is a non-relational Realism: he declines, with good reason, to postulate a dyadic universal of instantiation to bind particulars to their universals' (Lewis 1983, 354). The 'good reason', again, is that embracing a non-relational Realism allows Armstrong to avoid the Third Man regress by avoiding the relation between a universal and its particular. Various particulars may thus instantiate a certain universal, but the dyadic relation between universal and particular that launches the regress is halted because universals are not distinct and separable from the particulars that instantiate them. Armstrong can therefore be seen to embrace a non-extensional understanding of composition: universals, as Armstrong understands them, are non-mereological, non-spatiotemporal parts of the particulars that exemplify them. Given the traditional philosophical understanding of extension as being that which occupies space, and a space that can be subdivided into yet smaller extensional parts, Armstrong endorses the contrasting, non-extensional, non-mereological view whereby wholes – facts and states of affairs for Armstrong – may be composed of parts, but parts that cannot be divided off or separated from the wholes they are a part of.

Armstrong's approach does provide us with an answer to the question with which we began this section – namely, how do we know whether an object falls under a predicate or not? For Armstrong universals provide us with the answer. We are applying a predicate correctly if the sameness of type is seen, as a Moorean fact, to be recurring throughout a series of particulars. If several penguins waddle past a camera stationed at a remote research location, the (Moorean) fact that these penguins are all seen as instances of the same type – whether the name we give for this type be penguin or not – is evidence that these objects or particulars do indeed all fall under the same predicate. Lewis recognises that Armstrong's theory of universals does indeed provide an account of the Moorean fact regarding the sameness of type one sees as being shared among a number of particulars, but he adds that there are two other alternative approaches to consider: one is to deny that such Moorean facts exist, despite Armstrong's pleas to the contrary; the other is simply to accept sameness of type as a primitive, as something not needing an account by way of universals (see Lewis 1983, 352). Lewis adopts the latter approach in what he calls an 'adequate Nominalism'. In the spirit of the traditional debate between nominalists and realists, Lewis adopts the nominalist position, in contrast to Armstrong's realist position, and thus argues that we do not need to add an extra entity to our ontology – namely, universals – in order to understand and account for how and why we categorise and conceptualise particulars in the way that we do. For Lewis an adequate nominalism will do the job, and what makes it adequate is that it accepts as a primitive the distinction between natural and unnatural properties, with natural properties doing the work of Armstrong's universals while avoiding the need for the ontological furniture of universals. Before exploring Lewis's nominalism, let us first see why he did not adopt the other options, such as Armstrong's.

4. Lewis on Universals and Natural Properties

In *On the Plurality of Worlds*, Lewis further develops the arguments begun in his 'New Work for a Theory of Universals' (1983). After admitting that he would 'willingly accept the distinction [between natural and unnatural properties] as primitive' if it were the only option available, he recognises that there are 'two attractive alternatives' (Lewis 1986a, 63). The first alternative is Armstrong's theory of universals, and the second is the theory of tropes as found in D.C. Williams' work (see Williams 1953a and b). Lewis claims to be 'undecided' with respect to the merits of these two theories (Lewis 1986a, 64). If we take a unit of positive charge, or what Lewis would call a 'perfectly natural property', then what could be understood to be present is an immanent universal in that 'wherever there is a charged particle, there the universal of charge, or else one of the tropes of charge [is present]'. This is not all that is present, however – 'For instance', Lewis notes, 'there will be a universal or trope of mass' (64). The difference between the theory of universals and the theory of tropes becomes evident when you consider two particles with positive charge. On Armstrong's theory, each particle contains the universal as a non-spatiotemporal part, and each particle contains the same universal, or as Lewis puts it, 'the same universal recurs; it is multiply located; it is wholly present in both particles, a shared common part whereby the two particles overlap'. According to the theory of tropes, there is no multiply located part but rather the 'charge-trope of one particle and the charge-trope of another particle are duplicate tropes' (64).

It is at this point that we can begin to see the difficulties Lewis has with Armstrong's theory. If we have two particles of positive charge which are both composed, in part, of the universals mass and charge, and perhaps other universals they share as well, then we need to account for the fact that the particles are different. As Lewis puts it, we need 'something else, something non-recurrent, that gives it [the particle] its particularity' (1986a, 65), and hence gives us the fact that we have two distinct particles. This is not an insurmountable problem for Armstrong, and it is one he addresses (see Armstrong 1980b and c), but it doesn't even arise for nominalists such as Lewis, for whom there are nothing but particulars and hence no need to account for the particularity of a given particle. This problem also doesn't arise for the proponent of tropes, for a second particle will not have the same tropes as the first but will have duplicate tropes. As Lewis puts it, 'It is an advantage of tropes over universals that we need no special thing to confer particularity – that is, non-recurrence – since the tropes are particular already' (1986a, 65). Lewis acknowledges that universals and tropes are both 'fine candidates for the role of properties', and yet he finds them both inadequate to satisfy the desire to account for 'uninstantiated properties alien to this world', what Lewis will call *possibilia*. The reason for this is rather straightforward – 'Universals and tropes are present in their instances, and so must have instances if they are to be present at all' (66). The motivation for Lewis's desire to offer a theory that allows for uninstantiated properties is to provide a Humean framework for thinking about worlds other than the actual world. To do this, Lewis proposes the principle of plenitude, meaning thereby that the various ways one might imagine the world to be are ways in which other possible worlds are. With this principle we have a statement of the modal realism Lewis is famous for (or notorious depending on your perspective). The reason Lewis accepts modal realism and its principle of plenitude is that it does not simply tie properties to the actual world, and so does not embrace a necessary connection between properties, such as the property of being bread connected to the property of being nourishing (from Hume 2005, 113-14, 4.16). Lewis, in short, embraces Hume's critique of necessary connections and allows for properties and connections that are alien to this world. Lewis is explicit on this point, and echoing Hume argues that 'Episodes of bread-eating are possible because actual; as are episodes of starvation ... It is no surprise that my principle prohibits strictly necessary connections between distinct existences' (1986a, 91). In accounting for his Humean modal realism and providing an adequate justification of *possibilia*, Lewis finds tropes and universals insufficient to the task and calls instead upon natural properties.

Another reason for Lewis's turn to natural properties is that universals are only truly effective and explanatory when they are sparse. As he puts it,

> universals or sets of duplicate tropes would be fine for the role of sparse properties, but the sparse properties are not enough. There may be no urgent need to quantify over all of the very abundant and very gruesome properties that modal realism has on offer as sets of *possibilia*. But certainly we want to go well beyond the perfectly natural properties. (Lewis 1986a, 66).

In other words, universals and tropes are effective in providing for the basic sameness of types that become integral to scientific accounts of the world. But surely, Lewis thinks, there are many more relevant properties than these. As an example of such a relevant property, Lewis offers us the bed that 'George Washington slept in'. It would be 'quite unbelievable', Lewis argues, to think that 'this property [of being the bed George Washington slept in] corresponds to some special non-spatiotemporal part of the bed!' With examples such as this, Lewis concludes that 'it is just absurd to think that a thing has non-spatiotemporal parts for all its countless abundant properties!' (1986a, 67). Lewis also argues that we need to move towards an acceptance of properties rather than universals and tropes if we are to 'provide an adequate supply of semantic values for linguistic expressions' (Lewis 1983, 348). In sentences such as 'red is a colour' or 'humility is a virtue', Lewis doubts there are any universals such as humility or the determinable red (for more on determinables, see §12). From a semantic point of view, there are many determinate shades of red that satisfy the determinable red and serve to make a variety of sentences true – i.e., the sentences 'this cherry red car is red', 'this scarlet scarf is red', and 'this crimson sweater is red' are each true if the car is cherry red, the scarf scarlet and the sweater crimson. Universals, by contrast, and on Lewis's reading of Armstrong's position, are non-spatiotemporal parts of *actual instances*, and thus of actually determinate shades – cherry red, scarlet and crimson – whereas determinables consist of sets of *possible instances* which may satisfy the determinable (the same applies to humility taken as a determinable). Lewis's understanding of properties as *possibilia*, and of natural properties as sets of *possibilia*, thus not only provides, in his view, a better account of the semantics of our sentences, but also allows, with the distinction between natural and unnatural properties, for a recognition of the abundance of properties that go beyond the perfectly natural. Lewis's theory of natural properties will echo, in important ways, the arguments we have made with respect to the nature of problematic Ideas, and so it is to Lewis's theory that we now turn.

The first thing to note is that for Lewis a property is importantly different from a universal. As Lewis summarises the key differences: a universal is one of 'those entities ... that mostly conform to Armstrong's account' (Lewis 1983, 344); namely, entities that recur in the many particular instances of which they are a non-spatiotemporal part. A property, by contrast, is for Lewis a class, and thus 'To have a property is to be a member of the class'; for example, 'the property of being a donkey ... is the class of all the donkeys'. This class of donkeys, moreover, is not restricted to actual donkeys, to the donkeys that instantiate universals, but includes these donkeys plus 'all the unactualized, otherworldly donkeys'. Secondly, for Lewis, a universal, as Armstrong argues, 'is supposed to be wholly present wherever it is instantiated' (Lewis 1983, 344). Wherever there is a charged particle, the universal of charge is wholly present in this particle as a non-spatiotemporal part, along with the universal of mass and perhaps other universals as well. If a universal were to be uninstantiated, Lewis argues, we would then need a 'second-order universal of universalhood with the instantiated ones ... and [this] leads straightaway to a Third Man regress' (Lewis 1986b, 45). A property, by contrast, 'is spread around', meaning if there is a property present in a particular then this property is only partly present in it. For instance, the 'property of being a donkey', to use Lewis's example, is only 'partly present wherever there is a donkey', not wholly present, and thus 'it is closer to the truth', Lewis argues, 'to say that the donkey is part of the property' rather than that the property is part of the donkey in the manner of a universal (1983, 344–5). To state this differently, if an animal has the property of being a donkey, then it is a member of the class of donkeys rather than the class or property being a non-spatiotemporal part of the donkey. A final difference between universals and properties understood as classes is that universals commit us to locality whereas properties do not. For instance, as Lewis summarises Armstrong's account of 'lawful necessitation', if Ga is caused by Fa, this 'involves only a, the universals F and G that are present in a, and the second-order lawmaking universal that is present in turn in (or between) these two universals' (366). We have locality for universals, on Armstrong's theory, meaning that universals are wholly present in the particular instances (of a for example) that instantiate them. With properties, however, Lewis admits that 'locality is lost. For properties are classes with their membership spread around the worlds, and are not wholly present in a' (366). Lewis is nonetheless willing to sacrifice locality for he embraces a 'regularity theory of law' – that is, a Humean theory – which by its nature does away with locality.

5. Classes and Individuals

We will return to the theme of locality below, but first it is important to clarify the distinction between classes and individuals that is at work in Lewis's theory of natural properties, as this will have important consequences for understanding the relationship between part and whole. In *Parts of Classes* (1991), Lewis is quite clear that classes have members, not individuals, and individuals do not have members. For example, the class of cats, he claims, 'has all and only cats as members'. The cats themselves have parts – whiskers, cells, quarks, etc. – which are parts of the members of the class of cats, but these parts 'are not themselves members of it [the class of cats]' (Lewis 1991, 2). Lewis makes this distinction in order to maintain an analogous relationship between sub-classes to classes and parts to wholes. In both cases, transitivity applies – for instance, a cell that is part of a whisker that is part of a cat is a cell that is part of a cat; analogously a cat that is a member of the class of cats – a class that is a subset of the class of mammals, which in turn is a subset of the class of vertebrate animals – is a cat that is a member of the class of vertebrate animals. The analogy breaks down, however, precisely at the point when we consider the parts of individuals, individuals that are members of a class. The tail of a cat is a part of a cat, but a cat tail is not a mammal. A member of a class, therefore, is to be considered a determinate, homogeneous whole and unity, and thus the class of cats has 'all and only cats as members'. Individuals, by contrast, 'are members, but do not themselves have members' (4), and, as Lewis adds a few pages later, 'they're made of various smaller individuals, and nothing else' (9). These smaller individuals may become members of other classes, the class of cat parts, etc., but it is the individual as a determinate unity that is a member of a class, not the many sub-individuals and parts of the individual. This distinction between classes and individuals reveals a core assumption at work in Lewis's philosophy (and in Armstrong's too, as we will see), which is what I will call the primacy of the determinate. In short, what is presupposed as the unquestioned given, the point where one's spade is turned, is that reality is fundamentally determinate, and it is this determinate reality that forms the basis for the theories and philosophies that represent this reality. It is precisely this primacy of the determinate that the arguments for problematic Ideas seek to undermine.

6. The Trouble with Singletons

We can see the importance of the determinate for Lewis in his account of singletons. A singleton, defined simply, is a unit class, a class with a single member. In my house, we have two cats, Mila and Charlie. Although Mila and Charlie are each individuals, and individuals with their many parts – tail, whiskers, etc. – they are also each members of a class that has only themselves as a member. For Mila there is thus the singleton or unit class that has only Mila as a member, and for Charlie there is the singleton or unit class that has only Charlie as a member. If we take the set that includes both Charlie and Mila, and their singletons, then there is a singleton for that set, with the only member being the set of Mila, Charlie and their singletons. As Lewis states this point, 'every individual has a singleton, and so does every set. The only things that lack singletons are the proper classes – classes that are not members of anything, and a fortiori not members of the singleton' (Lewis 1991, 12). Moreover, we can begin with any individual and generate an infinite number of singletons – for example, we can begin with Mila and the singleton of Mila, the unit class distinct from Mila the individual; from there we get the singleton of the set that includes Mila the individual and Mila's singleton, and then the singleton of the singleton of Mila and Mila's singleton, and so on ad infinitum. This infinite series of singletons is sufficient, Lewis argues, to provide us with 'enough modelling clay to make the whole of mathematics' (12), in a manner he acknowledges mirrors the set-theoretic foundations of mathematics (see 109–10) in that his discussion of singletons parallels the set-theoretic arguments for the successor function (see Halmos 1974, 43–4), and hence for numbers and the foundations of mathematics. Lewis admits, however, that singletons are a mystery and a problem, but it is one he is willing to accept since we get mathematics as a result. Lewis is quite forthright on this point:

> Set theory is not innocent. Its trouble has nothing to do with gathering many into one. Instead, its trouble is that when we have one thing, then

somehow we have another wholly distinct thing, the singleton. And another, and another ... ad infinitum. But that's the price for mathematical power. Pay it. (Lewis 1991, 87).

The trouble with set theory, in short, is that the second we accept the possibility of a unit class that is distinct from an already determinate and distinct individual, we find ourselves upon an infinite regress, and a regress not unlike the Third Man regress, with the difference being that this is a regress of determinate individuals – singletons – rather than of universals. From Lewis's perspective, however, this regress is acceptable, for without it we would not have what we need for mathematics. However, since we should not base our mathematics on a single individual, on the contingent existence of my cat Mila for instance, Lewis, in what is probably the most original move of his book *Parts of Classes*, bases the regress on the null set, which is taken to be 'the fusion of all individuals' (1991, 14). For Lewis this is an intuitively plausible place to begin since, as he puts it, our inclination is to think of the null set as being in 'no place in particular', and thus as not linked to being or not being any individual in particular. For this reason, Lewis further clarifies his understanding of the null set by claiming that it is 'the fusion of all things that do not overlap the fusion of all singletons, which is to say that it is the mereological difference. Reality minus that fusion. It is what's left of Reality after all the singletons are removed' (17). If Reality is simply the mereological fusion of all singletons, including all actual as well as possible, otherworldly singletons (which is how Lewis understands Reality), then the null set is what we have when we have no singletons, in other words it is a set with no members. With this null set in hand, a set clearly not dependent upon the contingent existence of any particular individual, we can turn to the singleton of this set, and then to the singleton of this singleton and the null set, and so on *ad infinitum* until we have what we need for mathematics. This is a regress Lewis can live with.

7. Lewis and Regresses

Whereas Lewis is able to take the regress of relations between singletons and turn it into the 'modelling clay to make the whole of mathematics' (1991, 12), Armstrong seeks to avoid the regress of relations. In fact, Lewis claims that Armstrong repeatedly requires of a theory that there 'be no unanalyzed predication'; that is, the theory needs to avoid becoming 'victim to the "relation regress" [whereby] in the course of analyzing other predications the theory has resort to a new predicate that cannot, on pain of circularity, be analyzed along with rest' (Lewis 1983, 353). With Plato's theory of Forms, as we saw (see §5), the relationship between the Forms and the particulars that participate in them cannot be understood unless we have a third Form that accounts for the relationship between the Form and the particular. As Lewis puts it, with 'Transcendent, Platonic Realism ... predications of participation evade analysis' (353), for once one does an analysis of the predications of participation one immediately initiates the regress. 'Time and again', Lewis argues, one theory after another fails to live up to the requirement that it avoid relying upon an unanalysed predication, but the desire to do 'away with all unanalyzed predication is', Lewis claims, 'an unattainable aim, and so an unreasonable aim', and moreover it is one that Armstrong himself fails to satisfy (353).

To clarify Lewis's point, we can return to Armstrong and his defence of immanent universals, where he bites the bullet and claims 'we must just stick with this proposition: different particulars may have the same property ... Different particulars may be (wholly or partially) identical in nature. Such identity in nature is literally inexplicable, in the sense that it cannot be further explained' (Armstrong 1980b 108–9). What we have, in short, is the brute, Moorean fact regarding sameness of type we referred to above. This Moorean fact, however, avoids the requirement of not having an unanalysed predication for it is a fact that simply cannot be analysed – it is 'literally inexplicable'. For Lewis, by contrast, we need not rely upon an immanent universal whereby two particulars, 'a and b' for instance, 'have the same property (are of the same type), F-ness' (Lewis 1983, 354). For Lewis, simply stating 'a is F; b is F is analysis enough, once we give over the aim of doing without primitive predication' (355). In other words, a and b are both members of the class F, both have property F, but F is nothing over and above a and b. Rather, for Lewis the property is simply the mereological fusion of all the individuals that are F, just as the class of cats 'has all and only cats as members' (1991, 2), with class being 'nothing over and above the cats that compose it ... [whereby] If you draw up an inventory of Reality according to our scheme of things, it would be double counting to list the cats and then also list their fusion' (81). In other words, it would be needless double counting to list the a that is F, the b that is F, and then list the F-ness or type which is simply the fusion of all things that are F. F is nothing over and above the class of individuals that are F.

8. Natural Properties and Humean Supervenience

But have we answered the question concerning how we know whether or not we have correctly applied a predicate to a particular? If we say that 'a is F' and 'b is F', how do we know whether or not a and b are really F and not a member of some other class and thus more accurately referred to by another predicate? For Armstrong, since universals are sparse and ultimately present themselves as being inexplicably identical to the particulars of which they are the non-spatiotemporal part, this is not a particularly pressing question. For Lewis, however, properties are abundant, and there is a plenitude of properties not only for the way the world actually is but also for all the possible worlds and the ways in which they are. Lewis is aware of the problems this brings:

> Because properties are so abundant, they are undiscriminating. Any two things share infinitely many properties, and fail to share infinitely many others. That is so whether the two things are perfect duplicates or utterly dissimilar. Thus properties do nothing to capture facts of resemblance. That is work more suited to the sparse universals. (Lewis 1983, 346)

Whereas sparse universals can provide a basis for explaining how one applies, and applies correctly, a predicate to a particular thing, the abundance of properties Lewis calls for makes the task of correctly applying predicates, or of even knowing which predicates to apply, a nearly impossible venture. Fortunately for Lewis, we have 'not only the countless throng of all properties, but also an élite minority of special properties', special properties he calls 'natural properties' (346). Lewis takes the distinction between natural and non-natural properties, or what he calls unnatural properties, to be a primitive distinction. On this basis, a nominalist such as himself could do away with universals and could instead

> draw primitive distinctions among particulars. Most simply, a Nominalist could take it as a primitive fact that some classes of things are perfectly natural properties; others are less-than-perfectly natural to various degrees; and most are not at all natural. Such a Nominalist takes 'natural' as a primitive predicate, and offers no analysis of what he means in predicating it of classes. (1983, 347).

To this assumption that there are natural properties, Lewis adds his theory of Humean supervenience, which says that when one thing supervenes on another then 'there can be no difference in respect of so-and-so without difference in respect of such-and-such' (Lewis 1983, 358). Lewis argues that 'much of my work could be seen in hindsight as a campaign on behalf of "Humean Supervenience": the thesis that the whole truth about a world like ours supervenes on the spatiotemporal distribution of local qualities' (Lewis 1994, 473). As he states the thesis in *On the Plurality of Worlds*: 'The world has its laws of nature, its chances and causal relationships; and yet – perhaps! – all there is to the world is its point-by-point distribution of local qualitative character' (Lewis 1986a, 14). One way of characterising Lewis's work, therefore, is as an ongoing effort to remove the hesitation of the 'perhaps!' and replace it with a 'likely!' or 'yes, indeed!'

From the perspective of Humean supervenience, natural properties are the privileged or elite classes of properties that supervene on the 'spatiotemporal distribution of local qualities' in a way that will 'carve [nature] at the joints' (Lewis 1986a, 60, using Plato's famous expression from *Phaedrus* 265d-e). The natural properties are nothing over and above the local qualities they supervene upon, and thus there can be no change in the nature and distribution of the local points and qualities themselves without there also being a change in the properties that supervene upon them. The task of science, moreover, is to discover and represent these privileged classes, the natural properties, and this is indeed what Lewis argues: 'physics discovers properties. And not just any properties – natural properties' (Lewis 1983, 365). For both Lewis and Armstrong, therefore, what is primary is the determinate nature of reality, and it is this reality which accounts for our ability to apply predicates correctly to the things of the world. For Armstrong it is the determinate nature of universals themselves that accounts for the Moorean fact that we simply see, inexplicably, multiple particulars as all being of the same type. For Lewis it is the distribution of determinate, local matters and qualities that accounts for the natural properties that supervene upon and represent these local matters.

9. Primacy of the Determinate

By grounding their theories in the primacy of the determinate both Armstrong and Lewis presuppose that which the nature of the problematic Idea helps us to understand – namely, the conditions for the possibility of the determinate itself. It is for this reason that we have turned to Plato's theory of mixture as found in the *Philebus*. Rather than thinking of properties as classes which supervene on local matters – 'point-sized bits of matter or … local fields that are located there' (Lewis 1986a, 14); 'point-sized things and spacetime points' (Lewis 1994, 474) – or as determinate universals which recur as a non-spatiotemporal part of many determinate particulars, we have been following Plato's call to avoid 'mak[ing] the one and the many too quickly or too slowly, in haphazard fashion … [and] disregard[ing] all that lies between them' (*Philebus* 17a). For us this path between the one and the many has entailed setting forth a theory of problematic Ideas as multiplicities, as processual wholes that are neither extensive totalities nor determinate parts or elements which come to compose, through supervenience for instance, a larger whole or totality. Both Armstrong and Lewis remain committed to the primacy of the determinate, though Armstrong embraces, whereas Lewis does not, a non-extensional form of composition in that the immanent universals he argues for are non-spatiotemporal parts of particulars from which they cannot be separated. Problematic Ideas will also entail non-extensional composition, as we will see shortly, and this follows from carrying through on Plato's call to find the middle path between the one and the many.

10. *Philebus* and Lewis

Stephanie Gibbons and Cathy Legg have also heeded Plato's advice and in doing so have been led to part ways with Lewis's theory of Humean supervenience. Of particular interest to them is the manner in which Plato addresses the problem of how to establish the proper measure of pleasure and wisdom in order to attain virtue. As Plato puts it, and as discussed earlier (§5.7), 'we must seek the good, not in the unmixed but in the mixed life' (*Philebus* 61b), meaning a life where wisdom and pleasure are properly proportioned. Gibbons and Legg argue that the mixed life will bring wisdom and pleasure together into a new reality, the virtuous life, without changing the nature of either wisdom or pleasure. What 'Socrates suggests', they claim, is 'that we lack an adequate account of how an object can be sufficiently united that it comprises a genuine unity, while simultaneously being internally complex' (Gibbons and Legg 2013, 126). Gibbons and Legg refer to this as the 'combination problem', and another way of stating it is to ask 'How is it possible that by combining A [wisdom] and B [pleasure] one obtains something emergent, C [virtue], and yet A and B are *still present*?' (133). By only allowing for the Humean supervenience of mereological sums over local matters, Lewis does not allow for an emergent property that is other than the elements that give rise to this property. Natural properties, as we saw, are nothing over and above the local matters that they supervene upon. For this reason, Gibbons and Legg argue that 'Lewis' account falls at this problem [i.e., the combination problem], by failing to do justice to there being a C to speak of. (His mereological approach only allows the many, and gives no convincing account of a one)' (133). For Gibbons and Legg, however, things get even worse for Lewis's account when we see that for Plato we not only have virtue as an emergent property when wisdom and pleasure are properly mixed, a mixture that maintains the integrity of wisdom and pleasure; we also have improper mixtures which alter the elements being mixed and in turn alter the emergent properties this improper mixture gives rise to. To support this argument, Gibbons and Legg turn to the final pages of the *Philebus*:

> ... any kind of mixture that does not in some way or other possess measure or the nature of proportion will necessarily corrupt its ingredients and most of all itself. For there would be no blending in such cases at all but really an uncontrolled medley, the ruin of whatever happens to be contained in it. (*Philebus* 64d9-e3, cited in Gibbons and Legg 2013, 134).

Summarising the implications of this passage for Lewis's theory of Humean supervenience, Gibbons and Legg claim that 'The message here is that the nature of the combination can change everything in a mixture, in a way which is not at all like Lego, where one can rearrange the parts in all kinds of ways but they themselves remain the same' (134). The reference to Lego alludes to their argument that Lewis presupposes the already settled and determinate nature of reality – the local matters and qualities – upon which natural properties supervene. As they read Lewis, the nature of reality is simply an absolute plenitude of local matters and qualities, matters that do not change but rather enter into varied combinations and re-combinations over which natural properties may or may not supervene. What Gibbons and Legg argue, in effect, is that there is a reciprocal determination between the elements and the emergent properties these elements make possible. The elements do not remain unchanged during their mixing but can become changed if mixed poorly. It is only when one is virtuous, or when one is a musician, a grammarian, etc., as we saw earlier (see §5.7), that one hits the sweet spot in the mixture and has a taste for the relevant relations of the mixture, for what maintains the integrity and identity of the mixed elements, such as wisdom and pleasure, sound and beauty, etc. Stating this point in an Aristotelian manner, while there may only be a limited number of ways to get things right – to achieve virtue and excellence and thereby maintain the integrity of the ingredients of the mixed life – there are unlimited ways to mix the elements improperly, and hence mix them such that the mixture will in turn reciprocally alter and 'corrupt its ingredients'.

11. Problematic Ideas as Non-Mereological Parts of the Determinate

Returning to our response to Plato's call to adopt the method of mixture, we have also argued (see §8.3) that the elements that come to constitute the nature of problematic Ideas are reciprocally determined. These elements are precisely the differential elements – the Leibnizian differential unconscious – that involve reciprocal differentiations to infinity and become, at the limit, the determinate, differenciated elements that can then be taken up by a theory that supervenes upon such elements. It is for this reason as well that we adopted Plato's own terminology of the infinite and limits (*apeiron* and *peras* [πέρας]). The differential unconscious is the infinite series of differential elements, the infinite series that becomes, at the limit, a determinate element. We can thus see that problematic Ideas are indeed universals, in Plato's, Kant's and Armstrong's sense of the term, in that they are not to be confused with the spatiotemporal entities with which they come to be identified. To this extent, Armstrong was right to claim that a universal is a non-spatiotemporal part of a determinate instance. At the same time, however, Lewis is right to criticise Armstrong for strictly identifying universals with particulars that are already actualised and to argue instead for a principle of plenitude and for the classes that supervene in indefinite ways upon this plenitude. Problematic Ideas, however, are not classes that supervene upon an already determinate distribution of local matters; rather, they are non-spatiotemporal fields of non-extensional, non-mereological, pre-individual differentials that are the condition presupposed by the determinate elements which serve as solutions to the problematic nature of the Idea, solutions that do not do away with the nature of problematic Ideas. Problematic Ideas are the conditions that are not to be confused with the determinates they make possible, and thus they do not succumb to the transcendental illusion by accounting for the determinate in terms of something already determinate (as Lewis does). Stated differently, rather than accepting the primacy of the determinate, problematic Ideas entail the primacy of the determinable, if by determinable is meant a condition for the possibility of the determinate that is irreducible to the determinate. Understood in this way, what we are arguing for is the primacy of the determinable. This argument, in fact, has been made by Jessica Wilson (2012). To clarify our understanding of problematic Ideas, therefore, we will turn briefly to Wilson's arguments.

§12 Determinables and Determinates

1. The Problem of Emergence

To the arguments we have set forth in the previous section, David Lewis could respond by simply saying we have failed to justify our use of emergent properties to explain the phenomena under consideration. Lewis himself admits that emergent properties are not compatible with his approach, arguing that 'there might be emergent natural properties of more-than-point-sized things … It is not, alas, unintelligible that there might be suchlike rubbish … But if there is suchlike rubbish, say I, then there would have to be extra natural properties or relations that are altogether alien to this world' (Lewis 1986b, x). Lewis thus feels that emergent properties are unnecessary in accounting for and making sense of worlds like ours, much as he felt that we could do without universals. As was discussed in the previous section, if there were an A and B that remain the same while in turn giving rise to C as an emergent property, a C that is irreducible to A or B, then this would indeed violate Lewis's understanding of supervenience whereby a property (whether natural or not) is understood to be nothing over and above the class of local matters. If C is a new property irreducible to A and B, then C is not a property that is nothing over and above the elements A and B; it is something distinct from A and B. Lewis could argue that we have simply not properly sorted through all the properties involved in the process we are attempting to understand. The process whereby A and B give rise to C may well be capable of being understood in terms of laws that supervene upon local matters and hence be nothing over and above the patterned distribution of elements associated with A, B and C. The same is the case for the reciprocal determination of elements that occurs during improper mixtures that, as Plato argued and as Gibbons and Legg emphasised, corrupts elements if they are not properly mixed. This corruption of elements may in turn be amenable to a lawful explanation that likewise supervenes upon local matters that persist throughout the processes being explained. The key here is that an account in terms of determinate, local matters and lawful explanations that supervene upon these matters remains a possibility for Lewis; what needs to be shown is that an account based upon determinate elements is inadequate and something more is needed. Lewis could argue that we have failed to justify the inadequacy of his account and the adequacy of our move to emergent properties, or to the primacy of the determinable, as we referred to it.

2. Jessica Wilson and Fundamental Determinables

Jessica Wilson, most notably in her essay 'Fundamental Determinables' (2012), has set out to argue in defence of determinables, a defence that is at odds with much of the philosophical tradition that gives primacy to the determinate. The standard understanding of determinables is that determinates necessitate their corresponding determinables but the determinables do not necessitate their corresponding determinates. For instance, if I see a cerulean-coloured ball, I can say that I see a blue ball, and likewise if I see an indigo-coloured ball or an azure-coloured ball I may also simply say that I see a blue ball. If I tell someone I see a blue ball, however, they will not be led to any particular determinate shade of blue. These facts have led most philosophers to see determinates as metaphysically primary relative to determinables (see Prior 1949), as typified by Armstrong's claim that, 'because determinates entail the corresponding determinable, the determinable supervenes on the determinates, and so, apparently, is not something more than the determinates' (Armstrong 1997, 50; cited by Wilson 2012, 8). As Wilson notes, Armstrong's claim provides ammunition for many who think that we need simply the determinate to account for things such as causal powers. As Gillett and Rives argue, for instance, 'If determinable properties do not contribute causal powers to individuals, nor otherwise determine such powers, then it appears that they fail the Eleatic Principle and hence do not exist' (Gillett and Rives 2005, 487; cited by Wilson 2012, 6); the Eleatic Principle being the principle that requires an entity to have a causal power if it is to be considered an entity that exists.

Wilson will deploy what is known as the 'subset strategy' to defend the reality of determinables against the argument that they fail the Eleatic Principle (see Wilson 2011). On the surface, Wilson appears to agree with those who claim that determinables fail the Eleatic Principle, for she recognises that the powers of the determinable are nothing over and above the powers associated with the determinate. For example (from Wilson 2011), Sophie the pigeon has been trained to peck at determinate instances of the determinable red; when given a red patch, 'The patch's being red caused Sophie to peck ... But the patch's being scarlet also caused Sophie to peck – after all, to be scarlet just is to be red, in a specific way' (133). The power associated with pecking at a determinable, red, is nothing over and above the power of pecking at a determinate red, scarlet. 'Sophie's cousin Alice', however, Wilson continues, was 'trained to peck only at scarlet patches. Such cases suggest that the determinable type red has fewer powers than its determinate types' (134). The determinable type has fewer powers because it is nothing other than the power to peck at determinate instances of the determinable. Alice's ability to peck at scarlet patches does not bring with it an ability to peck at patches that entail the determinable red. Moreover, whereas Sophie may peck at red when presented with a scarlet patch, she may not peck at a red that shades ambiguously off into orange or purple, whereas another similarly trained pigeon may peck at this shade. The lesson to draw from this, for Wilson, is that a determinable type is to be understood as a 'multiply determinable' (134) subset of the determinate powers associated with the determinable. The subset of determinate powers associated with Sophie's pecking at red patches is different from the subset of the pigeon that pecks at the ambiguous shade, and yet they can each be said to be pecking at determinably red patches. A determinable thus does not contribute a new power separate from the determinate powers that are associated with it, but determinables are, for Wilson, 'associated with a *distinctive set of powers*, or *power profile*' (Wilson 2012, 7). There could be many ways in which a pigeon trained to peck at red patches may carry this out in determinate instances, and thus the determinable is for Wilson a subset of these determinate powers, or a subset of the determinate that is simply the way in which the powers of a determinable may be multiply realised. The conclusion Wilson draws from this subset strategy approach is that 'there is no need to "choose" which of the determinable and determinate are most appropriately deemed "the" cause; all that is required to accommodate the Eleatic principle is that determinables may be distinctively efficacious' (7).

3. Wilson and Deleuze

We can further clarify Wilson's arguments by turning to Deleuze's analysis of thirst from *Difference and Repetition*. Deleuze introduces the example of thirst in the context of discussing the importance of habit. Extending Hume's argument that '[r]epetition changes nothing in the object repeated, but does change something in the mind which contemplates it' (Deleuze 1994, 70), Deleuze reaffirms Hume's claim that habit, in what Deleuze calls a passive synthesis, is creative and brings about something new. For Hume this something new is the idea of necessary connexion that is brought about through repetition and habit (see Hume's *Treatise*, 1.3.14); for Deleuze likewise, in the context of thirst, it is the 'multiply realisable' subset of determinate behaviours associated with thirst. Thus, if we take the state of thirst, or the state whereby an animal actively seeks water as a means to satisfy its thirst, then according to Deleuze, but to state the point in Wilson's terms, the state of thirst is a multiply realisable determinable that is nothing over and above the determinate powers of the body that detects the absence and presence of water, a detection that causes the organism to seek water. The determinable habit that is thirst is only a subset of the determinate powers that thirsty organisms effect, for there are many determinate ways thirst may be realised in organisms, or thirst can be thought of as an emergent property. As Wilson argues, 'when a functionally characterized feature is multiply realizable', as the determinable state of thirst is, 'its *realizing types* will each have all the powers associated with the functional role, and more besides. Hence the powers of the *realized type* will be a proper subset of those of each of its *realizing types*' (Wilson 2011, 131). The determinable state of thirst is thus a *realising type* that is multiply *realisable*, or each of the many ways a realising type can be *realised* is each a proper subset of an indeterminate number of determinate, effectuating powers.

4. Uexküll's Ticks

We can clarify this point further by way of yet another well-known example – namely, Jakob von Uexküll's ticks. As Uexküll shows (in an example Deleuze also highlights), the tick has three determinate powers – it can detect light, which it uses to climb to perches from which to jump onto mammals; it can detect butyric acid which is emitted by all mammals; and it can detect the warmth associated with mammals which then prompts it to begin sucking blood from the mammal (see Uexküll 2010, 44–52). Each of these three determinate powers are to be understood, following Wilson, as the *realising types* or the determinables associated with the tick. As determinables they are multiply realisable in a proper subset of determinate behaviors since the actual circumstances of a tick, the type of mammal that passes by, etc., will constantly vary. This is also true of the determinate behaviours, for they too are habits that result from repetition, for example the repetition of butyric acid that becomes the determinable behaviour of jumping onto the source of the odour. This behaviour, as a determinable, is also multiply realisable in that the actual, determinate circumstances that prompt the behaviour will vary. The determinable type, or what, following Deleuze, Plato and Kant, I have referred to as Idea, is the result of a passive synthesis of elements (to use Deleuze's term for habit formation), such as the repetition of butyric acid, etc., that allows for the genesis of a generality irreducible to the determinate powers themselves while yet being nothing over and above these powers.

For this reason, Deleuze concludes that 'habit draws something new from repetition – namely, difference (in the first instance understood as generality)' (Deleuze 1994, 73). Stated differently, the something new that is drawn from habit is a determinable.

5. Metaphysical Indeterminacy and the Primacy of the Determinate

Have these arguments truly rescued us from the critical claim that determinables are metaphysically subordinate to the determinates that they supervene upon, where in this case the determinable supervenes upon the repetition of determinate instances? As Deleuze reads and follows Hume, the answer is an emphatic yes: habit does indeed draw 'something new from repetition'; it draws a determinable that is irreducible to the determinates from which it was drawn. This is exactly Jessica Wilson's argument as well. In one of her several defences of determinables, Wilson claims that they are, by virtue of their multiply realisable nature, modal facts that cannot be accounted for in terms of determinate facts alone. One of the tacit assumptions against determinables playing any fundamental role in metaphysics, according to Wilson, is 'that a (relatively) fundamental base need only ground the non-modal facts at a world' (Wilson 2012, 12). However, since 'it is a constitutive modal fact about every determinable instance that it is of a type whose instances might be differently determined', and since 'modal facts and features about entities at a world are also part of the world's inventory', Wilson concludes that 'no specific determinate instance seems suited to ground this [modal] fact [about determinables]', and thus 'determinables, in particular, also need a ground, which determinates, it seems, are not suited to provide' (12). In other words, determinates, as non-modal facts, are not sufficient to account for the modal fact that determinables entail a multiply realisable subset of determinates, for the determinates themselves are not multiply realisable but are what is realised. Yet another reason most philosophers have not looked to determinables as the fundamentals that ground the types of modal facts that are 'part of the world's inventory' – namely, the modal fact of multiple realisability – is the assumption that 'worldly entities are or must be precise', that the fundamental entities are or must be determinate, as Wilson puts it in her essay which provides a determinable-based argument in favour of metaphysical indeterminacy (see Wilson 2013). We have seen in the previous section that there is indeed a longstanding prejudice in favour of the determinate, a prejudice Wilson rejects in favour of fundamental determinables, arguing that these do equally well, if not better, in helping us to understand metaphysical indeterminacy (Wilson 2013).

The bias in favour of the primacy of the determinate at work in the debates regarding metaphysical indeterminacy is on full display in the broad number of arguments that adopt what Wilson calls a 'meta-level account' (2013, 361). In Parsons and Woodruff's reading of the problem of the many, for example, picking up on an argument initially put forward by Unger (1980), the question focuses on where boundaries are to be drawn. In Unger's presentation of the issue, the problem of indeterminacy arises when we attempt to draw, for instance, the boundaries of a cloud. As Unger puts it, 'when viewed from far away, certain puffy, "picture-postcard" clouds can give the appearance of rather a sharp boundary … [but] upon closer scrutiny … [the puffy clouds seem] to blend into their surrounding atmosphere' (Unger 1980, 413), and we do not know where to draw the boundary, or there are an indeterminate number of boundaries that could be drawn. In the Parsons and Woodruff example that Wilson addresses, much the same argument is put forward, this time concerning 'Tibbles-the-cat' rather than puffy clouds. At what point do we draw the boundaries of Tibbles? Upon closer scrutiny, we can ask the same questions about Tibbles that we asked about puffy clouds. The resulting problem of the many is that there are many cats, what Parsons and Woodruff call 'p-cats' (Parsons and Woodruff 1994, 172), that emerge as potential candidates to being identical with the one Tibbles-the-cat. As Wilson summarises the indeterminacy at issue here, 'the MI [metaphysical indeterminacy] of Tibbles explicitly involves its being indeterminate as to which of the various determinate (precise) p-cats Tibbles is identical' (Wilson 2013, 362). Wilson analyses several other accounts of metaphysical indeterminacy, and they will each adopt roughly the same approach – namely, indeterminacy arises when an identity becomes, upon analysis, a plurality of determinate identities wherein it is indeterminate or arbitrary to select one over the others as being the one identical to the worldly object in question, whether this be Tibbles or a puffy cloud. These accounts of indeterminacy, in short, continue to adhere to the primacy of the determinate thesis, and thus it is not the world itself that is indeterminate but rather the fact that there is 'an indeterminate array of (determinate) facts or things' (Wilson 2013, 363).

In her defence of metaphysical indeterminacy, Wilson will abandon the meta-level account, which continues to rely upon the primacy of the determinate, and argue instead for an 'object-level account' wherein determinables are taken to be the best way to go in 'characterizing MI' (Wilson 2013, 365). What this entails accepting, contrary to how this has been traditionally understood in philosophy, is that there may be an object that has a determinable property, but that this object fails to have a unique determinate of this property, or this determinable property has what Wilson calls 'a failure of unique determination' (366). Wilson develops this argument in two steps. In the first step, she offers as an example the 'highly iridescent feathers of the hummingbird' (367), feathers whose colour will vary depending on the angle of light refraction relative to the viewer. The hummingbird feather thus has a determinable colour but no unique determinate colour that is *the* colour of the feather. One could argue, however, that there is a determinate for the determinable, just one that is relative to a particular context for each viewer. Here Wilson moves to the next step of her argument and claims that metaphysical indeterminacy can be understood in terms of a determinable that is 'not at all determined at a time, even as a relativized matter of fact, if none of the circumstances relevant to determining the determinable is present' (370). She points to quantum superpositions as an example of such a determinable that is 'not at all determined at a time', referring here to eigenstates of the operator that is needed to determine the spin of an electron, a spin that is not determined or determinate when the determinable state of the electron is without an eigenstate. As Wilson summarises the point, 'Quantum superpositions can thus be seen as involving undetermined determinables' (371). We need not turn to quantum physics, however, although this does lend weight to Wilson's view that determinables are routinely at work within scientific explanations (see also Wilson 2012, 5–6, where she argues for this point explicitly). We can instead turn to our perception of colours, whereby 'we experience determinable rather than maximally determinate shades of colors' (Wilson 2012, 5). To clarify by way of Deleuze's example (discussed earlier, §8.3) in his book on Leibniz, when we perceive the colour green, and more precisely perceive what we take to be a determinate shade of green, forest green for instance, what is properly perceived, Deleuze argues, is the determinate as conditioned by a determinable, or 'a determinable magnitude' wherein 'yellow and blue can surely be perceived, but if their perception vanishes by dint of progressive diminution, they enter into a differential relation that determines green' (Deleuze 1993, 88). In other words, as a determinable, green is not subordinate to determinates, whereby the determinates account for the nature of the determinable; rather, we have the infinite series of differentiating differentials that are not in themselves determinate but presuppose their own infinite series (which is why Deleuze adds that 'nothing impedes either yellow or blue [the differentials of green], each on its own account, from being already determined by the differential relation of two colors that we cannot detect, or of two degrees of chiaroscuro' [88]), and so on *ad infinitum*. In perceiving a particular colour, a cerulean-coloured ink for instance, what is primary, for Wilson and Deleuze, is not the determinate nature of this perception, the perception that can become the subject of a propositional statement, but rather the multiply realisable determinable that is the condition of possibility for this determinate experience. Deleuze thus provides further support for Wilson's determinable-based account of MI, and he would likely second Wilson's conclusion that 'On the determinable-based account [of MI], for a macro-object [such as Tibbles, a puffy cloud, or a perception of the determinable property green] to have an indeterminate boundary is for it to have a determinable boundary but (for some level of determination) no determinate of that boundary' (Wilson 2013, 377).

6. Determinables and Problematic Ideas

With Wilson's determinable-based account of metaphysical indeterminacy, along with her defence of determinables as being legitimately understood as fundamental (in order to account for modal facts), we can gain a clearer sense of the notion of problematic Ideas as I have developed it here. As we saw earlier (§10.1), in defence of his choice to adopt Plato's term Idea, Kant argued that the term was appropriate since an Idea is not to be confused with anything given in experience, or with the determinate as we are discussing this now. As Kant put it, an Idea is a problem without a solution; as such, problematic Ideas are not to be understood either as relative to an extensive totality that serves as a regulative ideal (as in Kant), or as being subordinate to the primacy of the determinate as in Armstrong and Lewis. Restating this now in Wilson's terms, we can say that problematic Ideas are undetermined determinables, or multiply realisable determinables that are not to be understood in terms of, or in subordination to, any specific determinate instance. Stated in terms that have been used throughout, a problem or problematic Idea is not to be confused with, or placed in subordination to, the multiply realisable solutions it makes possible. Wilson's work has done much, then, to clarify the manner in which we can begin to understand problematic Ideas, and do so without returning to many of the traditional philosophical tropes that have provided the traditional means of thinking through these problems. It is important, however, to highlight a crucial difference between Wilson's project and the metaphysics of problematic Ideas being developed here. Most significantly, a problematic Idea needs to be constructed (recall our earlier discussion of learning [§9, and §14 below]), and constructed in a way such that it allows for the emergence of something new. This is where the creativity of habit looms large for Deleuze – recall as well our earlier example of the monkey in search of food beneath boxes of a particular colour. The problem space, or problematic Idea, is to be understood in these contexts as that which is not to be confused with what it makes possible, the solutions or determinate existents (e.g., a learned behaviour as in the case of the monkey). Since problematic Ideas need to be constructed, they are not an already existent reality but a reality that is always in the process of being created and recreated. For Wilson, by contrast, fundamental determinables are not created; or, if they were, it would have been by God, as she herself acknowledges in the closing line of her 'Fundamental Determinables' essay: 'Going forward, it may be useful to keep in mind the basic picture of what God had to do to create a world, if what I have here argued is correct: at a minimum, God had to bring into being the *determined fundamental determinables*' (Wilson 2012, 25).

By turning to issues in the philosophy of science, we will begin to clarify the manner in which problematic Ideas are constructed, and how they always require limits if the differential unconscious that consists of problematic Ideas is to become subject to representational thought.

§13 The Limits of Representational Thought

1. Predicates as Determinates or Determinables?

Let us return to the question that guided (or perhaps haunted) much of the argument of the previous two sections – namely, the question of determining whether or not one is correctly applying a predicate to an object, or, stated differently, whether the property named by the predicate is indeed being correctly named by the predicate. We sometimes get it clearly wrong. When my daughters were young, younger than two, one of their first words was cat, or 'kittycat' as they would say it. We also had raccoons that would frequent our back patio, looking for the cat food we would often have outside, and the first time they saw a raccoon on our back patio the girls called it a 'kittycat'. We can understand the reason they did so. Having never seen a raccoon before, they immediately saw it in light of animals who most closely resemble a raccoon, and for each of my daughters that animal was a cat. We corrected their mistake, telling them this was a raccoon and not a cat, and it didn't take long before they could see the differences between raccoons and cats and correctly apply the predicates '… is a cat', '… is a raccoon' to the animals before them. For D.M. Armstrong and David Lewis, similarly, a key to applying predicates correctly is that they account for a resemblance between entities. A fundamental role that immanent universals play, Lewis argued, is that they can account for the resemblance of entities. To explain why certain entities resemble one another, we can, as Armstrong does, turn to a shared universal, as that which provides the explanation. Lewis, by contrast, accepted resemblance as a primitive, and on this basis argued instead that we do not need to postulate the existence of a universal as some shared entity but can simply refer to classes of individuals that resemble one another. For Lewis, however, some classes are more natural than others, constituting what he called natural properties, and these natural properties entail a resemblance, again taken as a primitive, among entities that carve nature at its joints. These resemblances and hence natural properties are what physics discovers – the resemblances among electrons, quarks, etc., are most natural because these classes of entities that resemble one another are classes (properties) fundamental to the nature of reality itself, as the way nature itself is carved up and divided.

With the turn to Jessica Wilson's work, we saw that a strong case can be made for taking determinables to be fundamental to reality. Rather than taking determinate universals, *à la* Armstrong, to be the shared entities that account for the resemblance among determinate particulars, and rather than assuming a primitive resemblance among classes of particular determinates, *à la* Lewis, Wilson argues that determinables with no unique corresponding determinates may well be what are fundamental. Where this leaves us with respect to the question of whether a predicate is correctly applied to a property or not is that we do not begin with a determinate property and then search for the most appropriate and relevant predicate. What we begin with, rather, are problematic Ideas, and it is only with the solutions to these problems that we then have a determinate particular that can be taken to be in relationship to a determinate predicate. In other words, the question regarding the correct application of a predicate to a property already presupposes a resolution to the problem which makes possible the differentiation between a determinate property and the predicate that is applied to this property. The question Wilson's work leaves us with, therefore, is not one of knowing whether or not we have correctly identified a given entity under a given predicate, but rather how problematic Ideas, or fundamental determinables for Wilson, are realised in the particular determinates that come to be given to us at all, and given such that determinate predicates come to be applied to them. It is thus not a matter of accounting for determinables on the basis of the determinates that are given to us – the traditional understanding of determinables, as Wilson pointed out – but rather a matter of accounting for the determinates that are given to us on the basis of the determinables or problematic Ideas. We are left not with a truth question, a what is X? question (recall the Introduction), such as *what is* the correct predicate for this determinate? We are left, rather, with relevance questions, with the questions of who, how, under what conditions, when, etc., does the determinable become determinate? These relevance questions are integral to Mark Wilson's project, and thus we can turn to his work to gain a better sense of how we might approach the question that Jessica Wilson's work leaves us with.

2. Mark Wilson on Predicates

The work by Mark Wilson most relevant to the question at hand is his essay 'Predicate Meets Property'. A guiding question of this essay is how precisely to track the process whereby a predicate comes to be applied to a property. The assumption for Wilson is not that there is an already determinate property that simply awaits its proper predicate; to the contrary, for him properties are best understood as problems, or problematic Ideas in my terms, which are open to a variety of possible solutions, none of which completely removes the problem. Wilson sets the stage for this approach to the analysis of the relationship between predicates and properties by referring to a humorous example from film:

> I saw a movie (*Island of Lost Women*) in which a colony of Druids drifted in ancient times to a South Sea island, where they were subsequently terrorized by cavemen and out-takes from *One Million B.C.* Their descendants, naturally, were able to speak a variety of English, albeit with miscellaneous archaic features. A B-52 full of regular American types landed on their uncharted island and the Druids exclaimed, 'Lo, a great silver bird falleth from the sky.' (Wilson 1982, 549)

We may find ourselves easily dismissing the relevance of this example, perhaps chuckling at the naivety with which the Druids categorise a plane as a bird. At the same time, their mistake, at least as we are likely to see it, makes perfect sense if we think of the predicate, '... is a bird', as applying to a set of physical attributes and properties that include such things as having wings, flying in the sky, descending and landing, etc. The circumstances could have been very different, however, and a different predicate could have been applied. Suppose, Wilson continues, 'the hapless visitors [in the movie] had crashed in the jungle unseen and were discovered by the Druids six months later as they camped discontentedly around the bomber's hulk, their Druid rescuers would have proclaimed, "Lo, a great silver house lieth in the jungle"' (Wilson 1982, 550). Do these Druids suffer from conceptual confusion, or do they think about the world differently (that is, have a different conceptual scheme)? Wilson argues that they do not, and the arguments he puts forth to justify this claim both challenge and extend a standard Fregean-Russellian understanding of concepts, and by extension Armstrong's and Lewis's as well. Most notably, Wilson challenges Frege's commitment to what I have called the primacy of the determinate, the assumption that 'it must be determinate for every object whether it falls under a concept or not; a concept word which does not meet this requirement on its *Bedeutung* [reference] is *bedeutungslos*' (Frege 1997, 178). What Wilson hopes to show by way of his example is that while from an outsider's perspective there appears to be conceptual confusion going on, in that the Druids place an object under a concept to which it does not belong, the Druids themselves, Wilson surmises, do not have the sense of being confused, or the sense of placing an object under a concept to which it does not belong.

Wilson need not rely on campy movies, however, for examples of the process that interests him. Captain Cook, in his voyages through the south seas, encountered a number of islanders who had never seen the animals or many of the other things Cook had brought with him aboard his ships. In one memorable anecdote, recounted by Dugald Stewart, the native islanders were found to be rather flexible in their application of predicates. As Stewart recounts Cook's story:

> 'The inhabitants', says he [Captain Cook], 'were afraid to come near our cows and horses, nor did they form the least conception of their nature. But the sheep and goats did not surpass the limits of their ideas; for they gave us to understand that they knew them to be birds...' [Stewart then offers his explanation for this seeming 'mistake':] But these people seemed to know nothing of the existence of any other land animals, besides hogs, dogs, and birds. Our sheep and goats, they could see, were very different creatures from the two first, and therefore they inferred that they must belong to the latter class, in which they knew that there is a considerable variety of species. (Stewart 1792, 153)

As with Wilson's example of the Druids, the predicate, '... is a bird', is applied to objects to which we, as outside observers, know it does not apply. But there is a critical difference. Whereas one can understand, on Wilson's account, the extension of the predicate bird to the plane because they share some similar attributes, in the case of the islanders, on Stewart's account, the extension of the predicate is based not on a set of similar attributes but rather on the known fact that there is 'a considerable variety of species of birds', and thus by a process of elimination they think of the sheep and goats as birds. The cows and horses *surpassed the limits* of their ideas and thus they could not 'form the least conception of their nature'. For cows and horses, therefore, the differences were too great to be accommodated by the known variety of birds – birds are not that varied! It is this process of working within limits in order to apply predicates that is important to Wilson. On the Fregean-Russellian account that Wilson seeks to extend and modify, when one grasps the sense of a concept one has in essence understood a rule that guides one's actions and leads one to connect a predicate to those objects that fall under the concept. For Wilson, by contrast, what allows us to connect a predicate to a set of attributes is not the sense, as it is for Frege, but rather that we 'should employ physical properties rather than concepts as the appropriate middle terms' (Wilson 1982, 559). But these physical properties, if we are to 'form the least conception of their nature', and hence apply a predicate to them, must fall within certain limits, though not the conceptual limits Frege argued for.

3. Hasok Chang on Inventing Temperature

To clarify this point about the necessity of limits if we are to apply a predicate, let us take the example of temperature. What the examples of Wilson's Druids and Cook's South Sea islanders point to is a flexibility in our application of predicates, or how predicates tend to wander from one object to another (recall as well my girls' use of 'kittycat' for racoons). Other predicates, we might think, are more clearly tied to the properties they name. Temperature may be thought to be one such example. As Hasok Chang has shown in his book *Inventing Temperature* (2004), however, the nature of the property to be predicated was quite resistant to the many efforts to nail it down. The very standardisation of temperature readings itself was riddled with difficulties. As Chang shows, one of the first steps in standardising temperature entailed establishing fixed points that would provide the parameters or limits from which a scale of temperature readings could be constructed. The obvious candidates for such fixed points were the temperatures at which water boils and freezes. For many different reasons, there was tremendous debate about whether a fixed point such as the temperature at which water boils even exists. Under conditions where much of the dissolved oxygen is removed from the water it will boil at temperatures well above 100 degrees centigrade, a phenomenon known as superheating (Chang 2004, 17–23). Scientists did in time converge upon the fixed points and limits that we now take for granted, but they were by no means determinate givens that one could easily attach predicates to – e.g., the predicate '... is the temperature at which water freezes'. For Wilson, similarly, the physical properties associated with temperature are not to be understood as already determinate givens that simply await the predicates that will represent their nature.

Wilson, like Chang, argues that what first needs to be done in order to apply a predicate is to determine the limits and parameters that make it possible to identify a given property by way of the predicates one wants to apply. If temperature, for instance, is taken to be mean kinetic energy – a view that Wilson claims is 'generally false' (Wilson 1985, 228), though it is widely held to be the case due to the influence of Ernest Nagel's philosophy of science (see Nagel 1961 [for more on Nagel and rise of analytic philosophy, see §13.6]) – then this is an assumption that is only relevant to a classical ideal gas at equilibrium and not to most other substances or to dynamic contexts. If we assume a thermometer measures temperature, we also need to overlook the fact that this is true only within certain limits and parameters. A mercury thermometer, Wilson points out, 'will not function properly in an environment full of shock waves or if applied to objects at extremely high or low temperatures' (Wilson 1982, 563). It is for this reason that Wilson argues that, 'Except in trivial cases, almost no universal detection devices exist; instruments which can detect the presence or absence of P in any object whatsoever in any context' (563). In other words, in order to identify a given property and correctly apply the appropriate predicate, what is first necessary is that the limits be drawn which make it possible to identify the given property. If these limits are exceeded – if shock waves are present or temperatures exceed the limits for a mercury thermometer for instance – then the property itself will elude detection. In the vein of the coherentism that Chang argues for, Wilson will likewise argue that what gives us a basis for claiming that there is indeed a set of real physical properties associated with temperature predicates is the convergence of operational and experimental results. It is only because 'we obtain approximately similar readings from such a wide variety of distinct devices, for example, gas thermometers, liquid in glass thermometers, thermocouples, so called "sonic" thermometers, etc.', that we are able to refer to the physical properties associated with temperature as being freed from their 'operational underpinnings' (Wilson 1985, 244). For Wilson, the problem is not simply that we have not managed to create a detection device capable of taking into consideration all possible variables and parameters; rather, reality itself resists the descriptive frameworks and predicates we use to lasso it. This is in fact the thesis of Wilson's *Wandering Significance*:

> The main consideration that drives the argument of the book is the thesis that the often quirky behaviors of ordinary descriptive predicates derive, not merely from controllable human inattention or carelessness, but from a basic unwillingness of the physical universe to sit still while we frame its descriptive picture. (Wilson 2006, 11)

To restate Wilson's 'main consideration' in the terms I have used here, our attempts to establish a clear, determinate link between a predicate and a set of physical properties forever encounter problematic Ideas that are *both* the condition for the possibility of creating the determinate links between predicates and properties *and* are irreducible to the limits and parameters necessary to relate predicates to their properties. As we will now see, Wilson's 'main consideration' also poses a challenge to some fundamental assumptions of analytic philosophy, assumptions it is now time to reconsider.

4. Mark Wilson on Theory Façades

One of the consequences, Wilson argues, of the 'basic unwillingness of the physical universe to sit still while we frame its descriptive picture' is that we very often take short cuts when framing that picture. One way in which we do this is to simplify a mathematically complicated entity by reducing it to smaller, mathematically 'tractable terms' (Wilson 2004, 274). In an example from *Wandering Significance*, Wilson shows that the equations mathematicians use to understand 'how a spray forms on the surface of a choppy ocean' only effectively describe a part of the process. When one extends the equations beyond the limits of the particular range, they no longer describe what happens. For instance, the 'governing equations' used to understand the droplets that emerge from the ocean will, Wilson argues, 'gradually extend small extrusions into long spindly stalks with a ball at their end ... [but] Unfortunately, our equations will prolong this state forever, continuing to plot an attached blob that never relinquishes its absurdly elongated umbilical tie to the mother.' What practitioners do as a result is to 'begin investigating two fluid configurations that run in parallel, one containing the still attached drop and the other describing a drop of similar shape detached from the ocean' (Wilson 2006, 210). By combining the two separate configurations, the result is a better description of what actually occurs, and yet the two configurations, or what Wilson calls 'patches' or 'façades', may well and often do involve incommensurable equations that do not fully account for the processes as they unfold. This exemplifies what Wilson calls 'physics avoidance in that we do not directly describe the molecular processes that lead to drop separation, but merely cover the relevant region with an interpolating patch' (210).

Another way in which we simplify a process in order to better describe a physical universe that won't sit still is by simply ignoring the intervening processes that occur when one event causes another – what Wilson calls in this instance 'causal history avoidance' (Wilson 2004, 278). When Jack and Jill take a fall and begin their tumbling descent down the hill, we could attempt to apply the mathematics whereby we can 'trace the convoluted process in which [Jack and Jill] will now engage', but since the mathematics is so complicated we can focus instead 'on a so-called "equilibrium" or final rest state', and thus wait for Jack and Jill 'at the bottom with a medical kit' (280). As Wilson summarises the reasoning behind engaging in 'causal history avoidance', 'Jack and Jill's bruised outcome can be augured well enough without needing to trace the causal history that led them there' (278). A similar act of 'causal history avoidance' occurs with Hume's famous example of colliding billiard balls. Rather than fully investigating what occurs at the impact of one billiard ball with another, we simply combine two patches – the motion of the ball before impact and the motion of the balls after impact – and proceed as if what happens at the point of impact is irrelevant; and yet it is precisely here where the impact of the one ball causes the other to move. The reason for the avoidance, Wilson claims, is that much of the mathematics necessary to describe the 'mutually induced distortions of the colliding balls ... had not been invented in Hume's era', and many aspects are still poorly understood today (278). Given these caveats, within the limits and ranges of most circumstances, one can engage in 'causal history avoidance' without incident, much as mercury thermometers will work in most circumstances; but beyond these limits what was once avoided suddenly looms large and becomes incredibly relevant. The point for Wilson, to return to the theme of the previous subsection, is that we need to have established limits and ranges – or a patchwork and series of façades – if we are to begin describing and representing a physical universe that refuses to sit still. Our patchworks and façades, however, are constructions, and for Wilson they are not to be confused with the reality they attempt to represent, much as a Hollywood set of Babylon, with its 'pasteboard cut-outs arranged to appear, from the camera's chosen angle, like an integral metropolis' (273), is not, as we all know, the city of Babylon but just a façade.

5. Husserl and the 'constitutive becoming of the world'

Edmund Husserl will also alert us to the mistake of confusing the methods one uses to describe the physical universe with the universe itself, with the fundamental reality that is ultimately, for Husserl, the target of scientific inquiry. In *The Crisis of European Sciences*, for example, discussing the origin of mathematical natural science, Husserl argues that while this science developed an impressive set of methodological tools which have been passed on down the generations, the 'true meaning' of these methods has 'not [been] necessarily handed down with [them]'. It is necessary, he argues, for the scientist 'to inquire back into the original meaning of all his meaning-structures and methods, i.e., into the historical meaning of their primal establishment, and especially into the meaning of all the inherited meanings, taken over unnoticed in this primal establishment' (Husserl 1970, 56). Husserl is not calling for a mere historical inquiry into one's own scientific discipline, a retracing of the steps whereby the tools one now uses were developed. Most scientists would probably find such an inquiry irrelevant to the problems they are working on, problems to which they apply the methods now in use, and do so with no concern for how these methods originated. Husserl, then, is not calling for a factual history of the sciences, but instead for what he calls a 'depth inquiry which goes beyond the usual factual history' (373). This depth inquiry, or what he will also call a 'regressive inquiry', will start, for instance, with 'geometry which is ready-made', and move beyond the facts about geometry, including its history, to engage in a 'radical self-investigation'

(Husserl 1988, 153) that moves from the facts to the constitutive condition for these facts. In *Ideas,* Husserl refers to this constitutive condition as the 'constitutive absolute consciousness' (Husserl 1980, 67), though in response to criticisms of this view – in particular, that it reduces science and logic to being simply a construct of human consciousness – he will refer to this condition as the 'constitutive becoming of the world' (Husserl 1988, 113). It is this 'constitutive becoming of the world' that tends to get confused, Husserl argues, with the methods and techniques that have been handed down to us. In short, we can see in the cautions of both Husserl and Wilson a recognition of the tendency to reify those techniques and methods that, while they may help, in patchwork fashion, with our descriptions and representations of the 'constitutive becoming of the world' that won't 'sit still', nevertheless as reified may come to be seen as corresponding to the way the world is.

6. Husserl and American Neo-realism; or, Hook and Nagel Invent Analytic Philosophy

If we are to avoid confusing our descriptive representations and façades of the universe with the universe itself, then what is the proper relationship between them and how will we know if and when this has been achieved? This question is at the core of the neo-Kantian project in philosophy, and one of the more notable contrasts in how this project has been carried out is evidenced by the analytic and continental traditions in philosophy, with Husserl frequently seen as a founding figure of the latter and Frege, Russell and Moore as founders of the former (recall §7). The neo-Kantian project itself, however, needs to be understood in the context of its opposition to Idealism, and on this front Husserl was initially seen as allied with Russell and Moore. In his recounting of his impressions of the philosophical scene in Germany in the late 1920s, Sidney Hook, for example, identifies the phenomenological tradition spearheaded by Husserl as 'the strongest analytical group in Germany and closest to the English and American school of neo-realism' (Hook 1930, 152). The reason Hook groups Husserl with the neo-realists is because 'the phenomenological school keep their eyes on the object' (152), or, as Husserl puts it, 'we must go back to the "things themselves"' (Husserl 2001, 168), rather than focus on mental abstractions and constructions as do the Idealists. It thus made sense to align Husserl with Russell's own efforts to challenge Bradley's Idealism, and it likewise made sense to align Husserl with the American neo-realists, including Ralph Barton Perry and W.P. Montague who, along with others, were signatories to the 1910 essay and manifesto, 'The Program and Platform of Six Realists' (see Holt et al. 1910; see also Holt et al. 1912). To understand how, since Hook's time, Husserl has come to be identified with a continental tradition that is now seen to be at odds with an analytic approach that traces its roots to Russell and the neo-realists, we need to clarify what 'going back to the things themselves' meant for Husserl.

We can do this by turning to one of Husserl's first American students, Dorion Cairns, who responded to what he saw as the misrepresentations of Husserl he found in Hook's impressions of German philosophy. As Cairns details in his brief autobiography (1973), he entered Harvard's philosophy graduate programme in 1923, when Ralph Barton Perry, one of the six realists (Holt et. al. 1910), was department chair. Cairns cites Raphael Demos as his most important mentor and influence in his first years at Harvard. Demos was himself heavily under the influence of Russell and would later become an important Plato scholar, and it may have been Demos, among others, that Cairns had in mind when he wrote: 'It was common in those days for people in the English speaking world to construe Husserl as a realist and in consequence of Russell's highly favourable remarks on Husserl for me to think that I would like to learn more about Husserl' (the Russell reference is likely to a letter Russell wrote to Husserl [letter dated 19 April 1920] regarding Husserl's *Logical Investigations*, which was one of the books Russell read while in Brixton Prison in 1918). In addition to Perry and Demos (and their realist take on Husserl), there was more importantly Cairns' connection with Winthrop Bell. A former student of Husserl's, Bell was a first-year lecturer at Harvard when Cairns started his graduate work there in 1923, and Cairns took Bell's course on a general theory of value, which was taught from a phenomenological point of view. With Cairns' interest in Husserl piqued, he took advantage of a Sheldon Fellowship in 1924 that enabled him to study abroad for a year. (Marvin Farber, founder and long-time editor of the journal *Philosophy and Phenomenological Research*, had the fellowship the year before Cairns.) Cairns had intended to meet with Paul Natorp first, but Natorp (whose influence on Husserl should not be underestimated) died while Cairns was traveling to Europe. He ended up meeting with Husserl, and thus began a fruitful period of study with him. During his two years with Husserl from 1923–25, Husserl was working on what would eventually be published, and translated by Cairns into English, as *Formal and Transcendental Logic* (1929). On a return trip to study with Husserl in Freiburg in 1931, Husserl had recently published his *Cartesian Meditations*, which Cairns would also translate into English. When Cairns thus responds to Hook's impressions of German philosophy, and Husserl and phenomenology in particular, he is perhaps the most qualified English-language philosopher at the time to write such a response.

His response was unforgiving. As a student in Perry's Harvard philosophy department in the 1920s, and as a protégé of Demos, Cairns was well-versed in the realist debates of the time, and thus it is unsurprising that Hook's claim that Husserl was close to the 'American school of neo-realism' becomes the focus of Cairns' response. In particular, Cairns focuses on the passage in Hook's 'Impressions' essay where he draws the conclusion that Husserl's call to keep 'one's eyes on the object' places him among those who share the methodology and approach of the neo-realists. Cairns argues, first, that 'keeping one's eyes on the object' is a bad definition of the phenomenological method, and, he adds, it is a bad definition of realism as well. As Cairns puts it, for Husserl the object is not 'the mere object, but the subjective act with its intentional correlate as such, which is the fundamental datum' (Cairns 1930, 394). This point then connects to Cairns' criticism of Hook's suggestion that Husserl's phenomenology offers 'a logicized version of pre-Lockean psychology' (Hook 1930, 152). This completely misunderstands Husserl's point, Cairns argues, for psychology 'deals with the actual nature of existent minds', whereas phenomenology 'deals with the necessary nature of acts, quite apart from the reality or unreality of their exemplifications' (Cairns 1930, 396). As Husserl himself might put it, Hook reads Husserl's methodology as scientific in a naive realist sense, where this means, for Husserl, that the sciences presuppose 'a universe of constituted transcendencies' (Husserl 1969, 251). Such a reading is understandable if one assumes that Husserl is correctly placed among the American neo-realists and adheres to their call to develop a methodology with 'a common technique, a common terminology, and so finally a common doctrine which will enjoy some measure of that authority which the natural sciences possess' (Holt et al. 1910, 394). The basic assumption that underlies the techniques and terminology to be developed here, and the first claim listed in the neo-realists' platform, is that the 'entities (objects, facts, etc.) under study in logic, mathematics, and the physical sciences are not mental in any usual or proper meaning of the word "mental"' (394). But the problem for Husserl, as Cairns well knew, is not a matter of how best to address, through newly developed techniques and terminology, 'constituted transcendencies' and entities (objects, facts, etc.), but rather the problem of the constitution of these transcendencies themselves. This is the problem the methods of transcendental phenomenology seek to address. Since Hook completely misses this point, Cairns concludes that his 'impression of Husserl's phenomenology seems largely erroneous' (Cairns 1930, 396).

In Hook's defence, one could argue that Husserl should have embraced the platform of the American neo-realists, and thus while Cairns' reading of Husserl may indeed be correct, that is all the worse for Husserl. This is, in effect, what Ernest Nagel will argue in his version of Hook's 'Impression' essay. In 1936 Nagel offered his own 'Impressions and Appraisals of Analytic Philosophy in Europe' (Nagel 1936a, 1936b), and he pulled no punches, claiming from the start that 'a romantic irrationalism has completely engulfed Europe' (Nagel 1936a, 5). Although Husserl is not named as one of the 'romantic irrationalists', and neither is Heidegger, Nagel likely had Heidegger's philosophy in mind, and perhaps by extension that of his teacher Husserl. Nagel was no doubt familiar with Hook's own damning criticism of Heidegger from his 'Impression' essay, where Hook claims that Heidegger's philosophy is nothing more than the culmination of a German tendency to produce a 'disguised metaphysical theology', whereby, 'Instead of creation by divine fiat, creation by the ego – natural or transcendental – took its place' (Hook 1930, 156); thus, Hook concludes, 'German philosophers constitute one great idealistic family' (144). It is then likely that Nagel does indeed have Heidegger (whose influence was on the rise at the time) in mind, and perhaps also Husserl, whose conception of the pure transcendental ego as the constitutive condition for the transcendencies (more on this below) fits with Hook's claim that German philosophers were one 'great idealistic family'. Furthermore, in his introduction to Husserl's *Paris Lectures*, Peter Koestenbaum recognises that 'Existentialism has been accused of irrationalism', and by extension Husserl as well, given his 'view that reason itself is constituted by the transcendental Ego ... [and thus] scientific, mathematical, logical, and other rational pursuits are particular projects of man' (Husserl 1998, xlii). Husserl's call to get back to the things themselves thus does not appear, for Hook, Nagel and others, to be on a par with the task of the sciences. This point becomes explicit in Nagel's later review of a book published in honour and memory of Husserl soon after his death. Here Nagel expresses scepticism regarding Husserl's call for the sciences to recapture the constitutive meaning of their disciplines by engaging in a 'depth inquiry'. Such an inquiry is supposed to get us back to the radical givenness and meaning of that which the sciences study, but Nagel doubts the need for or relevance of 'a historical-genetic account of science', as Nagel understands Husserl's project, and moreover he believes that such an account would likely contribute little or nothing at all towards 'the solution of the concrete problems connected with the use of geometry in the natural sciences' (Nagel 1941, 303). On Nagel's view, then, Husserl ought not to be placed with the American school of neo-realism, and all the worse for Husserl since his 'regressive analysis' approach does little to help the sciences. As a result his work is not in line with the 1910 platform of the neo-realists, a platform analytic philosophers have largely taken on as their own.

7. Heidegger, Carnap and the Purification of Everyday Language

What Nagel ultimately rejects in Husserl's project is the move to a pure transcendental Ego as the constitutive condition that accounts for the transcendencies that are made possible by this pure Ego. Although Jean-Paul Sartre will also famously reject Husserl's move (see Sartre 1960), Sartre's critique was motivated by a desire to defend and better articulate a view of human freedom, whereas Nagel is motivated by the neo-Kantian desire that the task of philosophy be one of justifying the possibility and unity of science, and doing so by limiting metaphysical claims to those that fall within the limits of possible experience (recall §10.7). With his recourse to a pure transcendental Ego, Husserl has in effect returned to the metaphysics of the pre-Kantian dogmatists, or perhaps the post-Kantian absolute idealists, by calling upon a supersensible reality or Spirit as the unconditioned ground of that which one seeks to account for. Working within the spirit of the neo-Kantian tradition, however, one should not turn to a metaphysics that relies upon a supersensible ground, an unconditioned that exceeds any and all possible experience.

Importantly, and somewhat surprisingly given what Hook and others had to say about Heidegger, Abraham Stone has convincingly shown that both Carnap and Heidegger are agreed on the need to avoid a metaphysics that relies upon a supersensible ground. For Stone, both Carnap and Heidegger believe that Husserl's effort to move beyond problems in Kant's thought – in particular, his notion of the *Ding an sich* (thing in itself) – in the end calls upon a pre-Kantian metaphysics when Husserl argues for the sphere of pure consciousness. Stone argues that, in continuing within the spirit of the neo-Kantian tradition, both Carnap and Heidegger set out to give philosophy the task of addressing the problem of 'what constitutes a responsible and therefore clear and significant use of language' (Stone 2006, 6). For Heidegger, on Stone's reading, this consists of attending to the historical and grammatical roots of the language we speak, carelessly, every day. Heidegger thus continues with Husserl's call for a regressive analysis that begins with a given, everyday cultural formation, such as a linguistic expression, and then sets out to uncover its deeper meaning through a historical, grammatical and hermeneutic analysis. Carnap's project consists of purifying our everyday language of its errors and contradictions through the construction of a formal language in what he calls pure semantics. Carnap believes that by doing this we can avoid the pseudo-problems we are naturally led into by the carelessness of everyday language. When Carnap famously refers to the passage from Heidegger's *What is Metaphysics?* which ends with the question and response, 'What about this Nothing? – The nothing itself nothings' (Carnap 1996, 69), his critique, Stone argues, is not that Heidegger has fallen into obscurantist nonsense. This was Hook's criticism of Heidegger, whose book *Being and Time* he dismissed as 'such a jungle of arbitrarily-invented technical terms, that only the natural belief that where there is so much smoke there must be at least a little fire, keeps the reader at the grueling task of trying to make sense out of its pages' (Hook 1930, 154). As Stone shows, Carnap was able to make perfect sense out of Heidegger's writing, and understood him at a very deep level since he saw in Heidegger a kindred spirit with respect to the effort to purify our everyday language while avoiding Husserl's mistake of falling into a metaphysics of the supersensible. What Carnap criticises Heidegger for is not conducting the purification task through a logical analysis. Heidegger's approach does not survive the test Carnap applies to determine whether philosophical statements are significant or not – that is, the test of whether they can be stated in a language of formal, pure semantics. Heidegger's phrase, 'What about this Nothing?', for instance, cannot be translated into a logical form since it cannot be expressed by way of the logical syntax of existential quantifiers – there is nothing to quantify over – and thus it is an example for Carnap of a 'metaphysical pseudo-statement' (Carnap 1996, 69).

On Stone's reading of what is going on in Carnap's discussion of Heidegger's text, we gain an important perspective on how to understand the emerging methodological differences that followed in Heidegger's and Carnap's wake, differences that are now identified with the difference between analytic and continental philosophy. On the one hand, there is the historico-grammatical analysis that derives from Heidegger; on the other, there is the logical analysis that derives from Carnap (and Schlick and the Vienna Circle [of which Nagel speaks highly in 1936b]). Examples of the first approach include Derrida, Foucault and many others in the continental tradition who undertake archaeologies, genealogies, hermeneutics, deconstructive analyses, etc., of discursive practices, texts, narratives and so on. Examples of the Carnap-inspired approach include Quine, Davidson, Kripke, Lewis and those who set forth formal languages and semantic theories that seek to rid everyday language of its ambiguities and contradictions while offering a robust account of the meanings (or intensions) of everyday language (for example, one of the benefits of possible world semantics, Lewis argued, was precisely that it could account for the meaningfulness of counterfactual claims [see §11.4]).

8. Husserl's Humean Phenomenology

We could continue from here with this narrative of the emergence of the continental–analytic divide, but there is an important question, as well as an assumption, regarding Husserl's project, both of which we must first address.

First the question: has Husserl moved to the pre-Kantian tradition in his effort to account for the meaningfulness of that which is handed to us from the past? The answer is yes, though his move is not to the metaphysical dogmatists but rather to Hume. In particular, Husserl claims that Hume 'was the first to grasp the universal concrete problem of transcendental phenomenology', which entails showing how 'the concreteness of purely egological internality' can be the genesis of the Objective itself (Husserl 1969, 256). As Husserl reads Hume's *Treatise*, Hume's problem of showing how the 'repetition of perfectly similar instances' – instances that in themselves 'can never give rise to an original idea', such as the idea of causal necessity – nonetheless does give rise to an original, new idea through reflection upon the ease of transition one feels that comes to be associated with the repetition (see Hume 2007, T 1.3.14). For Husserl, this is one of the 'constitutional problems' he refers to repeatedly throughout his *Formal and Transcendental Logic*. In his own way, Husserl's move to the 'concreteness of purely egological consciousness' is similarly a Humean effort that does not simply accept the determinate and given, including the categories and pure concepts Kant takes as a given, but instead takes on the constitutional problem of showing how formal logic itself is grounded in the nature of transcendental consciousness.

As for the neo-Kantian assumption that one must avoid a metaphysics which calls upon a supersensible, I will argue that it is precisely this assumption that has provided cover for the post-Kantian bias towards the primacy of the determinate. By showing that Husserl's moves are not problematic, we can show that the approach that moves towards a supersensible, or the determinable as problematic Ideas on my account, is not a move to be avoided.

9. Husserl and Regress of Consciousness

How then does Husserl set out to address the 'constitutional problems' Hume was the first to discover? He begins, as we have seen, with the determinate, with already established traditions and methodological practices, such as geometry. On this point, Heidegger and Carnap followed suit. Where they broke with Husserl was in what they took to be his continuing adherence to what one could call a fundamental, supersensible determinate, which in Husserl's case would be the pure transcendental Ego. As Heidegger argued in his *Introduction to Metaphysics*, if we truly ask the question 'why is there something rather than nothing?', or 'why there is anything determinate at all rather than nothing at all', we do not answer this question by claiming that God is the reason there is something rather than nothing. If God is understood to be something, and something capable of bringing about the rest of that which is, then we can simply ask the fundamental question again and wonder why there is a God rather than nothing (see Heidegger 1959, 8). The assumption for Heidegger, therefore, is that Husserl's pure Ego leaves the fundamental question similarly unanswered; for Carnap as well, as we saw, he would likely place Husserl's claims regarding the pure transcendental Ego, along with Heidegger's claims regarding the nothing that nothings, into the category of metaphysical pseudo-statements that cannot be logically constructed out of determinate givens. We are also reminded at this point of the contrasting approaches Heidegger and Carnap take to performing the task of purifying everyday language. Whereas Heidegger adopts a version of Husserl's regressive method and pursues a historical-grammatical analysis in order to uncover the deeper meanings buried beneath layers of sedimented habits, Carnap seeks to construct meaningful statements out of particulars, or the similarity relations that are 'unanalysable units', as he will discuss in his *Aufbau* (Carnap 2003, 109–11). Carnap's approach thus follows in the footsteps of Russell, or more generally in the footsteps of the analytic philosophers in their response to the Bradley regresses (as discussed above, see §7.1): in order to avoid an infinite regress of relations it is accepted that certain relations and brute facts must be taken to be primitives that do not need to be accounted for or explained. These brute facts then become the basis of the Method of Intuition (MI) that Michael Della Rocca has shown to be so central to much of analytic philosophy (see §7.7)

Husserl does not follow the Moore-Russell game plan. He accepts the infinity opened up by the regresses and is untroubled by the lack of a determinate ground from which to construct an account of the determinate itself. To state Husserl's point succinctly: whereas Kant sought to avoid the antinomies opened up by infinite regresses, regresses which undermined the possibility of ideas that can be experienced since the infinite could not be synthesised into a determinate totality, Husserl accepts a regress of consciousness, or the fact that consciousness can always reflect on its intentional acts, thereby making this reflexive act an object for another intentional act, an act which in turn can be an object for yet another act, and so on. For Husserl, however, this does not give rise to 'endless regresses that are infected with difficulties of any kind (to say nothing of absurdities), despite the evident possibility of reiterable transcendental reflections and criticisms' (Husserl 1988, 152). The very act, moreover, whereby a constitutive consciousness intends an object, or an intentional correlate of the consciousness as Husserl refers to it, is precisely the act that is constitutive of determinately given objects, and yet that act itself is infinitely reiterable. This infinite reiterability, however, is not a problem for Husserl, since it is what makes possible the givenness of determinate objects for consciousness and it opens up for natural science 'the infinite pursuit of its method' (Husserl 1970, 56n21), meaning the infinite pursuit of the methods whereby what is constituted are the determinate givens which provide the material necessary for the meaningful fulfilment of scientific inquiry. Husserl thus anticipates Lewis's own embrace of the infinite series generated by the relations of singletons to individuals and to their own singletons, even though Lewis admitted that the relation between a singleton and its individual is a mystery, a mystery he accepted because the infinite series of singletons provided 'enough modelling clay to make the whole of mathematics' (Lewis 1991, 12 [discussed earlier, §15]).

10. Husserl and the Problem of Singletons

We are now at the point where we can begin to resolve the mystery Lewis finds in his account of the relationship between an individual and its singleton, and we can do so through an extension of Husserl's own account. The reason Husserl's account is appropriate in this context is because his theory of an infinitely reflexive consciousness as the condition for determinate content – the content that provides the material necessary for the meaningful fulfilment of scientific inquiry – leaves us with the question as to how this content becomes determinate and individuated in the first place. This question does not arise for Lewis precisely because he presupposes a determinate individual as a given, a presupposition in line with the primacy of the determinate bias. The answer that Husserl develops in response to this question, which is again for Husserl simply the constitutional problem Hume discovered, is to appeal to dual poles of the constitutive, generative acts of consciousness. On the one hand there is the object meant or intended, what Husserl calls the object-pole, 'a pole of identity, always meant expectantly as having a sense yet to be actualized'; on the other hand there is the subject-pole that points to 'a noetic intentionality that pertains to it according to its sense, an intentionality that can be asked for and explicated' (Husserl 1988, 45–6). The subject-pole, moreover, can become yet another object or pole of identity, meant expectantly, and again pointing to another intentionality, an intentionality that entails its own subject-pole or 'Ego as identical pole of the subjective processes' (66), which can in turn be asked for and explicated, and so on. The reason for the necessity of these poles, according to Husserl, is rather straightforward: without them there would be no unity, and hence no determinately given object or subject. The object-pole is that which, as Husserl puts it, '"polarizes" the multiplicities of actual and possible consciousness toward identical objects, accordingly in relation to objects as poles, synthetic unities' (66). The many varied perceptual perspectives one can take on a given object are synthesised by virtue of a pole of identity which is the tendency towards complete, exhaustive givenness, but a tendency that is never completed – it is an infinite task. Similarly for the Ego, there is 'a second polarization, a second kind of synthesis, which embraces all the particular multiplicities of *cogitationes* collectively and in its own manner, namely as belonging to the identical Ego, who, as the active and affected subject of consciousness, lives in all processes of consciousness and is related, through them, to all object-poles' (66). In short, it is by virtue of the Ego-pole and object-pole that the infinitely reflexive consciousness is able to encounter an object that is infinitely open, both objectively and subjectively, to a process of continual determination. And it is this process of continual determination that gives to natural science 'the infinite pursuit of its method' (Husserl 1970, 56 n21), which results in the generation of determinate individuals, individuals given to further inspection and possible transformation.

11. Husserl and Lebensphilosophie

We can probably hear Heidegger at this point, or even Sartre in his *Transcendence of the Ego*, accusing Husserl of presupposing that which he seeks to explain. By presupposing an Ego-pole and an object-pole, Husserl appears to presuppose a determinate identity, these poles themselves, in his very effort to account for the emergence of determinate identities. Perhaps Lewis's approach is best and easiest – simply accept that we are given, from the start, determinate identities, and proceed to offer accounts and explanations that build upon these or related identities (related if, for example, physicists discover that a given identity is itself to be accounted for in terms of more fundamental identities, or natural properties for Lewis). Husserl was certainly sensitive to these types of criticisms. Ronald Bruzina, for example, in his Translator's introduction to Eugen Fink's *Sixth Cartesian Meditation*, recounts Husserl's study of Heidegger's *Being and Time* and *Kant and the Problem of Metaphysics* as well as Georg Misch's *Lebensphilosphie und Phänomenologie*. As a result of having studied these works, Husserl concluded, as he expressed it in a letter 'to Roman Ingarden written towards the end of 1929, that "I cannot include [Heidegger's] work within the framework of my phenomenology … that I must reject it entirely as to its method and in the essentials of its content"' (Fink 1995, xi). What was more distressing to Husserl, however, than Heidegger's wayward philosophical development was the characterisation of Husserl's own work by Misch. As Bruzina describes it, Misch's book

> showed that the misunderstanding and critique of Husserl's phenomenology went beyond what Heidegger said of it. In treating Dilthey's philosophy

of life as standing in stark contrast to Husserl's philosophy, Misch touched upon matters at the core of Husserl's thinking. Misch emphasized in Dilthey's program the theme of living historical movement in human existence and thought, as against what he took to be the strongly logic-centered intellectualism of Husserl's works. Equally distressing on top of this was surely Misch's linking of Heidegger's analysis of 'Dasein' with this positive feature of Dilthey's position and therefore the ascription to Heidegger's work of a value beyond Husserl's. (Fink 1995, xii–xiii)

It is not surprising that Misch would stress Dilthey's philosophy of life, since he had been Dilthey's student (and was his son-in-law as well), but from Husserl's own perspective he himself had sought to do just what Misch found in both Dilthey and Heidegger. Criticisms such as Misch's therefore led Husserl to reformulate aspects of the *Cartesian Meditations*, the results of which became evident in his work throughout the 1930s. One key aspect of this change is that Husserl will no longer stress the constitutive role of the Ego-pole and the object-pole and will emphasise instead the transcendental life of the world. In the *Sixth Cartesian Mediation*, Fink will refer to the fact that the worldly, naive realism of the natural attitude misses the 'constitutive becoming of the world in the sense-performances of transcendental life' (Fink 1995, 4). This theme becomes even more prominent in Husserl's late book, *The Crisis of European Sciences*, where he will stress the importance of the 'life-world' throughout. In this new reformulation, the Ego-pole is rethought as a particular relation to the transcendental life-world, a relation that gives rise to the constituted and determinate givens of this 'life-world', including the givens that go by the names 'I', 'you' and 'we' (see Husserl 1970, 184). Husserl thus pushes back against the characterisation of his philosophy as engaging in 'strongly logic-centered intellectualism'. What he offers instead is a transcendental life-world with dual-tendencies, one tendency being that of the *epochē* and a rethought understanding of the Ego-pole, the Ego now being a process or life that is not to be confused with the determinate givens of the world itself, including the 'I', 'you', 'we' and all the other determinate givens that become the subject of the natural sciences. The other tendency is towards the determinate itself, towards the determination of that which is given in and through the transcendental life-world.

12. Problematic Ideas and Singletons

To clarify these dual tendencies, and return finally to the mystery Lewis finds in accounting for the relationship between an individual and its singleton, we can bring in the theory of problematic Ideas. Put simply, the dual tendencies of problematic Ideas are 1) the dedifferentiating tendency that is not to be confused with anything determinate, and 2) the differentiating tendency that further differentiates the extensive, determinate realities that become solutions to the problems, but solutions that are inseparable from and do not eliminate the reality of the problems themselves. In short, reality is nothing less than a multiplicity of processes of individuation involving problematic, intensive processes that are non-mereologically complete – meaning that as dedifferentiating they are not a totality that can be divided into determinate, extensive parts, but they are complete as a process, in the sense, discussed earlier, that Turner's paintings are art conceived as 'a process without goal, but that attains completion as such' (Deleuze and Guattari 1977, 370; see also §9.10). Processes of individuation also involve the tendency towards determination, or the differentiating tendency towards extensive actualisations that emerge as the determinate solutions relevant to the problematic Ideas that are the condition for the possibility of such solutions. These dual de/differentiating tendencies are how we will rethink Husserl's transcendental phenomenology. Moreover, this rethinking of Husserl will show that Deleuze also continues the Husserlian project, or that his 'transcendental empiricism', as he calls it, is in fact an example of what one might call Humean phenomenology. We will turn to this theme shortly, but first let us return to Lewis.

With our discussion of problematic Ideas as processes of individuation, which we will elaborate more fully below, we can now shed further light on the mystery of singletons. As we saw earlier, the mereological fusion of individuals into larger sums is no mystery to Lewis. If I take my cats Mila and Charlie, I can then have the fusion of the two and thereby the class that includes Mila and Charlie as members. For Lewis, however, it was a mystery why a single individual, Mila let's say, should be a member of a unique unit-class, or singleton, a class with only one member, namely Mila. With this singleton in hand, however, we have the singleton of every other class as well, including the singleton of the class that includes Mila and Charlie as members, and then on to the infinities that give us 'enough modelling clay to make the whole of mathematics'. Despite the mystery surrounding the singleton of a single individual, for Lewis it was worth accepting in order to account for mathematics. With the concept of problematic Ideas, however, we can begin to shed some light on this mystery and still give Lewis what he needs to make the whole of mathematics. The reason for this is that we don't simply have a given individual, a determinate individual that serves as the brute fact upon which our logical constructions are built, or where MI (Method of Intuition, from §7.7) gets started; rather, every determinate individual is inseparable from individuating processes, and hence from problematic Ideas. As a result, every individual, as a determinate individual, is the relevant solution to a problematic Idea (on the theme of determinate individuals as *relevant* solutions, see §16, Truth and Relevance), and thus to a multiplicity of intensive processes and differential series that become, at the limit or threshold (recall §8.3), the determinate individual with which Lewis begins. From our perspective, therefore, the singleton as a unit-class is to be understood as the intensive process which is complete as a process and which is inseparable from but not to be confused with the determinate individual, in the same way that problematic Ideas are inseparable from but not to be confused with the solutions they make possible. Moreover, each singleton, as the completion of an intensive, differential series (or differential unconscious [see §8.4]), entails the infinite series that gives Lewis the mathematics he wants to account for.

13. Deleuze's Transcendental Empiricism

We can now, finally, come to an understanding of the motivations at work in the project Deleuze has called transcendental empiricism. On an initial encounter with the name for this project, one may justifiably experience cognitive dissonance, for how can we reconcile the transcendental project or critique, the project of Kant and many neo-Kantians to deduce the conditions for the possibility of experience, with the empirical project that sets out to derive all our knowledge from that which is given to experience? As we saw earlier (§10.4), for Kant we can only have an experience at all if it is already predetermined in accordance with the pure concepts and categories. These categories thus serve as the predetermining forms which lay out in advance the nature and type of determinate content that one can experience, although this does not give us in advance the determinate content itself – that, Kant argues, is acquired through experience. It is at this point that Deleuze's transcendental empiricism enters the scene, for Deleuze is interested in the conditions for the possibility of the determinate givens of real experience, or what provides the actual content that is subsumed under Kant's forms of possible experience. As we can now see, problematic Ideas and the processes of individuation are the conditions for the possibility of the determinate givens of actual, real experience. Deleuze's project is thus very much in the spirit of Husserl's, for just as Husserl argued that the unities of formal logic – namely, Kant's presupposed categories and pure concepts – need to be accounted for in terms of the constitutive conditions that made them possible (what Husserl identified as the 'constitutional problem' and addressed through the transcendental logic he developed in *Formal and Transcendental Logic*), so too does Deleuze think that the determinate givens of actual experience, the experience that is central and foundational to empiricism, likewise need to be accounted for in terms of their constitutive conditions, conditions that become the subject of a transcendental empiricism. For Deleuze, it is problematic Ideas and the processes of individuation that are the constitutive conditions for the nature of determinate reality, or for that which is given in actual, real experience. Deleuze, like Husserl, thus places Hume's 'constitutional problem' at the centre of his own project, and in doing so attempts to do for empiricism what Husserl sought to do for logic (for more on the influence of Husserl on Deleuze, see Bell 1998 and Hughes 2008). It seems fair to say, therefore, that Deleuze was a Humean phenomenologist.

It is now time to turn to the details of the process whereby the givens of actual, real experience are constituted, or how the processes of individuation express problematic Ideas. This will be the theme for the final three sections of this book. Let us begin with a cup of coffee.

§14 Learning from a Cup of Coffee

1. Mark Wilson, Temperature and Theory Façades

Let us return to Mark Wilson's work, with a perfectly brewed cup of coffee in hand. The coffee was brewed, let us say, at an ideal extraction temperature of 195°F (91°C). Leaving aside for the moment the qualitative judgment tied to the claim that the 195°F temperature is an 'ideal extraction temperature' (a judgment we will come back to shortly when we return to the conditions for actual, real experience), and sticking simply for now with the statement that this coffee was brewed with water at a temperature of 195°F, we have already seen that for Wilson such claims disguise an array of complexities. To summarise our earlier discussion, to identify a given property – such as the property of bearing heat or temperature, a property which we then name or categorise in accordance with a particular predicate, such as '… is 195°F' – presupposes a series of relationships that are only identifiable within certain ranges and limits. The understanding of temperature as the mean kinetic energy of a gas, for instance, is relevant only with respect to noble gases at equilibrium, but not for gases in dynamic, far from equilibrium states, or for most other substances; the point at which water boils is relevant to water at sea level, and to water that has not been supersaturated with oxygen or de-oxygenated (again, see Chang's 2004, 17–23, discussion); and the mercury thermometer itself only registers accurate readings within a certain range of temperatures and conditions, which is again true for the other measuring devices as well. The provisional conclusion we reached was that given the limits and range of relevant applicability, coupled to a convergence of different measuring devices upon similar readings, we can then with a fair degree of confidence accept the accuracy of the descriptive claims about, or the application of predicates to, a given property.

Where things become more complicated still, for Wilson, is when the accurate description of a phenomenon requires multiple descriptive frames, or façades as he calls them, each of which entails a range over which it provides accurate descriptions but beyond which it does not. The mistake Wilson cautions us against is to assume that the different descriptive frames or façades provide, in combination, a complete and unified account of the phenomena under study. They do not, and the image Wilson would like to hold up for those who wrongly think the different frames do come together to create a beautiful whole is that of an illustration he once saw in a children's book, 'in which the King's horses and men stood triumphantly arrayed around a patently gimcrack Humpty montage, daylight streaming through its cracks and with much leftover egg scattered on the ground' (Wilson 2004, 275). We found a similar caution in Husserl's work. In particular, Husserl warned the sciences not to mistake the methodologies and techniques they currently use, no matter their effectiveness and ability to provide accurate descriptions and predictions, with the ultimate underlying meaning of these methodologies and techniques, a meaning that entails the constitutive condition for the givenness of the given itself, and hence the condition for its accurate description and representation. In the *Sixth Cartesian Meditation*, Fink will refer to this constitutive condition as the 'constitutive becoming of the world' (Fink 1995, 4), in part as a response to Misch's critique and description of Husserl's project as 'strongly logic-centered intellectualism' (xiii). For Wilson as well, the condition that provides the ultimate basis for the sciences, and a basis that fails to be fully captured by the different descriptive frameworks and façades used to represent it, or the predicates we apply to the properties of the world, is simply the 'basic unwillingness of the physical universe to sit still while we frame its descriptive picture' (Wilson 2006, 11).

2. Transcendental Empiricism and Real Experience

Turning now to the cup of coffee before me, currently at a temperature a good bit below 195°F, we can begin to add Deleuze's transcendental empiricism into the mix. In an important respect, Deleuze's approach breaks with both Wilson's and Husserl's. Both Wilson and Husserl set out to understand the ranges and limits within which a representational account of the world can take hold. For Wilson these are the physical limits and ranges within which we can accurately apply a predicate to a property, or the range over which a descriptive frame or façade provides accurate tracking of phenomena; for Husserl the limits and ranges will be the constituted transcendencies of consciousness, the noematic correlates of consciousness as he puts it, that are themselves made possible by virtue of the object-pole and the Ego-pole, or the life-world as he later thinks of it. Both Wilson and Husserl are thus concerned with understanding the conditions for possible experience, or the ranges and limits within which representational thinking may occur. By rethinking Husserl's project in terms of problematic Ideas that are expressed in the actualisations that are their solutions, or 'incarnations' as Deleuze will sometimes put it (see Deleuze 1994, 182), we moved away from the two determinate poles, and hence away from the conditions of possible experience, and towards the conditions of actual or real experience. To clarify how understanding the conditions of real experience parts ways with Husserl's and Wilson's attempts to understand the conditions of possible experience, we will draw on two sources. The first will be Theodor Adorno's work, especially the theory of objectivity he sets forth in his *Negative Dialectics*. The second will be Kenneth Liberman's recent ethnomethodological studies on coffee tasting. Combined, these works will offer us a more fine-grained understanding of problematic Ideas and how they are the condition for the possibility of real experience, including the experience of tasting a cup of coffee.

3. Adorno's Negative Dialectics

It is appropriate to turn to Adorno at this point, for a number of reasons. First, Adorno takes up the 'constitutional problem', the problem of accounting for the constitutive conditions for the transcendencies that come to be identified as objectively real. Adorno, for instance, will speak of 'the so-called "constitutive problem"' as being the problem of explaining the 'abstract legality of the totality itself', meaning the 'coercive mechanism' associated with a universal or a concept that binds or forces a thought of a particular into being a thought of a universal or conceptual type (Adorno 1973, 47). Like Husserl, Adorno argues that this binding nature of concepts is not a given but is constituted. Adorno will part ways with Husserl, however, and with Heidegger who extends and transforms Husserl's approach (in a way Husserl rejected as we saw), because both, according to Adorno, each in their own way continue to uphold the traditional idealist adherence to the primacy of the subject, a subject whose thinking is integral to understanding what it is that is objectively real. Adorno will turn instead to an understanding of objectivity or materialism that drives the processes of thinking, rather than argue for a thought that autonomously generates its own realities, *à la* Kant, Fichte and the neo-Kantians among whom Adorno rightly includes Husserl and Heidegger. A consequence of this move, and this is the second key point, is that Adorno will provide added insights into the challenges we face when, as Wilson puts it, we attempt to frame the descriptive representations of a universe that will not sit still.

Adorno begins his approach to the 'constitutional problem' with Hegel, and a specific interpretation of Hegel's theory of contradiction. In particular, for Adorno 'contradiction is not what Hegel's absolute idealism was bound to transfigure it into: it is not of the essence in a Heraclitean sense' (Adorno 1973, 5); that is, contradiction is not, as it was for Hegel, the root and essence of the relationship between being and becoming, and thereby the essence of reality itself. For Adorno, rather, contradiction 'indicates the untruth of identity, the fact that the concept does not exhaust the thing conceived'. To think is precisely to identify something – 'To think is to identify', Adorno claims (5) – but this very thinking entails an 'untruth', or a reality that is not exhausted by the thinking that seeks to identify it. It is for this reason that Adorno 'identifies' his project as being a negative dialectics. In contrast to a traditional Hegelian dialectics whereby the subject comes to identify that it is what it is not, or comes to recognise 'identity in nonidentity' (meaning it comes to identify the subject in what is initially identified as nonidentical to the subject, such as Nature for Hegel), Adorno's negative dialectics will 'contrast the nonidentity in identity' (154), meaning that it is not the subject whose thoughts and concepts are primary and determinative, but rather the nonidentical, the nonconceptual. The resulting effort then, for Adorno, is 'To change this direction of conceptuality, to give it a turn toward nonidentity, [which] is the hinge of negative dialectics', in order to give us '[i]nsight into the constitutive character of the nonconceptual in the concept' (12).

Without delving at length into Adorno's discussion and critique of Heidegger (although this is discussed in *TCE*, §4.2.b), on at least one key theme he admits that Heidegger was moving in the right direction – namely, with the ontological difference between Being and beings. Heidegger argues that there is more to reality than beings, including the sum of all determinate entities, this something more being what he understands by Being, and Adorno agrees with respect to the implications this has for thinking about beings, or entities. As Adorno argues, closing with a pointed critique of Heidegger:

> Every entity is more than it is – as we are reminded by Being, in contrast to entity. There is no entity whose determination and self-determination does not require something else, something which the entity itself is not; for by itself alone it would not be definable. It therefore points beyond itself. 'Transmission' is simply another word for this. Yet Heidegger seeks to hold on to that which points beyond itself, and to leave behind, as rubble, that beyond which it points. (Adorno 1973, 102)

As Adorno will argue at length, Heidegger's attempt to move beyond any conceptual thinking that derives from entities has the 'result that things evaporate for him' (79). The reason for this is that Heidegger seeks to remove all determinate characteristics from the nature of Being; for Adorno, however, without any determinate characteristics, without beings, there can be no thought or thinking. He thus concludes that '[t]he true philosophical task, according to Heidegger, would be to conceive Being, yet Being resists any cogitative definition. This makes the appeal to conceive it a hollow one' (98). In moving purely beyond the entities and beings towards a Being that is irreducible to beings, Adorno finds Heidegger's call for us to think Being a paradoxical call, for 'To think is to identify' (5). The resulting philosophical task for Adorno, therefore, is to openly embrace the paradoxical goal of 'uttering the unutterable ... The work of philosophical self-reflection consists in unraveling that paradox' (9); in short, the task is to embrace the paradox of a subject that identifies and conceptualises a nonconceptual objectivity that is nonidentifiable. On Adorno's reading of Heidegger, this paradoxical task is not embraced but is rather shunned in favour of a third reality – Being – that avoids the dual terms of subject and object that are paradoxically related. For Adorno 'We cannot', as Heidegger does with his understanding of Being, 'assume any position in which that separation of subject and object will directly vanish', and with this the paradoxical relation between them, 'for the separation is inherent in each thought; it is inherent in thinking itself' (85).

Adorno's negative dialectics is precisely the effort to understand thinking, or to detail the manner in which the identifications associated with thinking are made possible by an objectivity that is always something more. This something 'more' to thought and concepts is the hinge upon which Adorno's negative dialectics turns, or the reality that drives thinking in its very resistance to, and nonidentity with, thinking. Adorno thus begins with the assumption that 'What is, is more than it is', but in line with his negative dialectics he argues that 'This "more" is not imposed upon it but remains immanent to it, as that which has been pushed out of it. In that sense, the nonidentical would be the thing's own identity against its identifications' (Adorno 1973, 161). This is not to say that thinking is a hopeless task; to the contrary, thinking encounters the vertigo of the infinite, or of infinite series and regresses in our terms, in that everything that comes to be identified is identifiable precisely because it points beyond itself to others that may come to be identified; thus, to 'comprehend a thing itself', Adorno claims, 'is nothing but to perceive the individual moment in its immanent connection with others' (25), with others that in turn point beyond themselves, and so on. For this reason, Adorno concludes that 'a cognition that is to bear fruit will throw itself to the object *à fond perdu*. The vertigo which this causes is an *index veri*' (33). Adorno's approach is thus in line with the mixed approach we have been adopting in following Plato's call in the *Philebus* not to rush to the one or the many. Adorno is similarly motivated, though as he puts it we should rush to 'neither a system nor a contradiction' (11), meaning, on the one hand, neither a totality or system of elements, including a system or logical construction of brute facts, nor, on the other hand, the contradiction between a totality/system (universal) and elements or entities (particulars), or a contradiction between the determinate and the infinite that cannot be thought. What Adorno's negative dialectics calls for instead is to think of thinking as a process that engages with the nonidentifiable and nonconceptual in a way that generates predicates that assist in the identification of objective reality, but that does so without prioritising an overarching, systemic unity and without falling into contradiction. The model Adorno turns to in thinking through the nature of this process is music:

> The direct expression of the inexpressible is void: where the expression carried, as in great music, its seal was evanescence and transitoriness, and it was attached to the process, not to an indicative 'That's it.' Thoughts intended to think the inexpressible by abandoning thought falsify the inexpressible. (Adorno 1973, 110)

With great music, on Adorno's understanding of it (for more on his philosophy of music, see Adorno 2006 and 2002), the process is one that expresses the inexpressible, and it does so not by abandoning music but precisely by being musical, by being great music. Similarly, thinking and conceptualising the nonconceptual is done not by 'abandoning thought' but by thinking. There is an illuminating echo here of Nietzsche's claim, in *Human All-Too-Human*, that the goal of listening to a song is not to come to the end of the song. As Nietzsche states it, 'The end of a melody is not its goal; but nonetheless, if the melody had not reached its end it would not have reached its goal either. A parable' (Nietzsche 1996, 360). The song, for Nietzsche (and Adorno), is a process that is neither to be understood relative to the totality or unity of the song itself, nor reduced to, analysed and broken down into, the elements that constitute the song – namely, the notes and chords. In relation to thinking, this latter approach would indeed bring about the contradiction between what we are thinking and the elements that become the identifiable elements (brute facts) of analysis. To restate Nietzsche's parable in terms of Adorno's understanding of thinking, we could say that a thought – i.e., a conceptual identification – is not the end or goal of thinking, but a thinking that does not give rise to thoughts will not have attained its goal or purpose.

As Adorno comes to clarify this process of thinking, the goal or purpose is to provide provisional definitions for that which comes to be identified, definitions which go beyond that which is defined, beyond the defined to others that can be defined, and so on. For Adorno, what prompts the process of thinking is precisely the vertigo or infinite series of objectivity, 'the objectivity heteronomous to the subject, the objectivity behind that which the subject can experience' (Adorno 1973, 170). This objectivity, again, is the something 'more' that is nonconceptual and constitutes the passion of philosophical thinking for Adorno, a thinking that is much in line with art in that they both yearn to identify and bring into the light of day this 'more'. 'What the philosophical concept will not abandon', Adorno argues, 'is the yearning that animates the nonconceptual side of art' (15). Philosophical thinking thus yearns for the nonconceptual, and in this way it is 'a true sister of music' (109) and of art generally; likewise, as with a melody, this thinking is not itself the goal but as thinking it inevitably attains its goal and gives rise to concepts. But as Adorno goes on to warn us, 'The concept – the organon of thinking, and yet the wall between thinking and thought – negates that yearning.' The task for philosophy then, as he sees it, is that 'It must strive, by way of the concept, to transcend the concept' (109). Adorno's use of concepts, therefore, serves a critical function – namely, to transcend the concept – and with this effort we find the motivation for his critical theory. In pursuing this critical theory, moreover, philosophy will inevitably engage in a process of continually defining and redefining that which resists being defined, the universe that refuses to sit still.

4. Adorno's Non-conceptual Objectivity

The process of defining and redefining is one of embracing the differential unconscious, or, in Adorno's terms, the immanent nonidentity that is the condition for being able to identify and define, through language, that which has been identified. This is why Adorno argues that 'It is the matter, not the organizing drive of thought, that brings us to dialectics' (Adorno 1973, 144). In other words, it is the objective reality, the something 'more' that resists identification, which drives the process whereby one comes to continually define and redefine 'the matter'. What this process entails, for Adorno, is a discriminating observer, or as I would put it, one with a taste for problems. For Adorno, one who is to engage in critical theory, in his sense of the term, will be '[a] discriminating man ... who in the matter and its concept can distinguish even the infinitesimal, that which escapes the concept; discrimination alone gets down to the infinitesimal' (45). A discriminating coffee taster, for instance, may well be able to taste a particular quality that has yet to be identified, but in identifying it they are perceiving, as Adorno puts it, 'the individual moment in its immanent connection with others' (25), a moment not currently captured by the concepts already in use to identify the coffee they are tasting. The coffee taster then names this infinitesimal, describing it for instance in terms of a hint of pomegranate notes, a label or name that may then be picked up by other coffee tasters in their efforts to identify the nonconceptual matter that is the cup of coffee before them. As this example illustrates, language is critical to the process, and in fact for

Adorno 'No concept would be thinkable, indeed none would be possible without the "more" that makes a language of language' (106). In other words, what makes a language of language for Adorno is not a world of already existent entities to which we attach labels, but rather the infinitesimals (the differential unconscious) that escape our linguistic, conceptual categories, the matter that resists predication, or the universe that won't sit still. Language is therefore not a process whereby a subject attaches a name to an object, but it is indeed integral to the process of thinking itself, to its goal, namely that it lead to the discernment and identification of a nonconceptual matter that resists such identifications. Language, in other words, seeks nonidentity rather than identity, or it seeks to name and identify what has not yet been said. For this reason, Adorno argues that 'Nonidentity is the secret telos of identification. It is the part that can be salvaged; the mistake in traditional thinking is that identity is taken for the goal' (149). The goal of thinking, as we saw above, following Nietzsche's lead, is not one of creating terms and predicates by which we can identify a nonconceptual matter such as the tastes of a cup of coffee, but is rather a thinking that engages the nonconceptual as a process that often results, when one has learned something, in a name or predicate for a newly discerned attribute. This name or predicate, once identified, can then serve as a rule or guide for others. It can help another coffee taster, for instance, to identify the pomegranate notes in a particular coffee. Without thinking nonidentity, however, nothing new is learned, and no new terms are created to assist the thinking of others; thus if learning is to take precedence over already acquired knowledge, then our goal should indeed be nonidentity rather than identity.

The mistake we often make in thinking, however – as Adorno warns us, and as have Wilson and Husserl – is that we take the identities, concepts and definitions created to be representations of reality as it really is. The reason this is a mistake is that these representations mask the infinitesimals, the differential unconscious, the problematic Ideas that make possible the determinate identities that serve as provisional solutions to these problematic Ideas. By focusing solely on determinate concepts and representations, on identity, and not on the nonidentity that motivates thinking itself, one ultimately constrains and limits thinking. This process of constraining thinking will loom large in the political realm, as we will see in *TCE*, but in this context the mistake is one of failing to see or name realities that are discernible but escape detection because of an unconscious, habitual commitment to a current descriptive framework and set of descriptors and concepts. For Adorno, however, this process is not an all or nothing, and 'Definitions are not the be-all and end-all of cognition' (165). As determinate representations that identify an aspect of reality, definitions should not be the 'be-all and end-all of cognition' because this would again be to take identity rather than nonidentity as the goal of thinking. That said, Adorno goes on to acknowledge that 'A thinking whose course made us incapable of definition, unable even for moments to have a succinct language represent the thing, would be as sterile, probably, as a thinking gorged with verbal definitions' (165). The belief that definitions are in some sense primary, or that they satisfactorily grasp reality, even if only approximately and tentatively, reflects for Adorno a bias in favour of subjectivity – that is, a lingering idealism. Adorno admits that definitions 'make the object concrete', meaning they provide the conceptual unity whereby the object can be thought and identified, and iteratively so by many people in many different circumstances; but to assume that definitions are simply imposed upon an object is an assumption that 'applies only where the faith in the primacy of subjectivity remains unshaken' (187). The same faith in the primacy of subjectivity applies in the case of empiricists as well, Adorno argues, for here we have simple brute facts or impressions that are incapable of being defined in terms of anything else – as with Hume's impressions or Russell's particulars, they are simply that which stands 'entirely alone and completely self-subsistent ... [with] that sort of self-subsistence that used to belong to substance' (Russell 1970, 202).

Following Adorno's understanding of definitions as integral to and inseparable from thinking, what we end up with is a dialectical relationship between subject and object that is not resolved in a positive third, but rather forever spun by a nonidentity that leads to the reciprocal identification of subject and object. It is for this reason that Adorno claims 'the difference between subject and object cannot be simply negated. They are neither an ultimate duality nor a screen hiding ultimate unity' (Adorno 1973, 174). We thus do not have a positive dialectics, an ultimate unity in Hegel's sense, which guides the relation between subject and object. What we have instead is a situation wherein subject and object 'constitute one another as much as – by virtue of such constitution – they depart from each other' (174). In other words, both subject and object are each constituted by a process of nonidentity, a nonidentity that escapes yet motivates the constitution of the other. We thus have a negative dialectics, a dialectics where the identity of the subject leads to its nonidentity, and the same is the case for the identity of the object. We do not have a collapse or dissolution of identity. 'In truth', Adorno argues, what we have is a situation whereby 'the subject is never quite the subject, and the object never quite the object; and yet the two are not pieced out of any third that transcends them' (175). In other words, there is no Being, in Heidegger's sense, or Spirit or Notion in Hegel's sense of positive dialectics, which escapes the duality between subject and object, between the conceptual, determinate and identified on the one hand (i.e., subjectivity), and the nonconceptual, indeterminate and nonidentified on the other (i.e., objectivity). Rather, we have an ongoing process where identities forever presuppose the nonidentity that keeps them from ever being complete or fully determinate. We thus cannot eliminate the social or the natural, for to do so would again be to reassert, ironically, the idealist's faith in the primacy of subjectivity. The social, on this reading, would be the collective subject that imposes its conceptual forms and ideologies upon a reality that is largely of its making. This will be the view stressed by those who argue in favour of the social construction of reality (see Berger and Luckman 1967), as well as those who argue in favour of a strong reading of the social studies of knowledge (see Bloor 1983; Collins 1985; and Shapin and Schaffer 1985). Eliminating the social, however, and laying stress on the natural world alone, itself relies on a faith in the primacy of subjectivity, for in this case the natural world is taken to be a collection of brute facts that simply are what they are – 'self-subsistent' in Russell's sense – such that their ultimate nature is not open to interpretation or definition in terms of others, and most especially in terms of what subjects may think or experience. For Adorno, therefore, the process of thinking is one that is neither subjective nor objective, but one where each constitutes and undermines the identity of the other. This is the basis of what Adorno calls negative dialectics. As discussed here, this process is what I have claimed follows from the nature of problematic Ideas. To detail further the implications Adorno's reading has for our understanding of problematic Ideas, we can now turn briefly to Kenneth Liberman's use of Adorno's theory of objectivity in his ethnomethodological study of the processes involved as professional coffee tasters gather together in order to identify the tastes of a cup of coffee.

5. Ethnomethodology and the Taste of Coffee

Liberman's study of coffee tasters is part of his more recent work developing the field of ethnomethodology as initiated by Harold Garfinkel (see Garfinkel 1967; see also Sudnow 1978 for an ethnomethodological study of learning improvisational jazz, and Bell 2009, 24–6, for a discussion of this study). In this alternative approach to sociological studies, the everyday behaviours and interactions of people are subjected to detailed analysis and observation in order to shed light on the formation and execution of social norms. In one study, for instance, Liberman recorded several hours of individuals playing a board game for the first time, recordings that were then studied in order to detail the processes involved in learning the rules of the game (Liberman 2013, Chapter 3). As Liberman shows, this was not just a straightforward matter of applying the rules as provided; to the contrary, the process was much more dynamic and interactive among the participants, with the rules being taken up largely as the game went along (a frequent comment among the players was, 'Let's just play!' [84]). Liberman conducts a similar study of coffee tasters in order to examine the behaviours that create and support the judgments they make in the process of ensuring that a coffee tasted at a receiving wharf is given the same descriptor predicates that were used at the shipping wharf, e.g., 'chocolate', 'floral', etc. In his analysis, Liberman draws heavily upon Husserl, the social phenomenology of Alfred Schutz (especially Schutz 1967) and Adorno's theory of objectivity. In applying Adorno's theory, Liberman makes a distinction between two senses of objectivity, a distinction that will be central to his account of how coffee tasters come to identify the tastes of coffee. As he describes these two senses:

> The first is the real objectivity that is the actually existing taste of some coffee; this is the objectivity that always has some subjectivity attached to it. There is another sense of objectivity that is a socially constituted objectivity, more abstract and less immanent, and which seeks to remove all traces of subjective experience. (Liberman 2013, 222)

The relationship between these two senses of objectivity, Liberman argues, is reciprocal. For instance, during a tasting, Liberman, an admitted novice at coffee tasting, decided that a particular coffee was 'fruity'. A more experienced taster corrected him, saying the proper term was 'floral'. In response to this correction, Liberman 're-tasted the coffee and at once recognized the greater accuracy of this descriptor. Taste descriptors not only describe the taste that they find, they find the tastes that they describe' (221). The objectivity in the first sense, the physical tasting of actually existing coffee, was, in this context, a problematic set of attributes, or problematic Ideas to use our term – the smell, varied tastes, etc. – all without a clear rule or concept to guide the application of descriptors to this set of attributes. When 'fruity' was replaced by 'floral', Liberman discovered a better way to connect the varied elements of the set. Such efforts to connect the varied elements to a predicate are always provisional, Liberman argues, for that which is being predicated, in this case the taste of coffee, forever 'evades the system of descriptors that attempts to lasso it into a preexisting, comprehensive system of identity: the taste is ultimately a non-identity in that it always and necessarily exceeds whatever one identifies' (223). Liberman is drawing from Adorno's negative dialectics at this point, and hence the objectivity of taste is the something 'more' Adorno refers to, the objectivity that is the nonidentity which is the driving force of thinking, in this case thinking through the taste of coffee in order to identify and name its various attributes.

In his discussion of the process the coffee tasters engage in, Liberman emphasises the resistance of the objectivity of taste to the descriptors the tasters use. The challenge this poses to them, as Liberman describes it, is that 'to be professional, tasters must give this resistance its due; however, as soon as they do so the coherency of the system (for example, the tasting schedule used to measure the flavours) is put in jeopardy' (Liberman 2013, 224). In other words, if a taster gives in too much to the resistance of taste to a determinate description, then this threatens to undermine the usefulness of the tasting schedule whereby, for example, a coffee taster in Rio de Janeiro agrees with a taster in New York that a particular coffee has a strong floral character. The resistance of taste is still there, however, and this becomes evident in actual practice as the coffee tasters work collaboratively around a table: 'it may take time', Liberman notes, 'for a group of tasters to bring their practice of applying a tasting schedule into harmony on any local occasion, but they generally can get their use of descriptors remarkably well coordinated in less than a day' (223). At times, however, a taste may continue to resist being described – it 'resists being said … resists being organized into their discourse', as Liberman puts it – and it is at times like these that the tasters 'focus their attention' (248). What the coffee tasters encounter at such times of resistance is the nonidentity of objectivity, as Adorno understands it, or the problematic Ideas that make it possible to attach a descriptor or predicate. Coffee tasters will point to such problematic encounters with taste, what Liberman refers to as aporia, as being integral to learning about coffee: 'At the point of one aporia, when the taste of coffee could not be determined in a sufficiently objective way, a taster whispered to me, "This is where I learn the most about coffee taste"' (247).

6. Objectivity and Problematic Ideas

As we leave Mark Wilson now, with his cooling cup of coffee, we have a better sense of the relationship between problematic Ideas and the predicates that identify various properties. As we have seen, both Wilson and Husserl are interested in the conditions necessary for the possibility of representational thought. For Wilson a descriptor will accurately represent a property only on the condition that certain ranges and limits are satisfied – a mercury thermometer, for instance, will accurately represent a property if it lies within the range of temperatures suitable to the thermometer. Much of the work of science, Wilson argues, entails parcelling the universe into segments with which one can gain descriptive traction by using the analytical tools (e.g., mathematical equations, etc.) at one's disposal. The result, for Wilson, is that we end up with a series of façades rather than a unified theory, and he cautions us not to mistake these façades for a definitive representation of reality. They are representations, nonetheless, and with our reading of Adorno's theory of objectivity as problematic Ideas we can now begin to see that representational thinking presupposes a nonrepresentational, nonconceptual reality, and we have a clearer sense as to the nature of this reality. First and foremost, problematic Ideas are not to be confused with the determinate, individuated entities, properties and realities that come to be named and identified by way of various predicates. This was why the use of the term Idea, following Plato, was appropriate, since Ideas are not to be thought of as on a par with the particular, determinate realities that are the subject of representational thinking. At the same time problematic Ideas are indeed 'related' to the determinate realities, and in a manner analogous to the relationship between determinables and determinates discussed earlier (see §12). With Adorno's negative dialectics and the example of music we turned to in order to clarify the goal of thinking, coupled with Liberman's emphasis on the resistance of objectivity to being represented, we have begun to see how problematic Ideas are 'related' to the determinate realities they make possible. In encountering the resistance of the objectivity of taste, the coffee taster is learning the most about coffee precisely when the taste most resists easy description, or when it is a problem. Moreover, in this case, the goal of thinking, as Adorno understands it, is not so much identifying the tastes of the coffee – though this is a consequence of thinking, since 'to think is to identify' as Adorno put it – but rather to learn from the coffee, or to engage with the nonidentity of the coffee. Thinking, therefore, is a process of learning, and the knowledge gained, the words one can knowingly apply to various properties, is subordinate to thinking as learning. This learning only occurs, however, when an already established link between objective reality *and* the concepts and words a subject imposes upon this objective reality is broken, or problematised. The process of learning, therefore, or life as problematic Idea (for more on life as a problem, see *TCE*), is the condition for the possibility of real experience, for the possibility of the determinate realities one can think, perceive and hence represent. What thus comes to be identifiably thought, perceived and known – and thereby also capable of being represented and named in language – is made possible by problematic Ideas that are the pre-individuated differential unconscious that resists identification and yet is immanent to, as a non-mereological part (see §15), that which is individuated and taken up in representational thinking. To restate the cautions with which Mark Wilson and Husserl leave us, we should not confuse learning with knowledge, for without learning nothing new will come to be known. Stated differently still, we should be careful not to confuse our knowledge of reality with reality, or our known solutions to problems with a reality that is, at bottom, problematic. This latter confusion will be the subject of the next section, as we explore the relationship between analytic philosophy and metaphysics.

§15 Carnap and the Fate of Metaphysics

1. Carnap's 'Elimination of Metaphysics'

As has been noted before (Mares 2010, 53), the difference between the analytic and continental traditions in philosophy can pretty well be summed up by the titles of two books – *The Logical Basis of Metaphysics* (1991), by Michael Dummett, and *Metaphysical Foundations of Logic* (1928), by Martin Heidegger. Picking up where we left off with our earlier discussion of the differing approaches Heidegger and Carnap took to purifying the errors that seep into everyday language (§13.7), we can begin to explore this difference further. For Heidegger, the destiny of metaphysics has been the forgetting of Being, or the turning away from Being as the condition for the possibility of the presence of beings, for that which is determinately given to thought. The scientific and logical modes of thought presuppose, on Heidegger's view, the presencing of Being, or the 'Nothing that nothings'. To base logic on the 'Nothing that nothings', however, is for Carnap to turn to the type of metaphysics he seeks to eliminate through logical analysis. As we highlighted in our earlier discussion, statements that cannot be logically constructed are for Carnap at best pseudo-statements. Logical constructions, moreover, must be founded on something determinate; to take Carnap's example, the word 'teavy' is a word where, '[i]f no criterion of application for [it] is stipulated, then nothing is asserted by the sentences in which it occurs, they are but pseudo-statements' (Carnap 1996, 64). The same is true as well, as we saw earlier, for Heidegger's terms 'Being' or the 'Nothing that nothings'. In particular, for Carnap, if a word is to have a meaning then it must be reducible to other words and sentences and ultimately 'to the words which occur in the so-called "observation sentences" or "protocol sentences". It is through this reduction that the word acquires its meaning' (63). On Carnap's view, therefore, Heidegger is indeed attempting to provide the *Metaphysical Foundations of Logic*, for Heidegger's claim that Being is the truth (*alethēia*) or reality of beings, as with the claims of metaphysicians in general, is not intended to convey an 'empirically observable relationship', a relationship between Being and beings that could be reducible to an observation or protocol sentence. 'For in that case', Carnap adds, 'his metaphysical theses would be merely empirical propositions of the same kind as those of physics' (65). By beginning with protocol sentences (more on these below), Carnap believes that the task of philosophy is to provide the formal, logical analysis that will account for the transformation of protocol sentences into what he identifies as the 'system language' of the sciences (Carnap 1987, 462). If we turn to physics in our effort to comprehend the nature of reality, then it is the task of philosophy to logically construct, on the basis of protocol sentences, the 'system language' of physics.

Since our earlier discussion of Heidegger and Carnap, however, we have come to see that attributing predicates to various properties, as evidenced in statements regarding temperature, the tastes of coffee, etc., is no simple matter. Although it might seem that sentences such as, 'the temperature of this coffee is 195°F', or 'this coffee has raspberry notes', might qualify as protocol sentences, or as the type of statements that provide the evidentiary basis upon which a system language might be constructed, we have seen that these statements themselves presuppose a dynamic process that eventually results, after a sufficient degree of convergence, in a statement that is then taken to refer accurately to something that is determinately given. As Adorno argued, the objectivity we seek to identify resists being named and identified, or, as Wilson put it, the universe refuses 'to sit still while we frame its descriptive picture' (Wilson 2006, 11). The caution Wilson, Adorno and others we have discussed leave us with, therefore, is to avoid the mistake of confusing the results of our efforts to frame a descriptive picture of reality with how things ultimately are. Whether this be Adorno's objectivity, Wilson's universe, Husserl's 'constitutive becoming of the world' or the problematic Ideas I have been arguing for here, there appears to be a clear metaphysical relationship between this reality and the descriptive framings that come to identify the determinate nature of this reality. This relationship is not a determinate relationship between a determinate, already given entity and a logically constructed system founded upon this and other givens; to the contrary, the reality being described ultimately resists (Adorno) and eludes (Liberman) description. In making this claim we seem, in fact, to be harbouring a vitalist metaphysics, a metaphysics that calls upon a life or élan vital (Bergson 1984, 87) that is the condition for that which is determinately given to representational thought, but a condition that cannot itself be reduced to a determinate given or thought. Deleuze will largely accept this vitalist metaphysics (hence his fondness for Bergson [see Deleuze 1988]), and in a late essay, 'Immanence: A Life', he will point out how in the *Cartesian Meditations* Husserl himself flirts with a vitalist metaphysics when he claims that 'all transcendence is constituted solely in the *life of consciousness*, as inseparably linked to that life' (Husserl 1988, 43; cited by Deleuze 2001, 33 n.5; emphasis in original). As Carnap might argue, however, if life is not to be thought of in terms of any determinate givens, any empirically verifiable evidence, then it would seem there is no 'criterion of application' for the word 'life' and hence we are dealing with a metaphysical pseudo-statement.

2. Regresses and Logical Analysis

To address the metaphysical implications of the relationship between a vitalist reality and the determinate givens that are conditioned by this reality, we can return to where we began, with the problem of accounting for something new. As we saw at the time, to account for something new in terms of current predicates and concepts would be to place the new in relationship to something that is already given. An obvious response to this problem is simply to deny that there ever is anything truly new, to claim that everything that is and comes to be is always something that can be accounted for in terms of conceptual categories or Ideas that are always already given. This is in fact the standard interpretation of Plato. If we accept this reading of Plato, however, then we come upon the difficulties of the Third Man Argument that Plato recognised in the *Parmenides*. What emerges in the *Philebus*, however (see §5.7), is what we have called the method of mixture, a method that can be used to avoid the TMA regress. While he continues to accept the Forms, the truths of ideal knowledge, as 'fixed and pure and true and what we call unalloyed knowledge [that] has to do with the things which are eternally the same without change or mixture' (*Philebus* 59c), Plato will argue that when it comes to the good life 'we must seek the good, not in the unmixed but in the mixed life' (61b), meaning a mixture of the one (Ideas as pure and unchanging) and the many (pleasures as infinite). In developing the implications of this approach, we have also followed Plato's advice not to rush to 'the one and the many too quickly or too slowly, in haphazard fashion … [and thereby] disregard all that lies between them' (17a). This has led us to argue for the concept of problematic Ideas, which consist of infinite, differential series that come to be actualised, at the limit or threshold, as determinate entities that are not to be confused with these infinite series even though the series are inseparable from them – they are what the series becomes, at the limit. In short, problematic Ideas, as mixtures, are precisely the infinite series and the limits of these series, limits that could be drawn or actualised in ways other than how they were, and thus problematic Ideas are multiply realisable determinables (recall §12).

To clarify this mixed nature of problematic Ideas further, let us return again to the founding response of analytic philosophy to Bradley's regresses, the response Michael Della Rocca calls the Method of Intuition (MI; see §7.7).

As Della Rocca describes this method, it entails taking one's 'immediately recognised' intuitions and regarding them 'as ordinary beliefs or as expressions of common sense (whatever that is) … [and/or] ordinary language (Della Rocca 2013, 180), and from there aiming 'to arrive at an overarching theory that somehow accommodates these intuitive responses as well as possible' (179). For Moore these intuitions were the immediately obvious facts of common sense – what has since come to be known as Moorean facts; for Russell they are the particulars we know by acquaintance that stand 'entirely alone and [are] completely self-subsistent' (Russell 1970, 202), a point Russell reiterates years later in his *Inquiry into Meaning and Truth* (1940), when he refers to these brute, self-dependent particulars as being 'my momentary epistemological premises', the only true premises, whereas 'the rest must be inferred' (Russell 1940, 127). 'The rest', following MI, must be inferred or logically constructed on the basis of that which is given through intuition: the brute facts that need no explanation, account or justification.

In developing his own philosophical approach in the spirit of Moore and Russell, Carnap will likewise argue that the task of philosophy is simply to provide the logical analysis that will show how a general scientific account, or any naturalistic account that is ultimately derived from observation sentences (or protocol sentences), is logically constructed. For Carnap this task entails a crucial distinction. As he puts it, 'the work in the system of science has the following form': first, 'Inside the system language there are universal sentences, the so-called "laws of nature", and concrete sentences' (Carnap 1987, 462). Among cosmologists, for instance, questions regarding the nature or reality of the strings in string theory – i.e., questions regarding 'concrete sentences' about what exists – are asked and answered using the 'system language' and 'universal sentences', including laws of nature, etc., that are currently accepted by cosmologists. These questions regarding the reality of strings will be what Carnap calls internal questions, questions asked within the 'system language' itself. However, in addition to, or 'outside the system language' as Carnap puts it, 'there are signals which are understood as "protocol sentences" of a "protocol language" of the machine or man in question' (462). Carnap provides the example of 'a machine which reacts in certain situations by displaying signal-disks' (458). For instance, if it is raining, the disk will show the number '1', if it is snowing, '2', and if lightly, '4', and if hard, '5'. Given this machine, 'we can translate certain signal combinations into sentences of our language, e.g., "1, 5", into "it is raining hard"' (459). Carnap then adds that we can go on to understand human language, in certain key respects, as a signalling machine, and thus if it is raining we may simply state, 'It is raining.' Whether they be signals of a machine or observation sentences of a human being, Carnap argues that 'The signals of the machine and the statements of the man are treated like sentences of a language in that translation rules are constructed for them. We call them therefore "protocol sentences" of the "protocol language" of the machine or of the foreign man and distinguish this language from the language of our system' (459).

Protocol sentences, however, are not absolutes for Carnap, for as he argues: 'Every concrete sentence of the physicalist system language can serve under certain circumstances as a protocol sentence' (Carnap 1987, 465). For example, a given concrete sentence of a system language may, 'with the help of other laws and logico-mathematical inference rules [lead to the derivation of] further concrete sentences ... until one arrives at sentences one wants to admit in the case at hand', meaning, as Carnap concludes, 'it is a matter of decision which sentences one wants to use at various times as such endpoints of reduction and thus as protocol sentences' (465). In other words, in addressing questions or matters external to the system language, or external questions as Carnap will define them, one may use the 'logico-mathematical inference rules' of the system language in order to achieve the goal of providing an account that ultimately translates, through the logical transformation rules of the system language, into the end point external to the system language – that is, the protocol sentences. Carnap will also refer to these transformation rules as 'the "logical syntax" of a language (i.e., the system language)', adding that 'The formation and transformation of propositions resembles chess: like chess figures words are here combined and manipulated according to definite rules' (Carnap 1984, 9–10). Like a chess player, therefore, an analytic philosopher, on Carnap's understanding of their task, sets out to address the 'question, whether a certain proposition is an inference (entailment) of certain other propositions or not ... [just as a chess player addresses] the question whether a certain position in chess can be played from another or not' (11). In chess, the question is 'answered by chess theory, i.e. a combinatorial or mathematical investigation which is based on the chess rules' (11); the entailment questions of a system language in its relation to protocol sentences are likewise answered through a logical analysis based on 'logico-mathematical inference rules'. Ernest Nagel stresses this point as well in his appraisal of analytic philosophy in Europe during the 1930s, which included a favourable nod to Carnap and the logical positivists. The benefits of the analytic philosophy Nagel saw being practised in Europe at this time were twofold. First, it provided 'quiet green pastures for intellectual analysis, wherein its practitioners can find refuge from a troubled world and cultivate intellectual games with chess-like indifference to its course' (Nagel 1936a, 9); second, the tools of 'chess-like' logical analysis serve as a 'shining sword helping to dispel irrational beliefs and to make evident the structure of ideas' (9). Turning away from the troubling political, moral and ethical issues of the day, or of any day, analytic philosophers can instead 'find refuge' in an 'intellectual analysis' that makes use of its 'chess-like indifference' in order to demonstrate and brush aside the 'romantic irrationalism' Nagel believed had 'completely engulfed Europe' (5).

We could question Nagel's characterisation of analytic philosophy at this point. After all, ethical and political issues were not ignored by the logical positivists. Moritz Schlick, the founding member of the Vienna Circle (and hence of the logical positivism this spawned), wrote a book on ethics (Schlick 1939), and many of the other members of the Vienna Circle were politically active and did not see their philosophy as a refuge from their political commitments. Otto Neurath, for instance, wrote on economics and social planning (Neurath 2004), and was involved in a number of political movements throughout the 1930s. We will address the political implications of analytic philosophy in *TCE*, but for the moment let us first address three key arguments against the presuppositions of analytic philosophy, presuppositions that will allow us to clarify further the metaphysical implications of problematic Ideas. First, we will discuss Wilfrid Sellars' 'Myth of the Given' argument, which casts doubt on the very idea that there is something given to thought, something that might verify a thought in the manner of a protocol statement and thereby make statements meaningful. We will then show how John McDowell extends Sellars' Myth of the Given argument, and how Hubert Dreyfus challenges McDowell's position. In reviewing this debate we will set the stage for the second key argument, namely Huw Price's recent claim that Quine's critique of Carnap's anti-metaphysical arguments are not nearly as conclusive as has been widely assumed. The supposed success of Quine's arguments helped to pave the way for the recent upsurge in analytic metaphysics, as best exemplified by the work of David Lewis (one of Quine's students). Price's argument will allow us to return to Della Rocca's critique of MI (also discussed earlier [see §7.7–8]), and in doing so prepare the way for the third key argument, that of Donald Davidson (in §16), an argument that can be seen as an introduction to the political implications of problematic Ideas.

3. Wilfrid Sellars and the Myth of the Given

In *Empiricism and the Philosophy of Mind*, Wilfrid Sellars develops a famous argument that challenges one of the central assumptions of Humean empiricism – namely, the claim that knowledge is founded upon the givens of experience, whether these be Hume's impressions, Russell's particulars or Carnap's observation/protocol sentences. When asked how I know that the shirt I'm wearing is yellow, I can say, following Hume, that I see that it is yellow, or, more precisely, that it is given to me in my experience as a sense impression which I have come, through habituation, to associate with the word 'yellow'. Similarly for Carnap, who acknowledges adopting Hume's 'antimetaphysical position' (Carnap 1984, 7), if no criterion for the use of a word can be given, if for the word 'teavy' (to use Carnap's own example again [1996, 64]) one cannot point to a given instance where one can or cannot use the word, then the word is meaningless, and statements using such words, no matter how syntactically correct or meaningful they may appear to be, are pseudo-statements. Thus, as with Hume's call to consign 'to the flames' any text that does not 'contain any experimental reasoning concerning matter of fact and existence' (Hume 2005, 213), so too for Carnap we ought to abandon any philosophy that trades in pseudo-statements. The key to overcoming metaphysics, therefore, from the perspective of the Humean empiricism that Carnap adopts, is to make sure that any statements we make regarding the world are supported by something that is given to and in experience. It is precisely this assumption that Sellars challenges.

To challenge the Myth of the Given, Sellars calls upon the aid of another myth, the myth of Jones, 'our fictitious ancestor [who] has developed a theory that overt verbal behavior is the expression of thoughts' (Sellars 1997, 106). In other words, if I tell my wife that I am sad, then according to Jones' theory my verbal statement expresses a thought, the thought of being sad. Moreover, if such expressions regarding being sad are seen to be associated with overt behaviour, then on Jones' theory we can take the behaviour before us – e.g., the sombre facial expressions, tone of voice, etc. – as a reason for claiming that a person is sad. Once this mythical Jones has popularised his theory, and people have come to learn to apply it to the evidence before them, then my wife, for instance, may see my quiet, sullen demeanour as a reason to believe that I am sad, and I may in turn recognise this statement as an accurate description of what is going on with me. As Sellars puts it, 'when Tom, watching Dick, has behavioral evidence which warrants the use of the sentence (in the language of [Jones'] theory) "Dick is thinking 'p'" ... Dick, using the same behavioral evidence, can say, in the language of the theory, "I am thinking 'p'"' (106). The use of such theories, however, is on Sellars' account 'an intersubjective achievement' in that such theories and uses of language are 'learned in intersubjective contexts', a point Sellars admits to having in common with B.F. Skinner, Carnap and Wittgenstein, among others (106). In other words, the reason we come to apply the language of thoughts to ourselves and others is precisely because we have learned to apply Jones' theory, according to the myth, and in the language of Jones' theory thoughts are logically connected to, or provide reasons for, the overt behaviours we see, much as, Sellars argues, 'the observable behavior of gases is evidence for molecular episodes [and] is built into the very logic of molecule talk' (107). When an overt behaviour we witness leads us to infer and speak of what someone is thinking, including ourselves, then this happens not because the thoughts themselves are given to us to see; it is rather a consequence of the theory that logically entails a relation between particular thoughts and certain observable behaviours. We are thus in what John McDowell, Robert Brandom and others have called, following and developing Sellars, the 'space of reasons', meaning that our empirical statements, statements of what we see to be the case, are not pointing to a given – in this case, a thought – but rather are providing a reason for inferring one statement from another. In other words, the overt behaviours, and the statements describing them, provide a reason for statements about the thoughts these behaviours are assumed (on Jones' theory) to be expressions of.

With the myth of Jones' theory in hand, Sellars believes 'We are now ready for the problem of the status of concepts pertaining to immediate experience' (Sellars 1997, 107); that is, we are ready to take on the Myth of the Given. As with Jones' theory regarding the relationship of overt behaviours to the thoughts these behaviours express, the Myth of the Given also entails a theory. In this case, Sellars argues that 'the hero of my myth [the Myth of the Given] postulates a class of inner – theoretical – episodes which he calls, say, impressions, and which are the end results of the impingement of physical objects and processes on various parts of the body' (109). When I say, therefore, that I know I am wearing a yellow shirt because I see that it is so, the assumption, on this theory, is that this claim about seeing that this shirt is yellow is evidence for being given a yellow impression. Prior to such theories, Sellars argues, 'the only concepts our fictitious ancestors had of perceptual episodes were those of overt verbal reports' (108). If asked why I see my shirt as yellow, my fictitious ancestor would claim that my saying that I see my shirt as yellow is sufficient reason for asserting that it is yellow. These ancestors would not rely on the Myth of the Given theory, for they had not yet learned it, had not yet learned to see that one's observational statements are evidence for a content that is given, but given in a way that is beyond the expression of language itself, a non-propositional content that accounts for what it is I see, and ultimately for the statements I make regarding what I see. This effort to move beyond language, and beyond the space of reasons that come with the concepts that are inseparable from language, is a key motivation behind the Myth of the Given, Sellars argues. It may well be a feature, not a bug, of human nature. This can be seen in Sellars' closing lines to *Empiricism and the Philosophy of Mind*:

> I have used a myth to kill a myth – the Myth of the Given. But is my myth really a myth? Or does the reader not recognize Jones as Man himself in the

middle of his journey from the grunts and groans of the cave to the subtle and polydimensional discourse of the drawing room, the laboratory, and the study, the language of Henry and William James, of Einstein and of the philosophers who, in their efforts to break out of discourse to an *arché* beyond discourse, have provided the most curious dimension of all. (Sellars 1997, 117)

4. McDowell and World-Disclosing Experience

Sellars' critique of our human 'efforts to break out of discourse to an *arché* beyond discourse' has been extremely influential over the past few decades among philosophers in both analytic and continental traditions (see, for instance, McDowell 1994; Brandom 1994, 2000; and Brassier 2007). A key theme that has been most widely discussed is Sellars' basic claim that we cannot get outside the space of reasons, outside the inferential relations essential to a conceptually laden experience, and hence we cannot get to a non-propositional given that would lay the solid foundation for a privileged discourse, such as Carnap's 'protocol language' (Carnap 1987, 459) or Russell's 'primary language' (Russell 1940, 19). John McDowell, for instance, adopts Heidegger's distinction 'between being open to a world and merely inhabiting an environment' (McDowell 2007, 343), and argues that humans, unlike most animals, do not inhabit an environment but are open to a world, and as a result humans are 'animals whose natural being is permeated with rationality' (McDowell 1994, 85), including their 'world-disclosing' (McDowell 2007, 348) perceptual experience whose content is not given in a non-propositional form but is, to the contrary, 'present in a form in which it is suitable to constitute the content of a conceptual capacity' (346). The difficulty with this move of extending our conceptual capacity all the way to our perceptual experience is in accounting for what it is that provides resistance, if anything, to our conceptual formations. If our conceptual capacities are at work throughout our experience, including our perceptual experience, then how can we determine whether or not the content of our experience is independent and real, or simply a product of our understanding itself? In full recognition of this problem, a problem that was central to Descartes' *Meditations*, McDowell admits, 'We need to conceive this expansive spontaneity [of conceptual understanding] as subject to control from outside our thinking, on pain of representing the operations of spontaneity as a frictionless spinning in a void' (McDowell 1994, 11). 'The Given', he also admits, 'seems to supply that external control'. Following Sellars, however, McDowell will call upon a 'world-disclosing' experience rather than a non-propositional given to provide the friction that will constrain our conceptual spontaneity. As McDowell states his approach,

> The position I am urging appeals to receptivity to ensure friction, like the Myth of the Given, but it is unlike the Myth of the Given in that it takes capacities of spontaneity to be in play all the way out to the ultimate grounds of empirical judgments. That is what enables us to reinstate friction without undermining the very idea of ultimate grounds, as the Myth of the Given does. (McDowell 1994, 67)

The Myth of the Given undermines 'the very idea of ultimate grounds', for if the content of perceptual experience is to provide a reason for our inferential, conceptual claims, then it must already, according to McDowell (and Sellars and Brandom as well), be given in a manner suitable to our conceptual capacities. This is precisely what McDowell argues when he claims that the content of our perceptual experience comes in a form 'suitable to constitute the content of a conceptual capacity'. A non-propositional content, however, a content that is given, but given as 'an *arché* beyond discourse', undermines the possibility of providing grounds or reasons for it can only provide a reason or grounds once it has been taken up in accordance with our conceptual capacities, which includes the capacity for giving and asking for reasons. The world-disclosing nature of human perceptual experience, however, provides the friction McDowell seeks, since, in it, the world is given as an '"outer experience"' (67), but the content of this world-disclosing experience 'hangs together with other aspects of its content in a unity of the sort Kant identifies as categorial' (McDowell 2007, 346); in other words, 'its content has a distinctive form' (348), namely, the form of the categorial and hence a form congenial to our conceptual capacities and our ability to provide reasons and grounds.

5. Dreyfus on McDowell; or, on Non-conceptual Experience

In his critique of McDowell, Hubert Dreyfus argues that McDowell's efforts, following Sellars, to extend our conceptual capacities to the furthest reaches of our experience are doomed to failure for they do not recognise that key aspects of our experience are non-propositional and therefore always already beyond discourse and our conceptual understanding. Dreyfus will ask, rhetorically, 'can we accept McDowell's Sellarsian claim that perception is conceptual "all the way out", thereby denying the more basic perceptual capacities we seem to share with prelinguistic infants and higher animals?' (Dreyfus 2005, 47). For Dreyfus, the answer is a clear no. At the heart of his argument is the assumption that a conceptual understanding entails an abstraction from concrete experiences and an abstraction that enables one to use concepts to segregate and categorise one's varied experiences. This is comparable to Wilson's reading of Russell's and Frege's understanding of what grasping a concept entails, with Wilson arguing that for Frege and Russell a concept 'plays a causal role in guiding human classification, rather as a template steers the activity of a machine' (Wilson 1982, 556). When I have grasped what a gardenia is, I have in essence grasped an abstract rule that can then serve to guide my behaviour. If my wife asks me to water the gardenias, my understanding of what a gardenia is will lead me to water only the gardenias. It is this sense of conceptual understanding or rule-following that Dreyfus likely has in mind when he highlights the 'unexpected problem' the pioneering AI researcher Marvin Minsky encountered when he found that '[c]omputers couldn't comprehend the simple stories understood by four-year-olds' (Dreyfus 2005, 48). On Dreyfus's account, a computer is a machine that follows rules (programs), much as the activity of one who understands a concept does. Frege and Russell thus seem to support Dreyfus's reading of conceptual understanding, and Carnap's writing lends its support as well when he stresses the advent of 'modern symbolic logic' as being instrumental to our ability to derive a 'conclusion ... mechanically from the premises' (Carnap 1984, 10). What the computer's inability to understand a story alerts Dreyfus to, however, is that understanding a story is not a matter of categorising data in terms of abstract categories and rules; rather, it entails an ability to determine which facts in the story are relevant to the grasp of the story as a whole. But to grasp relevance entails a frame of reference. The resulting problem, as Dreyfus puts it, is to understand how 'the computer [could] determine which of the millions of facts in its database were relevant for recognizing the relevant frame' – that is, the frame relevant to understanding the story – but 'any AI program using frames to solve the story-understanding problem by organizing millions of facts was going to be caught in a regress' (Dreyfus 2005, 48). In other words, if we program a computer to use frames to determine which facts are relevant, the resulting problem is to know which frames are relevant for understanding the story at hand, a problem that brings in the need for yet more frames, and so on. Dreyfus, however, points out that we need not succumb to this regress: 'Happily', he argues, 'we are, as Martin Heidegger and Maurice Merleau-Ponty put it, always already in a world that is organized in terms of our bodies and interests and thus permeated by relevance' (49). For this reason, a four-year-old can understand a story that a computer cannot.

On Dreyfus's account of living in a world 'permeated by relevance', even the prototypical example of a rule-based activity – namely, chess – is understood to involve, at the highest levels of expertise, an experience that cannot be explained simply by reference to abstract concepts and rules. As we have seen, both Carnap and Nagel single out chess as a favoured example of a rule-based activity, an activity they set forth as an aspirational model for analytic philosophy. For Carnap the task of philosophy is to spell out the logical rules that transform protocol sentences into the system languages of the sciences. In undertaking this task, philosophers work with propositions and statements much as chess players work with chess pieces, and 'like chess figures', Carnap argues, 'words are here combined and manipulated according to definite rules' (Carnap 1984, 9–10). For Nagel too, analytic philosophers ought to ignore the issues that plague a troubled world and instead 'cultivate intellectual games with chess-like indifference to its [the world's] course' (Nagel 1936a, 9). For Dreyfus, by contrast, while chess is indeed a game based upon rules, and rules that may be programmed into computers that can analyse millions of moves per second, 'what is given to the chess master in his experience of the board' is not 'a bare Given'; rather, 'the chess master has a take on "the layout of reality"' (Dreyfus 2005, 55). Dreyfus is referring here to McDowell's claim that 'Experience enables the layout of reality itself to exert a rational influence on what a subject thinks' (McDowell 1994, 26), and Dreyfus's point is that the chess master's experience of the board, an experience permeated with relevance, is not to be thought of as just the '"bare Given" and the "thinkable" [for these] are not our only alternatives'; rather, the chess master's experience is of 'a meaningful Given – a Given that is nonconceptual but not bare' (Dreyfus 2005, 55). The chess master neither sees the pieces as a bare Given needing to be interpreted, nor do they simply think through what needs to be done. They simply see, without having to think it through, the relevant moves to make given the layout of the board. As chess grandmaster and world champion Magnus Carlsen put it in an interview:

> When a computer looks at a position it will consider all the possibilities and it will calculate them many, many moves ahead. For me, it's more about seeing the right [i.e., *relevant*] possibilities, finding the right ideas and evaluating them correctly ... I think it's partly subconscious, because sometimes there will be a decision-making process in my mind and then suddenly I make a move and I really don't know why I did that. (Carlsen 2015)

It appears then that Carlsen would likely accept Dreyfus's claim that what makes an expert's actions possible involves, in part at least, 'the sort of features that the expert could not be aware of and would not be able to think' (Dreyfus 2005, 58). Dreyfus will extend this point beyond chess, however, and argue that this is largely the default basis for an experience that is permeated by relevance. Our everyday navigation of the world is to be understood, according to Dreyfus, as entailing the same processes that allow the chess master to navigate the layout of the chess board. He makes this point explicitly, claiming that 'mastery requires a rich perceptual repertoire

... but it requires no conceptual repertoire at all. This holds true for such refined skills as chess, jazz improvisation, sports, martial arts, etc., but equally for everyday skills such as cooking dinner, crossing a busy street, carrying on a conversation, or just getting around the world' (58). Contrary, therefore, to McDowell's claim that perceptual experience always already comes with a categorial form – a form that enables us, implicitly at least, to place this experience into the space of reasons where it can then be stated explicitly as a reason for indeterminately many other inferential claims (see Brandom 1994 for a thorough development of this account) – Dreyfus argues that 'masterful action', or perhaps even just 'crossing a busy street', 'does not seem to require or even to allow placement in the space of reasons' (58). Dreyfus's argument carries an echo of Adorno's negative dialectics, especially Adorno's claim that 'the concept does not exhaust the thing conceived' (Adorno 1973, 5). Our engaged, meaningful experience of the world, as Dreyfus understands it, is one whereby the relevance of our experience cannot be reduced to abstract conceptual rules; it is given neither as a bare Given nor as something thinkable in terms of concepts. What is given, as Adorno would put it, is an objectivity that resists being conceptualised, an objectivity that is not exhausted by the concepts used to identify it; nor is it a determinate, nonconceptual given. McDowell's version of Sellars' Myth of the Given argument thus appears to remain committed to the primacy of the determinate, with the determinate being for McDowell the conceptual, world-disclosing form that provides the basis for experiences that find their *determinate* place within the space of reasons.

6. McDowell Replies, and Jason Stanley on Skill

In his reply to these criticisms, McDowell takes issue with Dreyfus's characterisation of rationality, or more precisely with what he thinks our conceptual capacities entail. As McDowell understands him, 'Dreyfus pictures rationality as detached from particular situations – as able to relate to particular situations only by subsuming them under content determinately expressible in abstraction from any situation' (McDowell 2007, 339). When Dreyfus argues, for instance, that the chess master's abilities, along with our everyday abilities and experiences in a world permeated with relevance, involve 'the sort of features that the expert could not be aware of and would not be able to think' (Dreyfus 2005, 58), he certainly does seem to presuppose that being able to think and be aware of what one is doing involves a determinate concept, a concept under which the particular behaviour or action is subsumed, and a concept which can be stated or expressed. McDowell argues that Dreyfus is wrong on this point. 'Contrary to what Dreyfus implies', McDowell argues, 'the domain of conceptual articulation includes thoughts that are not intelligible in abstraction from particular situations' (McDowell 2007, 342). As we have seen, for McDowell our human experience of the world is a 'world-disclosing' experience, and thus we are open to a world rather than simply inhabiting an environment. This experience of openness to the world is indeed one that McDowell claims has a 'distinctive form' (348), namely, a categorial form that allows us to place the experience within the space of reasons, but he adds that 'openness to the world, which is rationality at work, is intelligible only in a context that includes embodied coping skills' (344). In other words, integral to our experience of being open to a world are precisely those 'coping skills' that cannot be conceptualised or articulated in the determinate terms or categories that Dreyfus seems to think are essential to rational thinking. To the contrary, McDowell is quite clear that 'We do not need to have words for all the content that is conceptually available to us' (348), including, presumably, the content of the experiences of chess masters such as Carlsen, who will make decisions without being able to state or even know why they are making the moves they make.

This point has been reiterated and reinforced by Jason Stanley. Stanley, in a well-known argument (Stanley 2001), has argued against Gilbert Ryle's distinction between knowing how and knowing that, the key to Ryle's distinction being that one can state, in propositional form, what it is *that* one knows but cannot state in propositional form *how* one can perform certain skills, such as riding a bike. Knowing how, Ryle argues, is fundamentally different in kind from knowing that (see Ryle 1946). For Stanley, by contrast, knowing how is reducible to knowing that, and thus Ryle's distinction is wrong. Despite his commitment to this position, however – to the idea that knowing how to do something such as riding a bike involves 'a state with propositional content … [and content] that is suitable for us in guiding action (Stanley and Krakauer 2013, 1) – Stanley (and his co-author Krakauer) recognise that although someone who knows how to ride a bike, swim, cross a busy street, etc., possesses the 'knowledge of what to do to initiate an action … some manifestations of this knowledge are by agents who cannot verbally articulate its content' (3). Both Stanley and McDowell, therefore, can accept Dreyfus's claim that many embodied skills entail an experience that one 'cannot verbally articulate', and it is for this reason that Dreyfus's critique, McDowell argues, brings to the table its own presuppositions, or what McDowell calls 'The Myth of the Disembodied Intellect' (McDowell 2007, 349). This myth, as McDowell sees it, is quite common and 'familiar in philosophy', and it entails the assumption that 'the pervasiveness of conceptual rationality will not cohere with giving proper weight to the bodily character of our lives' (349). As McDowell believes he has shown in his reply to Dreyfus, this assumption could not be further from the truth. For McDowell, and for Stanley though for different reasons, we can perfectly well understand our lives as embodied and involved in skills and activities the content of which cannot be 'verbally articulated', and yet our experience, as openness to a world, also involves a particular form in that it all 'hangs together ... in a unity of the sort Kant identifies as categorial' (346). It is this categorial form that provides the friction necessary to ensure that the spontaneity of our understanding does not become a 'frictionless spinning in a void' (McDowell 1994, 11). This categorial form not only allows us to be open to a world but also allows us to see how the world hangs together, or to see how one thing is inferentially related to another; in short, our embodied experience opens us to the space of reasons.

7. MacFarlane on McDowell; or, the Problem of Mathematical Experience

John MacFarlane (2004) has taken issue with this latter point – namely, with McDowell's claim that our openness to the world involves 'a unity of the sort Kant identifies as categorial', meaning, as MacFarlane reads McDowell, that whatever the content of our experience of the world may be, this experience can be taken up as the content of a conceptual understanding. The problem with this approach, as MacFarlane sees it, is that while McDowell rejects, and rightfully so according to MacFarlane, Kant's efforts to account for mathematics in terms of the form of sensibility, McDowell nonetheless accepts a Kantian form of openness to the world in everything but the mathematical realm. McDowell thus holds to what MacFarlane will call the 'Weak Kantian Thesis', which is committed to the view that '[i]n order to have content, *empirical* concepts must have some relation to intuition' (MacFarlane 2004, 4), but not the 'Strong Kantian Thesis' (or simply Kant's position) which is committed to the view that 'In order to have content, concepts must have some relation to intuition' (3), and this includes mathematical concepts. McDowell's attempt to uphold the weak rather than the strong Kantian thesis leaves MacFarlane with a question: 'can McDowell coherently retain Kant's insight about empirical content while rejecting his view of mathematical content? Does the Kantian package come apart so neatly into independent modules?' (5). For MacFarlane, the answer is no.

Critical to MacFarlane's concerns is McDowell's effort to account for that which constrains thought, that which keeps thought from generating its own realities without check (i.e., the 'frictionless spinning in the void'). McDowell follows a common strategy in his account, arguing that it is what thought is about, the object of thought itself, which constrains thought and keeps it from slipping into a process of unchecked abstraction and conceptualisation. As MacFarlane notes, this puts McDowell's approach at odds with Donald Davidson's coherence theory of truth (we will discuss Davidson further in §16). While MacFarlane is committed 'to explaining how thought can be rationally constrained by the things it is about … [this] is precisely what Davidson denies is possible, on the ground that sensations, which "connect the world and our beliefs" [Davidson 1989, 311], are not propositional' (MacFarlane 2004, 8). McDowell, by contrast, on MacFarlane's reading, is committed to the position that 'What carries empirical thought to its objects … is experience, conceived as the passive actualization of concepts in sensory receptivity' (8). In other words, in our openness to the world, the world itself is precisely what thought is about, the outside that provides the constraints for the inferential connections we establish within the space of reasons. This is why MacFarlane believes that McDowell could only commit himself to the Weak Kantian Thesis, for if mathematical thought is also constrained by the nature of the objects of mathematical thought, and 'not just by more mathematical thought', then we would be left having to show 'the mechanism by which mathematical objects are made manifest to us' (10). For MacFarlane this cannot be done through the *a priori* form of sensory experience, or in the Strong Kantian Thesis manner, for Kant did not have, as MacFarlane puts it, the '*logical* resources for representing infinite mathematical structures' (5), structures that have been common in mathematics since Cantor. McDowell would also reject mathematical empiricism on the grounds that this would remain committed to the view that 'the language of theory can indeed be held separate from the language of observation' (McDowell 1994, 161), which is precisely the view that McDowell, following Sellars, rejects.

Whereas Russell and Carnap will draw philosophical inspiration from Hume's distinction between impressions and ideas and incorporate this into their own thought in terms of object sentences (Russell) and protocol sentences (Carnap) on the one hand, and a language of theory on the other, McDowell rejects the notion that there is a separation between an observation language (a language of the Given) and theory language. All language claims that are meaningful are within the space of reasons, or expressions of our openness to the world. If this is true of our experience in general, for McDowell, then it should be true of our mathematical experience as well, but thanks to Cantor and others who have given us transfinite numbers, it seems highly unlikely that mathematical empiricism is going to be the way in which 'mathematical objects are made manifest to us'. At this point McDowell could follow Gödel and accept a 'special mathematical form of receptivity distinct from sensory experience, like Gödel's "mathematical intuition'" (McDowell 1994, 10; citing Gödel 1947, 518), but this would result in a division at the heart of our world-disclosing experience and hence be at odds with McDowell's arguments upholding the Kantian categorial unity of this experience.

A third and final way out for McDowell, according to MacFarlane, would be to accept a formalist account of mathematics. On the formalist approach, the manner in which the content of mathematical concepts become manifest is no longer a problem, since formalists simply deny that there is any such content. According to them, as MacFarlane summarises their position, 'Mathematics has no content, either because it is just a game with symbols or because it is somehow a "by-product" of our understanding of language' (MacFarlane 2004, 6). MacFarlane traces this position to Wittgenstein (see Wittgenstein 1976) and A.J. Ayer (see Ayer 1971). McDowell could hold this view with respect to mathematics, given what MacFarlane takes to be his commitment to the Weak Kantian Thesis, and thus accept that empirical concepts have content while mathematical concepts do not. The problem with taking this line, MacFarlane argues, is that with respect to McDowell's project it 'ultimately threatens to undermine McDowell's thinking about empirical content as well' (MacFarlane 2004, 4). In short, as MacFarlane puts it, if we 'could make sense of mathematical content without invoking experience', as McDowell seems committed to, and if we were to argue along formalist lines that a 'holistic inferential articulation is sufficient for mathematical content, [then] why not for empirical content as well?' (13). If we could account for mathematical concepts along formalist lines, and thus without having to concern ourselves with the content of mathematical concepts or the nature of the object being thought through these concepts, then unless McDowell can satisfactorily segregate the formalist approach towards mathematical concepts from his approach to empirical concepts, we could just as well end up with a formalist account of empirical content as well and thus be left without an object being thought, an outside that serves to constrain our thinking – in other words, we would be left with a 'frictionless spinning in the void'.

At this point we could take up McDowell's reply to MacFarlane's concerns with his project (see McDowell 2004), or even turn to the extensive literature related to the issues in the foundations of mathematics that MacFarlane raises, but for the sake of time, and in order to return to the problematic Ideas that are our concern, I want to address the problem of accounting for the content of mathematical concepts, most notably the concepts that involve infinite mathematical structures. One of the primary reasons for segregating the content of mathematical concepts from the content of empirical concepts is that mathematicians routinely deal with infinite mathematical structures. The assumption behind the segregation of mathematical from empirical concepts, presumably, is that an infinite mathematical object could never be the content of an empirical concept. The content of an empirical concept, so it has been assumed, must be a determinate, finite and limited content; something that can be taken up in a representational thought. If we cannot experience the infinite, then we cannot experience the infinite nature of certain mathematical objects, and thus if we are to account for the content of mathematics, we will have to look elsewhere than our empirical concepts. It is at this point that we can either adopt Gödel's special form of mathematical intuition to account for the content of mathematical concepts, or we can adopt a formalist approach. With the relationship between problematic Ideas and transcendental empiricism I have been developing here, however, we have another possibility, and one that begins by rejecting the assumption that the infinite cannot be the content of an empirical concept.

8. Lewis and Singletons, Again

We have already encountered the mystery David Lewis claims confronts us when we attempt to explain the relationship between an individual and that individual's singleton (see §11.6). On the one hand, sets (or classes, since Lewis, as we saw, distinguishes between sets [which may have no members, like the null set] and classes [which do have members]) are unproblematic. If I take my two cats, then we can have the set that includes both Mila and Charlie. Thinking of a set as a gathering or collection of individuals, therefore, seems perfectly natural. But on the other hand, why would we think of an individual as being the unique member of its own set, its singleton? Moreover, things become stranger, Lewis notes, for we also have the set that includes Mila and Mila's singleton, a set that has its own singleton; and then we have the set that includes this new singleton plus Mila and Mila's singleton, and the singleton of this new set; and so on *ad infinitum*. If we allow for any determinate individual to be the unique member of its own set, its own singleton, and if we allow that sets themselves are determinate individuals in that they too can become members of their own unit-sets (singletons), then suddenly we have, from a single determinate individual, an infinite series. Set theory thus involves, as Lewis readily admits, a mysterious relationship that is far from unproblematic. As we have seen, for Lewis the trouble with set theory 'is that when we have one thing, then somehow we have another wholly distinct thing, the singleton. And another, and another ... *ad infinitum*. But that's the price for mathematical power. Pay it' (Lewis

1991, 87). In other words, the trouble with set theory is that we can start from any determinate individual, meaning the very type of determinate individual that can become the content of an empirical concept, and from there we can generate an infinity of other determinate individuals – namely, the singletons. An infinite series is thus in some way inseparable from each and every determinate individual, and yet it is a mystery for Lewis how this is so. It is a mystery he is willing to accept, however, or a price he is willing to pay, for with the infinite series of singletons we are given 'enough modelling clay to make the whole of mathematics' (12). With the concept of problematic Ideas we have shed some light on this mystery, since problematic Ideas are precisely the differential unconscious of infinite series that become, at the limit, the determinate individuals with which Lewis begins. The mystery of the relationship between the infinite series of singletons and the determinate individual begins when one attempts to account for the infinite series on the basis of the determinate individual, rather than accounting, as is the case with problematic Ideas or the transcendental empiricism Deleuze deploys, for determinate individuals on the basis of an infinite series of pre-individual differentials (the differential unconscious [see §8.4]).

9. Meillassoux, Contingency and Mathematics

We can further clarify these issues by turning to Quentin Meillassoux's work, and in particular to his 2012 Berlin lecture, 'Iteration, Reiteration, Repetition: A Speculative Analysis of the Meaningless Sign'. In this lecture, Meillassoux takes up a number of themes, most notably the critique of correlationism that was a central concern of his book *After Finitude* (Meillassoux 2010). Correlationism, as Meillassoux understands it, is the philosophical position that 'maintains the impossibility of acceding through thought to a being independent of thought' (Meillassoux 2012, 2). Speculative philosophy, of the sort Meillassoux seeks to develop, aspires to move beyond 'the closure of thought upon itself ... [and] attain an absolute outside of it [thought]' (2). The problem, in short, is to understand the nature of a reality (the absolute) that is not relative to, or correlated with, a thought, consciousness or subjective process (individual or social) to which this reality would be given. It is at this point in his argument that Meillassoux turns to mathematics.

In his discussion on the philosophical foundations of mathematics, Meillassoux begins with the formalism of Hilbert, and then turns to a version of the formalist alternative MacFarlane lists as one of the possible ways to understand mathematical concepts. Of most importance to Meillassoux is set theory, and this for the same reason Lewis turned to it – namely, set theory is foundational for mathematics itself. Meillassoux states this point explicitly, noting that 'Set theory … is a theory capable, notably, of constructing both numbers (ordinals and cardinals) and functions (which are a certain type of set, a set of ordered pairs) – and thus a theory that is foundational for mathematics (foundational in a non-philosophical sense), in that it constructs its two principal objects: numbers and functions' (Meillassoux 2012, 20–1). The importance of Hilbert for Meillassoux is that Hilbert's formalist understanding of set theory does not, as does the formal axiomatic of Euclid's *Elements*, '*begin with any initial definition*' (21; see Hilbert 2013). Whereas Euclid's *Elements* begins with definitions of a point, a line, the extremities of a line, a straight line, and so on (see Euclid 1908, 153), Hilbert's formal axiomatic begins with axioms where 'one posits relations between terms that themselves are not defined' (Meillassoux 2012, 21). For Meillassoux the key move here is to think of sets as signs, and to name these signs – as α, β, γ, etc. (what Meillassoux calls 'base-signs'); 'but to name them', Meillassoux adds, 'is not to define them. In set theory, we never get involved in defining what a set is.' What set theory works with instead of definitions, according to Meillassoux's reading of Hilbert, is simply sets understood as signs 'devoid of meaning, and *a fortiori* of any reference. And this is the initial object of mathematics, in so far as the latter is "founded" on set theory: the pure and simple sign that refers only to itself' (21).

At this point Meillassoux meets Lewis. For Lewis, as we saw, the singleton is problematic for we cannot understand how or why an individual should be a member of its own unique set (the singleton), a singleton that thereby generates the infinities from which we can found mathematics. For Meillassoux, the problem with singletons is that we are attempting to give them a meaning, or define them, and in doing so come to an understanding of that which accounts for their reality. From Meillassoux's perspective, however, the reality of the singleton is no longer problematic if we understand it to be simply a meaningless sign. But what is a meaningless sign? For one thing, 'a meaningless sign', Meillassoux insists, '*is* still a sign' (Meillassoux 2012, 24). With this claim, Meillassoux recognises that he is parting ways with 'most modern analyses of the sign, which, setting out from the linguistic sign or index, do not conceive of it outside its capacity *to refer to something*: to a meaning, an object, a reference'. But it is precisely the advantage of Hilbert's mathematical formalism that there exists a sign that 'refers to nothing other than itself as sign; a sign that is not the index of any reality outside of it' (24). We can now see that a singleton is a meaningless sign. The singleton of Mila, for instance, is a sign, but a sign that refers to nothing other than itself as a sign. The singleton is thus not to be understood as a sign which refers to Mila, even though the singleton is a singleton of nothing other than Mila.

That is, a singleton is not, as Meillassoux puts it, an 'index of any reality outside of it'. The singleton of Mila does not point beyond itself to the reality of Mila, to the reality it includes as the unique member that we could then use to define or understand the sense and meaning of the singleton; rather, for Meillassoux the singleton could be seen to be simply the contingency of the sign itself due to the fact that it could be any other or all other individuals from which the infinities that a singleton generates are spun.

With this last point we come to one of the central claims of Meillassoux's Berlin lecture, a claim that is also central to his metaphysics. Meillassoux states it as the following thesis: *'it is because I can intuit in every entity its eternal contingency, that I can intuit a meaningless sign'* (Meillassoux 2012, 35). What is driving this claim is Meillassoux's rejection of the principle of sufficient reason (PSR). As we saw earlier (see §7.4), Bradley affirmed the PSR, and as a result every relation needed to be accounted for. The problem, however, is that if we accept the PSR and thereby attempt to account for the nature of relations, we end up, Bradley claims, with either an arbitrary account – e.g., arbitrarily accounting for the relation between A and B in terms of A rather than B – or we generate a regress of relations and end up with no account of the relationship we initially sought to understand. We can avoid the regress by claiming, as Bradley does, that relations are merely appearances of a single Absolute reality; or we can follow Russell, reject the PSR and accept certain facts as brute facts that need no account or explanation. Meillassoux's rejection of the PSR is similar to but importantly different from Russell's. Like Russell, Meillassoux accepts that there are things that cannot be accounted for or explained, things for which we cannot give a reason why they are this way rather than another – they simply are this way. For Russell, however, among the brute facts that need no explanation are logical relations and universals – such as the logical transitivity of the greater than or equal to relation, $\geq$, so that if $a \geq b$ and $b \geq c$, then $a \geq c$. For Russell, this relation needs no account or justification – it is a brute fact, perhaps even a Moorean fact. He will thus begin with these brute facts (what he calls 'particulars' and 'atomic facts') and then, in accordance with his logical atomism, set out to provide for the logical construction of the claims that may be derived from these facts, including the claims associated with the sciences. Meillassoux, by contrast, will embrace a thorough, all-encompassing contingency, and argue that there is no reason why any entity is the way it is and not otherwise. Even brute facts, on this reading, could be other than they are, and thus any logical construction based upon them could be other than it is as well. In *After Finitude*, Meillassoux will refer to this metaphysical state of complete and absolute contingency as 'hyper-Chaos'. In fact, hyper-Chaos is how Meillassoux understands the absolute, the reality that is independent of and irreducible to any form of thought or thinking: 'Our absolute, in effect, is nothing other than an extreme form of chaos, a *hyper-Chaos*, for which nothing is or would seem to be, impossible, not even the unthinkable' (Meillassoux 2010, 64). For Meillassoux, therefore, there is no reason why any entity is the way it is and not otherwise, and it is this absolute contingency, this hyper-Chaos, that makes the meaningless sign of mathematics possible, the meaningless sign of the singleton for instance. This was precisely Meillassoux's thesis, and a consequence of this absolute contingency, for him, is that

> whereas normally we grasp things through their properties, and secondarily through their contingency (unless we see them from the speculative [that is, Meillassoux's] point of view), we are constrained to grasp these same things through their speculative contingency (their arbitrariness) once they are seen as signs ... Now it is precisely at the moment when we flip from the grasping of contingent things to the grasping of the contingency of things ... that we immediately iterate them without limit. (Meillassoux 2010, 36–7)

To restate Meillassoux's point in the terms we have been developing: our normal, everyday perspective entails thinking in terms of that which is determinate and individuated, and individuated in terms of its identifiable properties. To identify the properties of things, such as a cup of coffee, is, as Adorno argued, precisely what it is to think, but in doing so we encounter an objective world (with objectivity taken in Adorno's sense) that resists our efforts to think it. Once things are seen as signs, however, and as meaningless signs that could be other than they are and refer, as signs, to nothing other than themselves, then we move beyond thinking of determinate things to the eternal contingency and indeterminacy of things. Moreover, this move to the eternal contingency of things brings an iteration without limit, since there is no determinate thing being repeated, and thereby no determinate limit to the nature of a meaningless sign. The iteration of signs will also come without limit, or without a determinate point where the contingency becomes something, something that we may think of as being contingent. In this sense, then, the meaningless sign, as made possible by absolute contingency, brings the infinite in its wake, just as Lewis recognised with respect to the singleton (itself a meaningless sign).

For reasons to be discussed in the next section, we will not stress, as Meillassoux does, the absolute contingency of problematic Ideas. The reason for not doing so is that contingency, I will argue, presupposes a *determinate* difference that problematic Ideas make possible – namely, the difference between being and non-being, whereas reality is to be thought of, and as a consequence of problematic Ideas, as mixed (in accordance with Plato's call not to rush to the One or the Infinite). It is thus neither all or nothing, being or non-being, but rather relative, mixed existence; or, to state this slightly differently, and in the manner of Adorno, we neither completely have being or non-being. That said, Meillassoux has provided a perspective from which we can further dissipate the mystery Lewis felt surrounded the appearance of singletons. With this perspective, however, we have come quite far from Carnap's attempt to eliminate metaphysics. With Meillassoux's appeal to hyper-Chaos as the absolute that appears through the meaningless signs of mathematics, we have an appeal Carnap would probably see as relying on pseudo-statements. Hyper-Chaos would likely be seen by him, along with Being, the Nothing that nothings, etc., as yet another metaphysical term that cannot be provided with a determinate 'criterion of application' (Carnap 1996, 64). Without explicitly saying so, Meillassoux may well be fine with his metaphysics of absolute contingency because with it we get the full autonomy and independence of mathematics, just as Lewis was willing to pay the price for the difficulties that come with the singleton in order to have 'enough modelling clay to make the whole of mathematics' (Lewis 1991, 12). By paying this price, however, Lewis has paved the way in recent decades for a resurgence of metaphysical discussions among analytic philosophers. In fact, most contemporary philosophers are likely to argue that, after Quine's influential critique of Carnap, the latter's own critique of metaphysics is no longer seen to be as powerful as it was once thought to be. Huw Price has recently argued that this view is mistaken. Carnap's critique of metaphysics is still relevant, and contemporary analytic philosophers would do well, he argues, to consider the extent to which their own metaphysical commitments may be subject to a Carnap-style critique. Given the metaphysical nature of my own project – 'problematic Idea' is an admittedly metaphysical term – it would do us well to address Price's arguments.

10. Huw Price, Pragmatic Relevance and the Fate of Metaphysics

Huw Price offers a rather straightforward thesis in his essay, 'Metaphysics after Carnap' (Price 2009), a thesis intended to prompt a rethinking of the history of analytic philosophy since the 1950s. Price's argument, in short, is that it is mistaken to continue to believe the widely held narrative that Quine's essay 'On What There Is' (1948) 'gave Ontology a life-saving transfusion', and that his 'Two Dogmas of Empiricism' (1951) 'drove a stake through the heart of Carnap's "Empiricism, Semantics and Ontology" [1950]' (Price 2009, 3), and thus through Carnap's arguments against metaphysics. The key issue in the 'skirmish' between Carnap and Quine, as Price puts it, centres on Carnap's well-known distinction between internal and external questions.

In the 'Frameworks of Entities' section of his 'Empiricism, Semantics and Ontology', Carnap argues that internal questions are those that arise within a given language, or within a given framework in this context. If we are within the framework of 'everyday language', Carnap argues, then questions such as '"Is there a white piece of paper on my desk?", "Did King Arthur actually live?", "Are unicorns and centaurs real or merely imaginary?", and the like [are] questions to be answered by empirical investigation' (Carnap 1952, 210); that is, they are to be addressed within the framework of what Carnap calls 'thing-language'. Within a different framework, such as the 'system of numbers' (212), there will be different internal questions and different corresponding procedures for addressing these questions. With internal questions such as 'Is there a prime number greater than one hundred?', Carnap argues that 'the answers are found, not by empirical investigation based on observations, but by logical analysis based on the rules for the new expression' (212). As Price summarises Carnap's point, internal questions are 'questions that arise within the framework, and their nature depends on the framework in question' (Price 2009, 4). External questions, by contrast, ask about the reality of entities independent of their role within a framework. An external question relative to the thing-language framework thus asks about 'the reality of the thing world itself' (Carnap 1952, 210). For Carnap this is a question 'raised neither by the man in the street nor by scientists, but only by philosophers' (210). It is the question asked by Meillassoux, for instance, when he asks about the nature of reality (or things) independent of any thought or process that experiences, verifies and thinks these things. In *After Finitude*, Meillassoux refers to this question as the problem of ancestrality, the problem of showing how 'a being [can] manifest being's anteriority to manifestation' (Meillassoux 2010, 26). As Carnap understands the motivation behind this question, it is 'a matter of a practical decision concerning the structure of our language' – that is, it is concerned with our choice of 'whether or not to accept and use the forms of expression for the framework in question' (Carnap 1952, 211). In short, it is a question of whether or not to adopt the framework at all, and thus it is a pragmatic question along the lines, as Price puts it, of 'Should we adopt this framework? Would it be useful?' (Price 2009, 4).

This distinction between internal and external questions plays a key role in Carnap's critique of metaphysics. Put briefly, one engages in metaphysics when one uses language in a manner suited to a particular framework but then uses it outside that framework. As we saw earlier, Abraham Stone (2006) shows that Carnap and Heidegger were both immensely concerned to purify everyday language of the errors that creep into it over time. For Heidegger, this involves a grammatical-historico analysis of language, leading ultimately to Heidegger's ontological difference between Being – the 'Nothing that nothings' — and beings, and metaphysics arises, for Heidegger, when one forgets Being and thinks solely in terms of beings. Carnap attempts to clean up language by eliminating pseudo-statements, or statements that cannot be logically constructed on the basis of protocol sentences. Heidegger's use of the word 'Nothing' in the question 'What about this Nothing?' is an example, for Carnap, of using a word outside of the framework where it would normally have meaning (see Carnap 1996, 70). In the statement, 'Nothing is outside', for instance, 'Nothing' is to be understood within a logical framework where it is expressed by way of a negative existential quantifier; namely, as $\sim(\exists x)\cdot Ou(x)$, to be read as: it is not the case that there is an x, and x is outside. In the question 'What about this Nothing?', by contrast, nothing is used in an entirely different way, as a word in the thing-language framework for instance. This is where the errors of metaphysics come in for Carnap, and his method of logical analysis, as we have seen, was an attempt to set philosophy on the right track by pointing out such errors. As long as the language we use remains within the appropriate framework, there will come with this framework an already accepted criterion for the appropriate use of a word, and for the internal questions these words and criteria help us to address. Once we step back and outside the framework, however, and ask a question that does not fall within the criterion of the framework, then we have begun to walk down the path of metaphysics, especially if we claim that these entities exist independently of the internal questions to which they are appropriate. To ask, for instance, whether numbers exist or not, in the same way that tables, cats and clouds exist, would be to step outside the system of numbers framework (and thus outside the accepted criterion for the use and application of number words), and into metaphysics if we were to answer the now external question in the affirmative.

It is at this point that Quine enters the narrative. With his famous critique of the analytic-synthetic distinction in his 'Two Dogmas of Empiricism' essay, Quine in essence argues that the collapse of that distinction also dooms the internal/external questions distinction. As Price states it, 'Quine argues that in virtue of the failure of the analytic-synthetic distinction, even internal questions are ultimately pragmatic ... there are no purely internal issues, in Carnap's sense' (Price 2009, 6). As Quine reads Carnap, he claims that 'Carnap maintains that ontological questions ... are questions not of fact but of choosing a convenient scheme or framework for science; and with this I agree only if the same be conceded for every scientific hypothesis' (Quine 1966, 'On Carnap's Views on Ontology', 134; cited by Price 2009, 7). In other words, whenever a scientific hypothesis is put forth, there inevitably comes with it a practical question, the question of whether to accept a given hypothesis that is on a par with Carnap's external questions regarding whether or not to accept a given framework. Quine is thus 'embracing', as Price sees it, 'a more thoroughgoing post-positivist pragmatism', and thus, 'far from blocking Carnap's drive towards a more pragmatic, less metaphysical destination, Quine simply overtakes him, and pushes further in the same direction' (Price 2009, 7). A consequence of Quine's 'more thoroughgoing post-positivist pragmatism' is that he will cast doubt on the pluralism that is integral to Carnap's approach. Whereas Carnap will see a plurality of frameworks – e.g., a system of numbers framework and a thing-language framework, among others (perhaps ethical, religious frameworks, etc.) – Quine adopts a holistic position and argues instead for an all-encompassing web of belief (see Quine 1970). As Price summarises Quine's position on this point: 'Quine is arguing that there is no principled basis for Carnap's distinction of language into frameworks, where this is to be understood in terms of the introduction of new quantifiers, ranging over distinct domains of entities' (Price 2009, 9).

It is with Quine's argument against Carnap's pluralism that Price challenges the traditional narrative regarding the vanquishing of Carnap by Quine. The 'Tradition seems to assume', Price argues, 'that Quine has an argument for the opposing view – an argument for monism, where Carnap requires pluralism, as it were. I want to show that this is a mistake, and rests on a confusion between two theoretical issues concerning language' (Price 2009, 10). The confusion Price refers to is between the two levels at which Carnap's pluralism operates. At the first level, there is the pluralism of 'distinct linguistic frameworks' that Quine no doubt has in mind when he refers to 'a particular style of bound variables' (Quine 1966, 130; Price 2009, 10). There is, however, a second level, Price argues, which is the 'pragmatic or functional pluralism that provides its [the pluralism of linguistic frameworks'] motivation'. For Price, the construction of the distinct linguistic frameworks 'reflects this [pragmatic] assumption'. Quine's criticism of Carnap is directed towards the first level pluralism, the logico-syntactical level, and Price argues that 'we can allow that Quine is right about this, while insisting that it makes no difference at all to the issue that really matters: viz., whether Carnap is right about the underlying functional distinctions' (Price 2009, 10). Price accepts that Quine is right to assert that when we talk about tables and when we talk about beliefs, we are not talking about 'any difference in the notions of existence involved', and thus 'we should concede to Quine that there is a single logico-syntactic device of existential quantification' (11). That said, however, Price follows Gilbert Ryle's functional approach to language, an approach that will 'lead us to focus on the difference between the functions of talk of beliefs and talk of tables; on the issue of what the two kinds of talk are for, rather than that of what they are about' (11). Thus, despite the fact that Quine is right about there being a single 'logico-syntactic device of existential quantification', Price insists that 'this device has application in a range of cases, whose functional origins are sufficiently distinct that naturalism is guilty of a serious error, in attempting to treat them as all on a par' (12–13). Such functional questions arise, for instance, in talking about tables and chairs. Price grants, for instance, that 'talk of chairs serves a different function from talk of tables, simply because chairs and tables are different kinds of furniture'. I may, for instance, be concerned with the comfort of the chair given the use to which it will be put, and given these practical constraints I may prefer one chair over another, whereas the functional issues regarding tables will be different. Despite this difference, Price goes on to say that 'Ryle (and I) don't want to say that "chair" and "table" belong to different logical categories. So we need a story about which functional differences are the important ones' (14). Satisfying the need for this story, however, brings its own questions, what I have called relevance questions, and 'Much of analytic philosophy came to forget about Wittgenstein, Carnap and Ryle', who were concerned with addressing just these questions. Quine, at the very least, should not reject such questions, even if, as Price notes, 'The issue is one for science. It is the anthropologist, or perhaps the biologist, who asks, "What does this linguistic construction do for these people?"' (14). Price will continue to call upon science to help us address these key functional questions (see, especially, Price et al. 2013), but they are nonetheless questions that continue to show that the motivation behind Carnap's critique of metaphysics – namely, the functional pluralism of linguistic frameworks – remains largely intact.

One consequence of the blind eye that much of analytic philosophy has turned, in recent decades, to the functional questions that were the concern of Wittgenstein, Carnap and Ryle, is that Quine is given undue credit for the upsurge of metaphysics in analytic philosophy, and for the unproblematic nature of this trend. This becomes clear as we trace the consequences of what has come to be called the 'Quine-Putnam indispensability argument'. Put briefly: since we need to speak in terms of mathematical entities when we do mathematics, science, etc., we have, as Hartry Field puts it, an 'excellent reason for supposing that that kind of entity exists' (Field 2001, 329; cited by Price 2009, 16). But we need to be wary of the conclusion we draw from this argument. As Price argues, 'it doesn't imply that there is an argument *from* the needs of science *to* ontological conclusions – *for* realism' (18). Appealing to the functional benefits a linguistic framework provides, to continue with Carnap's distinction, is no argument in favour of the existence of entities independent of this framework. To assume that this is so is to continue to confuse the two levels of pluralism that were at work in Carnap's criticism of metaphysics, and yet this is precisely the tendency that has occurred, Price argues, and largely because functional or external questions regarding linguistic frameworks have been pushed to the side, or at least are no longer thought to be an issue thanks to Quine.

This tendency is evident in one of Quine's most famous students, David Lewis. Lewis, for example, will employ the indispensability argument in defence of his claim that there are possible worlds that are real. There is a world, for instance, where I become a geologist and work for my father's geotechnical firm, and this world is just as real as the actual world where I am a philosopher. I simply do not, Lewis argues, have access to this possible world. In defence of this proposal, one that admittedly led to many 'incredulous stares', Lewis will answer the question he feels many must have: 'Why believe in [such] a plurality of worlds? Because the hypothesis is serviceable, and that is a reason to think that it is true' (Lewis 1986a, 3). Or, as Lewis also states his case: there are 'many ways in which systematic philosophy goes more easily if we may presuppose modal realism in our analysis. I take this to be a good reason to think that modal realism is true, *just as the utility of set theory in mathematics is a good reason to believe that there are sets*' (1986a, viii, emphasis added; cited by Price 2009, 20). For Price, 'a Carnapian might accept that the utility of talk of possible worlds (or sets) is a good pragmatic reason for adopting the vocabulary in question, without reading this in any sense as an argument for the truth of a metaphysical conclusion' (20). In other words, answering the external question regarding the utility of adopting a given framework does not, according to Carnap's critique of metaphysics, support the claim that the entities presupposed by a framework exist independently of the role they play within the framework itself. As Price draws his arguments to a close, he claims that Lewis, and perhaps many others who feel Quine has vindicated their forays into metaphysics, are 'blind to the distinction between what we might call a metaphysical stance with respect to a vocabulary ... and a genealogical or anthropological stance, which is interested in why creatures like us come to employ the vocabulary in the first place' (23). The latter stance, Price argues, accounts for the pragmatic motivations that in turn account for why adopting a particular framework is relevant. The truth of statements within a linguistic framework thus depends, Price concludes, on the conditions of relevance that led to adopting the framework at all.

At this point in our argument, we can introduce Price to Dreyfus. As we saw in Dreyfus's critique of McDowell, the problem with emphasising the conceptual capacities of human beings to the exclusion of their non-conceptual capacities, the capacities they 'share with prelinguistic infants and higher animals' (Dreyfus 2005, 47), is that it paints an impoverished picture of human experience. In support of this claim, Dreyfus cites the difficulty AI researchers have had in getting computers to 'comprehend the simple stories understood by four-year-olds' (48). What is lacking here is not a capacity to filter, sort and categorise data in accordance with rules – which is what Dreyfus (as McDowell points out in his critical response) seems to think our conceptual capacity consists of – rather, what is missing is the relevant framework to use in doing the filtering and sorting in the first place. One must adopt the relevant framework in order to determine which facts are relevant to understanding a story. Not just any framework will do, and if we attempt to program the computer we will end up with a regress problem, Dreyfus argues, for how do we determine which framework is the relevant one to use without another framework to guide us, a framework in need of yet another framework to guide us, and so on *ad infinitum*? For Dreyfus the solution is there in plain sight, in that we are, as Heidegger and Merleau-Ponty both recognised, 'always already in a world that is organized in terms of our bodies and interests and thus permeated by relevance' (49). As we have seen, on the basis of the relevance our embodied experience provides, Dreyfus claims that much of what we do 'requires no conceptual repertoire at all. This holds true for such refined skills as chess, jazz improvisation, sports, martial arts, etc., but equally for everyday skills such as cooking dinner, crossing a busy street, carrying on a conversation, or just getting around the world' (58).

Carnap, as we have seen Price read him, is also aware of and interested in investigating the functional and pragmatic frameworks that provide the relevance for the plurality of linguistic frameworks we come to use. For Carnap as well there is the pragmatic question of knowing which framework is the relevant one to use. As we saw, talk of chairs and talk of tables do differ because chairs and tables each serve different practical functions; for Price, however, following Ryle, chairs and tables fall into the same logical category, whereas beliefs, mathematics, etc., fall into different frameworks. What is the functional, pragmatic basis for how we determine which linguistic and logical framework to use? For Price this is a question the scientists will answer, especially the anthropologist and the biologist, though I would add the critical existentialist as well, which is the theme of *TCE*. What the anthropologist et al. are concerned with is precisely the question, 'What does this linguistic construction do for these people?' (Price 2009, 14), and in addressing this question the conditions of relevance will be key, or the relevance questions with which we began this book (recall the Introduction). Quine would agree that conditions of relevance are important. One of the most serious difficulties he had with Carnap's distinction between internal and external questions, which followed similarly from his difficulties with the analytic-synthetic distinction, was that he doubted whether internal questions could ever be insulated from external questions. It is for this reason that Price refers to Quine's position as an example of post-positivist pragmatism. Carnap, on Quine's reading, simply didn't push the pragmatic questions far enough. The deeper reason for Quine's criticism of Carnap, however, is that while Carnap accepts a form of pluralism, Quine embraces a form of monism, a holism of the web of belief.

We raised the question of whether to adopt pluralism or monism earlier, when we saw how Michael Della Rocca employs a Bradley-inspired argument to counter many of the key motivations behind analytic philosophy – in particular, the Method of Intuition (MI). In this context, Della Rocca found an ally in Quine. Quine's criticism of the analytic-synthetic distinction, and by extension of Carnap's internal/external questions distinction, is that in the end they are distinctions that are arbitrarily drawn. As Quine famously put it in 'Two Dogmas of Empiricism', 'Any statement can be held true come what may, if we make drastic enough statements elsewhere in the system' (Quine 1980, 43). Given the holistic web of beliefs in which all our statements are related, no statement, according to Quine, is immune from being reconsidered given a willingness to make adjustments elsewhere in the web of our beliefs. Wherever we draw the line between analytic and synthetic statements, therefore, it will be arbitrary – there will be no ultimate reason for drawing the line there rather than elsewhere. The lesson Della Rocca draws from this, following Bradley, is that if there is no reason for the distinction, if it is arbitrarily drawn, then it is not a real distinction. Quine's monism, therefore, stems, as Della Rocca sees it, from a concern to avoid arbitrary distinctions that are simply assumed to be immune to change. This assumption is the central dogma that Quine challenges in his 'Two Dogmas of Empiricism'.

Despite Quine's monistic challenge to Carnap's pluralism, Price maintains that a plurality of functional frameworks persists, and it is to the detriment of philosophers to ignore them. By relying solely on the relevance of entities *within* a linguistic framework, assuming that if they are indispensable to that framework then they must exist, many philosophers have overlooked the functionality of the frameworks themselves, the questions of relevance that these linguistic frameworks answer to, and hence why one framework is more suitable than another. We have already seen, in our discussion of Mark Wilson's work (see §13.2, 4), that a thorough picture of physical phenomena requires a plurality of frameworks (or what Wilson calls façades) to gain representational traction with what is occurring. Since the universe will not 'sit still while we frame its descriptive picture' (Wilson 2006, 11), we come to depend on these façades to help us piece together an account of a universe that escapes the plurality of façades we have come to depend upon. Wilson's pluralism, moreover, can be seen to be a consequence of his monism – that is, the one universe is too dynamic and complicated for us to rely on a single framework to understand and describe what is going on, so we therefore need a plurality of façades to get the job done as best we can. Wilson also provides us with an answer to Quine's problem – namely, how do we determine which framework to adopt? In short, we adopt the one that works, the one that most accurately tracks the relevant phenomena. Price's appeal to the sciences is similarly motivated: the sciences will provide the functional frameworks that track the relations between the linguistic frameworks people use and what they do for the people who use them. We will discuss this theme more thoroughly in §16, and again throughout *TCE*, but the result will be, as it was for Wilson, a plurality of frameworks or façades.

11. Monism or Pluralism?

A final issue, before closing, that motivates the tension between Quine's monism and Price's (and Carnap's and Wilson's) pluralism is the role determinate distinctions play in determining relevance. Wilson argues, for instance, that the physical attribute of temperature can be tracked and measured only within a limited set of parameters. Beyond certain temperatures and conditions, for instance, standard measuring devices such as the mercury thermometer will not accurately track the phenomena. Wilson's pluralism of façades, therefore, is a consequence of the effort to track and measure determinate phenomena. But do these determinate phenomena provide a non-arbitrary basis for distinguishing the relevance of one framework from that of another? No matter how certain we may be that a given phenomenon or law may provide a basis for distinguishing the relevance of one framework from another, Quine's holistic-inspired doubts may seep in if we allow them to. As Quine himself noted, 'Revision even of the logical law of the excluded middle has been proposed as a means of simplifying quantum analysis' (Quine 1980, 43), and thus this law should not be taken as a true 'come what may' law on the basis of which we can differentiate the relevance of one framework from another. As McDowell picks up on these issues, he adopts Sellars' critique of the Myth of the Given to argue that there is no Given that could serve as the determinate check to our conceptual formations, allowing us to differentiate between those that are grounded and those that are not. In place of the given, McDowell calls upon our world-disclosing experience, an experience that is always already in a categorial form and hence able to be taken up explicitly within the space of reasons where claims are justified in their inferential relations to others. The problem MacFarlane had with McDowell's proposal was that it leaves us unable to account for the content of our mathematical concepts. Put briefly, the content of mathematical concepts cannot be incorporated into McDowell's approach since our world-disclosing experience is assumed to be determinate and limited in nature, and hence incompatible with the infinite mathematical structures that are the frequent subject of mathematics.

One of the reasons for McDowell's difficulty in accounting for mathematics is that he implicitly embraces – as do many others, as we have seen – the primacy of the determinate. That is, our basis for differentiating is to be grounded in that which is already determinate. How could differences not be determinate differences? It is this assumption that differences must be determinate differences, or differences between determinate things, that is at work in a number of the philosophers we have encountered so far. Adorno, however, is not one of them. In his negative dialectics (see §14.3), determination occurs not through an encounter with already determinate entities, an already determinate given for instance, but instead through an encounter with an objectivity Adorno claims resists all efforts to think it – that is, to identify it, given that for him 'To think is to identify' (Adorno 1973, 5). This objectivity is what we have called a problematic Idea, and rather than think of it as a negative, as that which we *cannot* think *à la* Adorno, we see it as the condition of relevance that is inseparable from each and every determinate phenomenon. As problematic Ideas have been discussed here, they are problems without a solution (following Kant's understanding of transcendental Ideas [see §10]), conditions of relevance without determinate relevance, or, to bring in the monism/pluralism debate, difference and multiplicity without determinate diversity and plurality. This is the reason behind Deleuze's claim that 'Difference is not diversity' (Deleuze 1994, 222). There is given to us in our experience a diversity of phenomena, and a plurality of frameworks is no doubt necessary to do justice to this diversity, as Carnap, Price, Wilson and others have shown. But this diversity, according to Deleuze, is made possible by a difference that is not a determinate difference, or a difference between determinate things (including a diversity of determinate things). Deleuze thus argues that 'Diversity is given, but difference is that by which the given is given, that by which the given is given as diverse' (222). To state this in the terms that will become the subject of the next section: problematic Ideas are the conditions of relevance by which the diversity of determinate phenomena is given, and given such that it can be represented in statements that are true.

§16 Truth and Relevance

1. Arbitrary Accounts and Infinite Regresses

A key approach that has been taken throughout this book has been to develop the implications of two related claims. First, it has been argued that an account, explanation or grounding that is arbitrary is not a real account, and as such it offers no explanation or grounding. We saw this first with Michael Della Rocca's arguments, following Bradley, that if we use A to account for the relationship between A and B, then this is an arbitrary account – why not B rather than A? – and as arbitrary the relationship is left unaccounted for. More recently we have seen Quine draw upon this argument in his critique of the analytic-synthetic distinction. An analytic statement, a statement that is true by definition, or come what may, could, with sufficient and radical enough revisions elsewhere in the web of beliefs, become a statement that is no longer true come what may. There is no non-arbitrary line to be drawn between analytic and synthetic statements, and hence the distinction itself is ungrounded and is therefore rejected by Quine. The second, related claim, is that an account or explanation which generates an infinite regress never provides the explanation or account it sets out to provide. If we attempt to ground the relationship between A and B in a unique quality shared by both A and B, and thus avoid the arbitrary account, we end up in the classic Bradley regress, for we now have a special relationship AB – this special quality that is related to both A and B – that now needs to be explained. If we appeal to yet another special relationship at this point to account for AB, then we are off on a regress and will never provide the explanation we sought. The Third Man Argument (TMA) is the most famous example of such a regress, and its problematic implications have long been recognised (e.g., by Plato in *Parmenides* [see §5.2]), as has been a guiding theme throughout this work.

2. Brute Facts or Spinozist Bullet?

Another theme that set the stage early on for much of what has been developed here is the arbitrary nature of a common solution to the regress problem – namely, the turn to brute facts and explanations that are self-sufficient and in no need of their own explanations. Both G.E. Moore and Bertrand Russell, for instance, recognise that Bradley's understanding of relations presents one with the problem of a regress; however, for both of them, and Russell in particular, the regress is avoided if we simply take certain facts and relations to be brute facts, facts needing no explanation or justification. Russell is unmoved by Bradley's critique, arguing that without external relations, relations that are simply given, as brute facts, mathematics would be 'inexplicable' (Russell 1959, 12). More importantly, by accepting brute simples, or the particulars Russell characterises as having the 'sort of self-subsistence that used to belong to substance' (Russell 1970, 202), we can avoid Bradley's regresses and accept the reality of diversity. In his essay 'On the Nature of Truth', for instance, Russell concludes that with brute, self-subsistent simples we can safely speak of 'a world of many things, with relations which are not to be deduced from a supposed "nature" or scholastic essence of the related thing. In this world, whatever is complex is composed of related simple things, and analysis is no longer confronted at every step by an endless regress' (Russell 1907, 44). What Russell sets out to avoid, in short, is Bradley's solution to the regress – to wit, adopt a monism and argue that there is only one absolute reality, with the consequence that diversity and relations are simply appearances of this one reality. This is precisely the Spinozist solution to the problems of arbitrary accounts and regresses. Hume, we saw, flirted with the implications of Spinoza's monism but refused to bite the Spinozist bullet and accept the fact that, as Della Rocca argues, 'the only consistent form of rationalism is one that accepts a form of monism and denies any multiplicity of distinct objects' (Della Rocca 2017, 479).

3. Davidson's Coherence Theory of Truth

Despite Quine's critique of the analytic-synthetic distinction, a critique that adopts the arbitrary distinction strategy Della Rocca will also use, and despite his move towards holism, Quine does not bite the Spinozist bullet and deny 'any multiplicity of distinct objects'. Quine rescues the reality of distinct objects by appealing, as did Carnap and Russell before him, to a diversity of facts that are given immediately and constitute the non-propositional content for the web of propositional claims and beliefs that interpret this content. In *Word and Object*, 'sensory stimulations' will be the term Quine uses to refer to this diverse content (see Quine 2013, 8–12). Although Donald Davidson will consider himself to be 'Quine's faithful student' (Davidson 1989, 157) with respect to Quine's holism and rejection of the analytic-synthetic distinction, Davidson will break with his teacher's position that 'whatever there is to meaning must be traced back somehow to experience, the given, or patterns of sensory stimulation, something intermediate between belief and the usual objects our beliefs are about' (158). What Davidson proposes, instead, is that Quine should have extended his scepticism regarding the line between analytic and synthetic statements, a line that Quine was right to point out was arbitrarily drawn, and extend that same scepticism to the line he himself draws between observation sentences and the sentences built upon them. As Davidson puts it:

> In my view, erasing the line between the analytic and synthetic saved philosophy of language as a serious subject by showing how it could be pursued without what there cannot be: determinate meanings. I now suggest also giving up the distinction between observation sentences and the rest. (Davidson 1989, 158)

Once we give up this distinction, Davidson believes, we are then ready to embrace a coherence theory of truth, since a 'major reason', he argues, 'for accepting a coherence theory is the unintelligibility of the dualism of a conceptual scheme and a "world" waiting to be coped with' (155). In one of his most influential essays, 'On the Very Idea of a Conceptual Scheme' (Davidson 2001), Davidson claims there is an 'unintelligibility of the dualism' between a conceptual scheme, as a web of propositional contents, and a diversity of sensory stimulations that are the givens for the various conceptual schemes. Davidson is quite forthright in his rejection of this dualism of 'scheme and content, of organizing system and something waiting to be organized'. Echoing Quine's famous essay, Davidson argues that this dualism 'is itself a dogma of empiricism, the third dogma' (189). For instance, if we were to divide up our experience into that which is to be organised, the diversity of observation sentences, Russell's particulars, etc., and the schemes that organise this diversity, then we have for Davidson the issue of first identifying that which is to be organised. This cannot be, Davidson argues, 'a single object (the world, nature, etc.) unless that object is understood to contain or consist in other objects' (192). As Davidson puts it, one 'would be bewildered' if one were told to organise one's closet but not the things that are in the closet (shoes, shirts, pants, etc.). To organise thus applies 'only to pluralities', Davidson concludes, but then 'whatever plurality we take experience to consist in – events like losing a button or stubbing a toe, having a sensation of warmth or hearing an oboe – we will have to individuate according to familiar principles. A language that organizes such entities must be a language very like our own' (192). In other words, whatever is taken to be a given content to be organised must first be identified and made determinate – individuated as Davidson puts it – but this process already presupposes a conceptual scheme. If we push this process back one step further, we would again encounter yet another individuating process, or 'a language very like our own' and thus a conceptual scheme and not a determinate content. On this point, Davidson agrees with Rorty's claim that 'nothing counts as justification unless by reference to what we already accept, and there is no way to get outside our beliefs and our language so as to find some test other than coherence' (Rorty 1979, 178). It should be no surprise that John McDowell finds an ally in Davidson, and he explicitly mentions Davidson as a kindred spirit in his efforts to do without the Myth of the Given (see McDowell 1994, xvi, where McDowell invokes Davidson). Where Davidson suspects he differs from Rorty (and by extension McDowell) is in his continued commitment to the view that 'we nevertheless can have knowledge of, and talk about, an objective public world which is not of our own making' (Davidson 1989, 310). It is at this point that Davidson's coherence theory of truth enters the scene.

For Davidson it is a natural move from rejecting the third dogma of empiricism to embracing a coherence theory of truth. If we do away with a determinate content that needs to be organised, and if all we have are the beliefs and propositions that are expressible in a language of some sort, then we are left with coherence theory, which Davidson defines as being 'simply the claim that nothing can count as a reason for holding a belief except another belief' (Davidson 1989, 310). This is not to say that a sensation is a belief. Sensations may cause beliefs, Davidson recognises, 'but a causal explanation of a belief does not show how or why the belief is justified' (311); only another belief can do this. It would be a mistake, however, Davidson argues, if we were to shift our search for a determinate given as the basis for justifying a true belief onto a search for a determinate belief or proposition as the basis for justifying our true beliefs. This would be yet another instance of what Davidson calls the 'confrontation between what we believe and reality', something that he thinks is 'absurd' (309). The reason Davidson thinks this is absurd is because, while he accepts the view 'that each of our views may be false', without our knowing or being able to determine which ones these may be (that is, we cannot confront each of our beliefs with a reality to determine whether it is a justified, true belief or not), nevertheless, integral to his coherence theory is the underlying assumption that not 'all of them [our beliefs] can be wrong' (309). In other words, a fundamental presupposition for Davidson is that 'belief is in its nature veridical' (314), or, more importantly, that we need to proceed with 'a general presumption of truth for the body of beliefs as a whole, but the interpreter does not need to presume each particular belief of someone else is true' (319). Some beliefs may indeed be false, but the best we can do here is to 'cope with error holistically, that is, we interpret so as to make an agent as intelligible as possible, given his actions, his utterances and his place in the world' (318). The reason 'the body of beliefs as a whole' is true, for Davidson, is precisely because they are about an 'objective public world which is not of our own making' (310). This is where Davidson's coherence theory of truth relies most heavily on Tarski's convention-T, which entails, as Tarski famously stated it, 'that "snow is white" is true if and only if snow is white' (see Tarski 1944). For Davidson, similarly, a sentence 'like "Grass is green" spoken by an English speaker, is true if and only if grass is green', and what is key here for Davidson, as it was for Tarski, is that 'the truth of an utterance depends on just two things: what the words as spoken mean, and how the world is arranged' (Davidson 1989, 309). What Davidson adds to Tarski's theory is the assumption that the body of our beliefs is on the whole true, and it is this general, holistic presumption of truth that makes it possible for us to determine both what another person means and whether any particular belief they express is true or false – in other words, the diversity of determinate meanings and truth claims is given by virtue of a general, holistic presumption of truth.

4. Davidson on Language

Davidson will apply a similar analysis to his understanding of language. Rather than begin with determinate words and their determinate meanings, or with the rules of language that would serve as a conceptual scheme that gets applied to some linguistic content, Davidson begins with a presumption of meaningful truthfulness – that is, a presumption that what we state we believe, and what we believe is generally true because it corresponds to some state of the world. It is this presumption that accounts, Davidson argues, for our surprising ability to quickly translate and understand malapropisms. In 'A Nice Derangement of Epitaphs', Davidson recognises that we readily translate malapropisms all the time and do so with ease. Given this sentence from Goodman Ace, 'In quest of this pinochle of success, I have often wrecked my brain for a clowning achievement' (Davidson 2005b, 89), or many others like it, we can generally, and without hesitation, understand what is being said and correctly and accurately translate what is meant. How do we do this? According to Davidson, what we do not do in circumstances such as this is translate based on our having learned a basic structure, system or rules of a language that account for the regularities of the language that we then apply to a given situation as we translate what is said. The malapropisms, Davidson argues, do not fit such a model. This leads him to this surprising conclusion:

> I conclude that there is no such thing as a language, not if a language is anything like what many philosophers and linguists have supposed. There is therefore no such thing to be learned, mastered, or born with. We must give up the idea of a clearly defined shared structure which language-users acquire and then apply to cases. And we should try again to say how convention in any important sense is involved in language; or, as I think, we should give up the attempt to illuminate how we communicate by appeal to conventions. (Davidson 2005b, 107)

Instead of appealing to a determinate set of rules or conventions to understand what occurs when we understand what another person means, Davidson proposes that we begin with a fundamentally shared presupposition, what we might call a fundamental convention or form of life (following Wittgenstein, and discussed further in *TCE*) that is neither a determinately shared language nor a determinate set of rules we learn to apply in given, concrete circumstances. If we think of language as a set of rules we learn, then 'there is no such thing as a language' for Davidson. It is for this reason, finally, that he reiterates his rejection of the third dogma of empiricism: 'For we have found no intelligible basis on which it can be said that schemes are different' (Davidson 2001, 198) – that is, there is no perspective outside our beliefs whereby we can definitively, non-arbitrarily differentiate one scheme from another. Similarly, Davidson also concludes that 'if we cannot intelligibly say that schemes are different, neither can we intelligibly say that they are one' (198). What we have instead is a fundamental convention (convention-T), or a guide to systematic interpretation that is not to be confused with anything determinate – Davidson is indeed doing 'without what there cannot be: determinate meanings' – and thus language is neither determinately one nor determinately plural.

5. Problematic Ideas; or, Pluralism = Monism

We can begin to contrast Davidson's approach to doing without 'determinate meanings' with the arguments we have developed here to support the move beyond the primacy of the determinate. In an important sense, Davidson's efforts are much in line with my own, for the arguments that led him to conclude that 'there is no such thing as a language' are motivated precisely by a rejection of the traditional effort to ground language and truth, for instance, in something else, with this something else being determinately given in some way. With our concept of problematic Ideas, we have also challenged the primacy of the determinate, and we have argued that the determinate is itself made possible by a fundamental determinable, or by problematic Ideas that cannot be reduced to the determinate entities they condition. Where my approach differs from Davidson is that for him the fundamental convention is an equilibrium state, a shared common condition that assures the possibility of our communicating with and understanding one another, including one another's malapropisms. It is for this reason that Davidson will refer frequently to a Bayesian analysis of beliefs that incorporates a probability of expectations as this comes to be established over time, through custom and habit. Although Davidson is certainly right to understand established practices along these lines, problematic Ideas are understood here to be the condition for the new, for that which cannot be placed within a current framework of expectations. Problematic Ideas are thus the condition for the limits a framework of expectations entails, and hence they account for a plurality of frameworks, or for the diversity of frameworks, and are the condition that accounts for the transformation of these frameworks into something other, something new. This is the sense in which, to repeat Deleuze's claim, 'difference is that by which the given is given, that by which the given is given as diverse' (Deleuze 1994, 222). Problematic Ideas are the difference irreducible to a difference among determinate entities, including a diversity of determinate entities, and yet problematic Ideas are the problems the diversity of determinate entities serve as solutions for. At the same time, problematic Ideas are inseparable from each and every determinate entity, each and every determinate framework, while not being exhausted by these determinate entities and frameworks. Problematic Ideas are precisely the universe that will not sit still, as Wilson understands it, the 'ultimate elements of nature' as Deleuze puts it (Deleuze 1994, 165), or the objectivity that both resists and motivates thinking as Adorno argues. In short, problematic Ideas account both for the pluralist, differentiating tendency (the Humean tendency), for the plurality of frameworks we saw in Carnap, or the multiple façades Wilson calls upon, and they account for the monist, dedifferentiating tendency (the Spinozist tendency) that remains unexhausted by, and is not to be confused with, each and every determinate entity and façade. It is this aspect of problematic Ideas that is expressed by Deleuze and Guattari when, in characterising the nature of rhizomes in their introduction to *A Thousand Plateaus*, they claim that rhizomes are 'the magic formula we seek – PLURALISM = MONISM' (Deleuze and Guattari 1987, 20).

6. Problematic Ideas and the Relevance of the Determinate

With problematic Ideas, and especially with what we have seen in our earlier discussions of Wilson, Chang, Adorno and Liberman, what comes to be seen as a determinate link between a predicate and a property is inseparable from numerous processes that are social as well as empirical. In his discussion of coffee tasters, for instance (see §14.5), Liberman shows that the tasting schedule whereby tasters apply various predicates to the attributes of the coffee they are tasting is itself the result of a dynamic social process in which the predicates help them to discover the tastes rather than simply identify them. Moreover, a taster learns the most from a coffee when they cannot find the predicate to apply, when there are no descriptors available; at this point a new predicate (descriptor) may emerge, and if other tasters find that the predicate helps them to identify the taste, then the tasting schedule may change. Adorno understands this process to be simply what occurs in our efforts to think objectivity, understood as that which resists our efforts to think it. These efforts to think objectivity are in turn shared efforts, involving interactions with other individuals and things. The same was true with Chang's discussion of the emergence of temperature. Here, too, the efforts were shared across a number of experimenters, and it was only due to a convergence of findings over time that a threshold point was attained and the modern temperature scale emerged along with various instruments to measure it. Mark Wilson also highlighted the difficulties associated with determining the temperature of a given substance, noting the need for a determinate range of applications for particular measuring devices if we are to be successful in tracking determinate phenomena. It is the convergence of multiple instruments in varying circumstances – though still within a limited, determinate range – that leads Wilson to claim that there is a property to be identified and measured. The point to be stressed here, and one that Huw Price makes as well in his discussion of Carnap's critique of metaphysics, is that the determinate measurements, frameworks, façades, etc., are the result of a process of engagement with an objectivity that is problematic – that is, with problematic Ideas – and it is precisely this encounter that provides the relevance for the determinate frameworks, façades, etc., that emerge as solutions to the problematic nature of the encounter.

7. Living the Problem; or, the Inescapable Social Field

What needs to be stressed, however, is that problematic Ideas are not abstract, decontextualised problems that are far removed from social, political and historical contexts. Our encounter with problematic Ideas is not amongst Ernest Nagel's 'quiet green pastures for intellectual analysis, wherein its practitioners can find refuge from a troubled world and cultivate intellectual games with chess-like indifference to its course' (Nagel 1936a, 9). In extending

Davidson's critique of the distinction between 'observation sentences and the rest', a distinction that is drawn arbitrarily (as we saw), I would argue that we cannot draw a clear, non-arbitrary distinction between social and intellectual problems. We may choose, as Carnap suggests we do, to ignore the fact that language is an intrinsically meaningful and social activity – we should 'avert methodically from meaning' he tells us, and look instead at words and propositions in the manner of 'chess figures ... combined and manipulated according to definite rules' (Carnap 1984, 10); but to do so comes at a cost, and as Price argues the cost is that we lose sight of the conditions of relevance that motivate the very determinate frameworks and linguistic systems that interest Carnap. In particular, by focusing upon the abstract systems and rules, as Nagel encourages us to do, we in effect mistake the conditioned for the conditions, as Husserl, Mark Wilson and others had warned us not to do. To encounter problematic Ideas, therefore, is to live a problem, or to think objectivity (in Adorno's sense), and consequently there is no determinate way to differentiate in advance between problems that are and are not social. Problematic Ideas are thus the determinable condition for differentiating between those problems that are social and those that are not, and the determinate differentiations that result are always provisional, open to being reworked and revised, in a process that is assured since problematic Ideas condition these determinate differentiations.

8. Meillassoux and the Primacy of the Determinate

We can now address the earlier concern expressed regarding Meillassoux's concept of hyper-Chaos. As we saw, key to this concept is the idea that everything that is could be other than it is, or not be at all. This is why Meillassoux rejects the principle of sufficient reason. Instead of endorsing the claim that there must be a reason why everything is the way it is rather than another way – i.e., rather than endorse the PSR – Meillassoux argues that there is no reason why anything is the way it is rather than any other imaginable way. Key to his argument, however, is that the PSR sets out on the basis of a determinate difference between being and non-being. Problematic Ideas, by contrast, are inseparable from determinate being, and for this reason determinate beings always presuppose alternatives that are *not other* than the determinate beings, but rather are alternatives in the finite, determinate beings themselves – this is the sense in which the problematic Idea is infinite, or *in*-finite. This point is crucial because we live a problem in our determinate experiences, including our experiences of applying determinate frameworks. The task of philosophy – or the task of making sense of life, as we will detail in TCE – is to remind us of our living condition, that our life is an unending encounter with a problem. To philosophise is thus a process of recollection, as Plato said; a recollection of a pure past, in the manner of Bergson (1988), but a past that was never a determinate present. This experience of life as a problem, therefore, is not a negation of determinate experience, the experience with which we think and identify (which are one and the same for Adorno), and thus it is not an experience of contingency in Meillassoux's sense, where what is – that is, the determinate – could be other than what it is, another determinate being or nothing at all. This determinate difference between being and non-being that is central to Meillassoux's conception of contingency is one that depends, as I have argued, on problematic Ideas. An experience of life as a problem, therefore, is not one of non-being that haunts being but rather of a real problem that subsists as a determinable or non-mereological part of the solution, and thus in the determinate experiences we think, represent and express in propositions. To philosophise, therefore, is an attempt to encounter the infinite in the finite, the eternal now in the determinate present; in doing so the recollection philosophy provokes may well transform current ways of thinking and being, ways that are simply the determinate solutions made possible by problematic Ideas.

9. Towards a Humean Political Theory

These issues become especially clear as we turn to politics. Understood in the terms we have developed here, we can take current social and political formations – institutional structures and the various activities, affects and beliefs that are inseparable from these structures – as solutions to our social-political life as a problem. We are not, to repeat, differentiating a definitive social and political life from its non-social and non-political alternative. Wherever we may draw the line between the quiet refuge of intellectual problems and the problems one finds in the troubled world will be arbitrary, and thus, in extending Davidson's Quinean arguments, as well as Della Rocca's Bradley-inspired arguments, we will resist accepting such distinctions. A consequence of doing this, however, is that social and political problems are not to be taken off the table, but quite to the contrary will become part of what a philosophical experience of and encounter with problematic Ideas will lead one to attempt to think. The task of philosophy and political theory will therefore be one of revealing the problematic Ideas inseparable from current formations, and, contrary to Davidson, it will not assume that the equilibrium state of current formations is the true criterion of what is real, and hence the criterion of the truth of the body of our beliefs that correspond to this reality. Stated simply, in *Towards a Critical Existentialism* we will take up life as a problem, beginning, as Aristotle does, with the problem of household maintenance, or οἰκονομία in Greek (from which we get the word economy); thus the problem will be precisely the social and economic problem that political formations and institutions respond to, and respond to as provisional solutions. Political formations and institutions, therefore, are always a form of political economy, and the task of political theory, or of critical existentialism as I will lay it out, will be one of becoming alert to the problematic Ideas that are inseparable from the social and political formations within which our daily lives are immersed. Deleuze and Guattari will refer to this effort of detecting the problematic Ideas in current formations as developing and using 'a higher "taste" as problematic faculty' (Deleuze and Guattari 1994, 133); that is, rather than setting out to detect that which is already determinately there to be identified, in the manner Hume calls for in his essay 'Of the Standard of Taste' (Hume 1985), we are instead to bring to the fore the problematic determinable, a problematic that may become multiply realised in a number of determinate ways that are not predetermined. In the event of political engagement, for instance, this will entail a critical approach that does not presume or predetermine the ends to which political and social processes ought to be directed. A critical existentialism, subsequently, will not be a matter of accommodating political and social processes with a predetermined goal of maximising our preferences, for instance, as rational choice theorists would argue (see Luce and Raiffa 1957, and Harsanyi 1966 for classic examples). The reason for this is straightforward: a ranking of preferences presupposes that one already knows one's preferences, or that one knows enough about one's current situation that one can determine in advance which ends will maximise the desired outcomes. A critical existentialism engaged with a 'higher "taste"' for problematic Ideas would be one concerned precisely with those situations where it is unknown what ends will maximise preferences or desirable outcomes.

In an important sense, however, this project will be a Humean project, and more precisely will entail developing a Humean political theory. The reason for this is that while Hume's thought is often cited as foundational for a rational choice model, wherein one calculates based on desires, preferences and known probabilities in relation to maximising one's preferences, this already assumes that one possesses the determinate knowledge of one's preferences and the probabilities associated with maximising them. Although there has been much work done on rational choice models under uncertainty, Hume's concerns lie deeper than this, as I have argued. In particular, a Humean political theory will be one that follows through on the constitutional problem Husserl claimed Hume was the first to discover. What this will entail, subsequently, is an interest above all in how a determinate possibility came to be constituted in the first place, a determinate possibility that can become the subject of one's desires and preferences that can then be maximised in accordance with a rational preference ranking. To turn to the formation of these determinate possibilities, or to the habits, customs and institutions that embody them, is to probe problematic Ideas – and this is the task of critical existentialism as I will develop it in *TCE*. In developing and beginning to carry out this task, we will gain a fuller understanding of the conditions of relevance that motivate our philosophical and scientific discourses, and the concerns for truth that are inseparable from these discourses.

Conclusion

Let us return to where we began, with Kant's admission that philosophy 'cannot, as other sciences, attain universal and lasting acclaim' (Kant 2014, 5). With this recognition, Kant began a philosophical project that has dominated much of philosophy for the past two centuries – namely, the task of reconciling philosophical inquiry with the success of the sciences. As we traced the implications of these efforts, we honed in on two dominant trends, what I called the monist, Spinozist tendency, and the pluralist, Humean tendency. Both can be seen to be carrying forward important aspects of Kant's project. The Spinozist tendency, as we saw, recognises that there is a reality that accounts for but is not to be confused with anything determinate, such as natural laws, universals or Ideas. The problem this leaves us with is the problem of accounting for how the determinate comes to be conditioned by that which is not to be confused with it. The Humean tendency, by contrast, accepts the reality of diverse phenomena, a reality that is fundamentally determinate and discrete, whether these be Hume's impressions, Russell's particulars or Lewis's singletons, among other examples we have discussed. The problem this leaves us with is accounting for the relationship between determinate phenomena, an account that Bradley argues ultimately leads us to a vicious regress which undermines the possibility of giving an account. The problems both tendencies lead to are exacerbated, I argued, by assuming that in the end an account must rely on something that is fundamentally determinate. It is this bias in favour of the primacy of the determinate that was challenged as I developed the arguments in favour of problematic Ideas.

Problematic Ideas entail the paradoxical tendency to be both dedifferentiating, and hence less and less differentiated to the point of becoming irreducible to anything determinate, *and* differentiating, or more and more differentiated as relationships become increasingly individuated. The primacy of the determinate largely adopts the latter approach, seeking to determine what is the case, locating the determinate reality that offers us an account and/or ends a regress. Problematic Ideas, however, never become fully determinate, and the determinate presupposes the problematic Ideas that make them possible; thus, whatever is determinate is at the same time inseparable from a problem that may come to be solved in other ways, ways that transform the determinate into another, and yet another, and so on. As we stated this contrast in the Introduction, and have developed it since, problematic Ideas come to be expressed in the form of two questions – truth questions and relevance questions. In our efforts to identify the determinate basis upon which to ground an account or explanation, whether a determinate totality and unity on the one hand (e.g., a universal, natural law, rule, etc.) or a determinate particular on the other (e.g., Russell's particulars, protocol statements, etc.), these efforts seek to address a truth question, a 'What is x?' question. As Bradley has shown, however, and as Della Rocca has also stressed and shown with respect to the history of analytic philosophy, the answers to such truth questions almost inevitably rely upon determinate facts that remain inexplicable, which then raises the spectre of arbitrariness – why draw the line between inexplicable and explicable facts there and not somewhere else? It is at this point that truth questions give way to relevance questions, the '"How much?", "How?", "In what cases?" and "Who?"' questions (Deleuze 1994, 188). To restate our earlier point, problematic Ideas therefore tend towards both relevance questions and truth questions.

Given our arguments regarding problematic Ideas as conditions for the possibility of the determinate, and the dual tendency they have towards relevance and truth questions, what are we to make now of the role philosophy has in this process, and its prospects for 'lasting acclaim'? Stated simply, we could say that philosophy, in the manner of Socrates, is tasked with being the gadfly in relation to our tendency to rest secure in the answers to our truth questions. To put this in yet another way, philosophy charts the limits of our reliance upon the determinate, of our answers to truth questions, but in a way that both accepts the inevitability of these questions and the provisional nature of the answers and solutions that respond to these questions, questions that express the nature of a problematic Idea. Moreover, by reminding us of the relevance questions that are inseparable from whatever determinate truths we arrive at, philosophy gives us the opportunity to inquire beyond the scope of that which falls within the range of concerns relevant to truth questions. As we saw in Huw Price's arguments concerning the continued relevance of Carnap's arguments against metaphysics, there continues to be a strong tendency to ignore the reasons why we adopt certain frameworks, or why we do not ask the relevance question that 'the anthropologist, or perhaps the biologist ... asks, "What does this linguistic construction do for these people?"' (Price 2009, 14). In short, we have forgotten the questions Price believes Wittgenstein, Carnap and Ryle raised, namely the relevance questions concerning who, how much and in what cases the 'linguistic construction' becomes relevant for satisfying truth questions. It was because such questions had been forgotten, Price claims, that much of analytic philosophy was led to conclude that the indispensability of a determinate entity or reality to the success of a linguistic construction was sufficient evidence for the existence of this entity (recall Lewis's argument for possible worlds). For Price however, and in a reminder of the lesson he draws from Carnap, we fall into metaphysics as soon as we ask and answer questions independent of the questions that are answerable within the linguistic constructions themselves – that is, we fall into metaphysics when we seek, as Carnap put it, to answer an external question rather than an internal question.

What our discussion of problematic Ideas has added to Carnap's arguments, with the help of Davidson, among others, is a focus on the arbitrary nature of where one may happen to draw the line between an internal and an external question. The metaphysics of problematic Ideas set forth here has been motivated in large part by the problem of arbitrariness associated with brute facts and brute, fundamental relations and distinctions, such as the analytic/synthetic or the internal/external distinction. Problematic Ideas both condition and resist the type of answer one ultimately seeks when one asks an external question rather than an internal one – asking a truth question while ignoring the relevance questions inseparable from this question – and problematic Ideas are also the condition for the possibility of drawing a line, if even provisionally so, between internal and external questions. In other words, Price is indeed right to stress the point that we ought to call upon the anthropologists, among others, to discern the relevance of the linguistic frameworks we use so that we may discern the role they play in our lives. In extending Price's point, we could say that the role of philosophy in this project, the role of philosophy as gadfly, is one of continually exploring the limits of life as a problem, or as the ceaseless expression of problematic Ideas. When one encounters such limits one is left, like the coffee taster discussed above, at a loss for words, but it is precisely this loss that creates an opportunity for learning, for the emergence of something new in our lives. As a result, whatever acclaim philosophy achieves will not be akin to the determinate successes of the sciences, noteworthy as these may be, but will come, as it should, from philosophy's ability to remind us of all that follows from the problems with which we began this book – such as the problem of the new – problems that are inseparable from our lives as lived. As will be clear by now, these problems have been a recurrent theme throughout the history of philosophy, and given their relevance to life itself – to how, when, with whom and in what circumstances we should do one thing or another – it is indeed unsurprising that philosophy continues to persist. As Kant encountered the lack of acclaim philosophy had received relative to the sciences, we could say now that it is just this encounter, and the questions it raised for Kant, that has given to philosophy its acclaim and will continue to do so into the future.

Bibliography

Adorno, Theodor W. 1973 [1966]. *Negative Dialectics*. Translated by E.B. Ashton. New York: Routledge.
Adorno, Theodor W. 2002. *Essays on Music*. Translated by Susan H. Gillespie. Berkeley: University of California Press.
Adorno, Theodor W. 2006 [1949]. *Philosophy of New Music*. Translated by Robert Hullot-Kentor. Minneapolis: University of Minnesota Press.
Agamben, Giorgio. 2009. *Potentialities*. Translated by Daniel Heller-Roazen. Stanford: Stanford University Press.
Algra, Keimpe, Jonathan Barnes, Jaap Mansfeld and Malcom Schofield, eds. 2008. *The Cambridge History of Hellenistic Philosophy*. Cambridge: Cambridge University Press.
Allison, Henry E. 1983. *Kant's Transcendental Idealism*. New Haven: Yale University Press.
Amadae, S.M. 2003. *Rationalizing Capitalist Democracy: The Cold War Origins of Rational Choice Liberalism*. Chicago: University of Chicago Press.
Anderson, Benedict. 1991. *Imagined Communities*. New York: Verso.
Aristotle. 1979. *Metaphysics*. Translated by Hippocrates Apostle. Grinnell: The Peripatetic Press.
Armstrong, D.M. 1974. 'Infinite Regress Arguments and the Problem of Universals'. *Australasian Journal of Philosophy* 52 (3):191–201.
Armstrong, D.M. 1980a. 'Against "Ostrich" Nominalism: A Reply to Michael Devitt'. *Pacific Philosophical Quarterly* 61 (4):440–9.
Armstrong, D.M. 1980b. *A Theory of Universals: Universals & Scientific Realism Volume I*. Cambridge: Cambridge University Press.
Armstrong, D.M. 1980c. *A Theory of Universals: Universals & Scientific Realism Volume II*. Cambridge: Cambridge University Press.
Armstrong, D.M. 1997. *A World of States of Affairs*. Cambridge: Cambridge University Press.
Armstrong, D.M. 2004. 'How Do Particulars Stand to Universals?' In *Oxford Studies in Metaphysics*. Edited by Dean Zimmerman. Oxford: Oxford University Press, 139–54.
Armstrong, Joshua, and Jason Stanley. 2011. 'Singular Thoughts and Singular Propositions'. *Philosophical Studies: An International Journal for Philosophy in the Analytic Tradition* 154 (2):205–22.
Arrighi, Giovanni. 1994. *The Long Twentieth Century: Money, Power, and the Origins of Our Times*. New York: Verso.
Arrighi, Giovanni. 2009. *Adam Smith in Beijing: Lineages of the 21st Century*. London: Verso.
Arrow, Kenneth J. 1977. 'Extended Sympathy and the Possibility of Social Choice'. *The American Economic Review* 67 (1):219–25.
Arrow, Kenneth J. 1982. 'Risk Perception in Psychology and Economics'. *Economic Inquiry* 20 (1):1–9.
Aune, Bruce. 1967. 'Statements and Propositions'. *Noûs* 1 (3):215–29.
Austin, J.L. 1961. *Philosophical Papers*. Oxford: Clarendon Press.
Austin, J.L. 1962. *How To Do Things With Words*. Oxford: Clarendon Press.
Ayache, Elie. 2010. *The Blank Swan: The End of Probability*. Chichester: John Wiley & Sons.
Ayache, Elie. 2015. *The Medium of Contingency: An Inverse View of the Market*. New York: Palgrave.

Ayer, A.J. 1971 [1936]. *Language, Truth and Logic*. New York: Penguin Books.
Badiou, Alain. 2004. *Theoretical Writings*. Translated by Ray Brassier and Alberto Toscano. London and New York: Continuum.
Baier, Annette C. 1991. *A Progress of Sentiments: Reflections on Hume's Treatise*. Cambridge, MA: Harvard University Press.
Baker, G.P., and P.M.S. Hacker. 2005a. *Wittgenstein: Understanding and Meaning, Part I: Essays*. Edited by P.M.S. Hacker. Vol. 1, *An Analytical Commentary on the Philosophical Investigations*. Oxford: Blackwell.
Baker, G.P. and P.M.S. Hacker. 2005b. *Wittgenstein: Understanding and Meaning, Part II: Exegesis §§1–184*. Edited by P.M.S. Hacker, *An Analytical Commentary on the Philosophical Investigations*. Oxford: Blackwell.
Baran, Paul, and Paul Sweezy. 1966. *Monopoly Capital: An Essay on the American Economic and Social Order*. New York: Modern Reader Paperbacks.
Bealer, George. 1998a. 'Propositions'. *Mind* 107 (425):1–32.
Bealer, George. 1998b. 'Intuition and the Autonomy of Philosophy'. In *Rethinking Intuition: The Psychology of Intuition and its Role in Philosophical Inquiry*. Edited by M. DePaul and W. Ramsey. Lanham: Rowman and Littlefield, 201–39.
Beard, Mary. 1986. 'Cicero and Divination: The Formation of a Latin Discourse'. *Journal of Roman Studies* 76:33–46.
Becker, Gary S., and Kevin M. Murphy. 1988. 'A Theory of Rational Addiction'. *Journal of Political Economy* 96 (4):675–700.
Beiser, Frederick C. 1987. *The Fate of Reason: German Philosophy from Kant to Fichte*. Cambridge, MA: Harvard University Press.
Beiser, Frederick C. 2002. *German Idealism: The Struggle against Subjectivism, 1781–1801*. Cambridge, MA: Harvard University Press.
Beiser, Frederick C. 2014. *The Genesis of Neo-Kantianism, 1796–1880*. Oxford: Oxford University Press.
Bell, Jeffrey A. 1998. *The Problem of Difference: Phenomenology and Poststructuralism*. Toronto: University of Toronto Press.
Bell, Jeffrey A. 2006. *Philosophy at the Edge of Chaos: Gilles Deleuze and the Philosophy of Difference*. Toronto: University of Toronto Press.
Bell, Jeffrey A. 2009. *Deleuze's Hume: Philosophy, Culture and the Scottish Enlightenment*. Edinburgh: Edinburgh University Press.
Bell, Jeffrey A. 2016. *Deleuze and Guattari's* What is Philosophy? *A Critical Introduction and Guide*. Edinburgh: Edinburgh University Press.
Bell, Jeffrey A. 2018a. 'Postulates of Linguistics'. In *A Thousand Plateaus and Philosophy*. Edited by Henry Somers-Hall, Jeffrey A. Bell and James Williams. Edinburgh: Edinburgh University Press, 64–82.
Bell, Jeffrey A. 2018b. 'Reading Problems: Literacy and the Dynamics of Thought'. *Open Philosophy* 1 (1):223–34.
Bell, Jeffrey A., Andrew Cutrofellow and Paul M. Livingtson, eds. 2015. *Beyond the Analytic–Continental Divide: Pluralist Philosophy in the Twenty-First Century*. New York: Routledge.
Benardete, José A. 1958. 'The Analytic a posteriori and the Foundations of Metaphysics'. *The Journal of Philosophy* 55 (12):503–14.
Benardete, José A. 1964. *Infinity: An Essay in Metaphysics*. Oxford: Clarendon Press.
Benardete, José A. 1980. 'Spinozistic Anomalies'. In *The Philosophy of Baruch Spinoza*. Edited by Richard Kennington. Washington, DC: The Catholic University of America Press, 53–72.
Benes, Jaromir, and Michael Kumhof. 2012. 'The Chicago Plan Revisited'. *IMF Working Paper* (WP/12/202):1–70.
Berger, Peter L., and Thomas Luckman. 1967. *The Social Construction of Reality*. New York: Anchor Books.

Bergmann, Gustav. 1944. 'Pure Semantics, Sentences, and Propositions'. *Mind* 53 (211):238–57.
Bergson, Henri. 1984 [1911]. *Creative Evolution*. Translated by Arthur Mitchell. New York: Henry Holt and Company.
Bergson, Henri. 1988 [1896]. *Matter and Memory*. Translated by Nancy Margaret Paul and W. Scott Palmer. New York: Zone Books.
Berman, Sheri. 2006. *The Primacy of Politics: Social Democracy and the Making of Europe's Twentieth Century*. Cambridge: Cambridge University Press.
Bhaskar, Roy. 1975. *A Realist Theory of Science*. Leeds: Leeds Books.
Bhaskar, Roy. 1989. *Reclaiming Reality*. London: Verso.
Bhaskar, Roy. 1994. *Plato, Etc.: The Problems of Philosophy, and Their Resolutions*. London: Verso.
Bjerg, Ole. 2014. *Making Money: The Philosophy of Crisis Capitalism*. London: Verso.
Bloor, David. 1983. *Wittgenstein: A Social Theory of Knowledge*. London: Macmillan.
Blyth, Mark. 2002. *Great Transformations: Economic Ideas and Institutional Change in the Twentieth Century*. Cambridge: Cambridge University Press.
Boolos, George. 1998. *Logic, Logic, and Logic*. Cambridge, MA.: Harvard University Press.
Bourdieu, Pierre. 1968. 'Intellectual Field and Creative Project'. *Social Science Information* 8 (2):89–119.
Bourdieu, Pierre. 1984 [1979]. *Distinction: A Social Critique of the Judgment of Taste*. Translated by Richard Nice. Cambridge, MA: Harvard University Press.
Bourdieu, Pierre. 1990. *In Other Words: Essays Towards a Reflexive Sociology*. Stanford: Stanford University Press.
Bourdieu, Pierre, and Loïc J.D. Wacquant. 1992. *An Invitation to Reflexive Sociology*. London: Polity Press.
Bradley, F.H. 1893. *Appearance and Reality*. London: George Allen & Unwin, Ltd.
Bradley, F.H. 1909. 'Coherence and Contradiction'. *Mind* 18 (72):489–508.
Bradley, F.H. 1910. 'On Appearance, Error and Contradiction'. *Mind* 19 (74):153–85.
Bradley, F.H. 1911. 'Reply to Mr. Russell's Explanations'. *Mind* 20 (77):74–6.
Brandom, Robert B. 1994. *Making it Explicit*. Cambridge, MA: Harvard University Press.
Brandom, Robert B. 2000. *Articulating Reasons: An Introduction to Inferentialism*. Cambridge, MA: Harvard University Press.
Brassier, Ray. 2007. *Nihil Unbound: Enlightenment and Extinction*. London: Palgrave.
Bridgman, Percy Williams. 1959. *The Way Things Are*. Cambridge, MA: Harvard University Press.
Bridgman, Percy Williams. 1961 [1927]. *The Logic of Physics*. New York: Macmillan.
Brooke, Christopher. 2012. *Philosophic Pride: Stoicism and Political Thought from Lipsius to Rousseau*. Princeton: Princeton University Press.
Bruner, Jerome. 1991a. 'The Narrative Construction of Reality'. *Critical Inquiry* 18 (1):1–21.
Bruner, Jerome. 1991b. *Acts of Meaning*. Cambridge, MA: Harvard University Press.
Burgess, Alexis G., and John P. Burgess. 2011. *Truth*. Edited by Scott Soames, *Princeton Foundations of Contemporary Philosophy*. Princeton: Princeton University Press.
Cairns, Dorion. 1930. 'Mr. Hook's Impression of Phenomenology'. *The Journal of Philosophy* 27 (15):393–6.
Cairns, Dorion. 1973. 'My Own Life'. In *Phenomenology: Continuation and Criticism*. Edited by Frederick Kersten and Richard Zaner. The Hague: Martinus Nijhoff, 1–13.
Call, Josep, and Michael Tomasello. 1999. 'A Nonverbal False Belief Task: The Performance of Children and Great Apes'. *Society for Research in Child Development* 70 (2):381–95.
Cameron, Lisa A. 1999. 'Raising the Stakes in the Ultimatum Game: Experimental Evidence from Indonesia'. *Economic Inquiry* 37 (1):47–59.
Candlish, Stewart. 2007. *The Russell/Bradley Dispute and its Significance for Twentieth-Century Philosophy*. New York: Palgrave Macmillan.

BIBLIOGRAPHY

Carlsen, Magnus. 2015. 'I Make A Move and I Really Don't Know Why'. In *Chess24.com*. Edited by Colin McGourty, at <https://chess24.com/en/read/news/carlsen-i-make-a-move-i-really-don-t-know-why>.

Carnap, Rudolf. 1952. 'Empiricism, Semantics, and Ontology'. In *Semantics and the Philosophy of Language*. Edited by Leonard Linsky. Urbana: University of Illinois Press, 208–30.

Carnap, Rudolf. 1956. *Meaning and Necessity: A Study in Semantics and Modal Logic*. Chicago: University of Chicago Press.

Carnap, Rudolf. 1984 [1934]. 'On the Character of Philosophic Problems'. *Philosophy of Science* 51 (1):5–19.

Carnap, Rudolf. 1987 [1932]. 'On Protocol Sentences'. *Noûs* 21:457–70.

Carnap, Rudolf. 1996 [1932]. 'The Elimination of Metaphysics Through Logical Analysis of Language'. In *Science and Philosophy in the Twentieth Century*. Edited by Sahotra Sarkar. New York: Garland Publishing, 60–81

Carnap, Rudolf. 2003 [1928]. *The Logical Structure of the World*. Translated by Rolf A. George. New York: Open Court.

Cartwright, Richard. 1987. 'Propositions'. In *Philosophical Essays*. Edited by Richard Cartwright. Cambridge, MA: The MIT Press, 33–54.

Cencini, Alvaro, and Sergio Rossi. 2015. *Economic and Financial Crises: A New Macroeconomic Analysis*. London: Palgrave Macmillan.

Chang, Hasok. 2004. *Inventing Temperature: Measurement and Scientific Progress*. Oxford: Oxford University Press.

Chisholm, Roderick. 1970. 'Events and Propositions'. *Noûs* 4 (1):15–24.

Chomsky, Noam. 2005. *Chomsky on Anarchism*. Oakland: AK Press.

Chomsky, Noam. 2013. *On Anarchism*. New York: The New Press.

Chomsky, Noam, and Edward S. Herman. 1988. *Manufacturing Consent: The Political Economy of the Mass Media*. New York: Pantheon Books.

Church, Alonzo. 1936. 'An Unsolvable Problem of Elementary Number Theory'. *American Journal of Mathematics* 58 (2):345–63.

Clark, Andy. 2017. 'A Nice Surprise? Predictive Processing and the Active Pursuit of Novelty'. *Phenomenology and the Cognitive Sciences* 17:521–34.

Clarke, Stephen V.O. 1967. *Central Bank Cooperation 1924–31*. New York: Federal Reserve Bank of New York.

Clastres, Pierre. 1987. *Society Against the State*. Translated by Robert Hurley. New York: Zone Books.

Clastres, Pierre. 1994. *Archaeology of Violence*. Translated by Jeanine Herman. New York: Semiotext(e).

Cole, Michael. 2005. 'Cross-Cultural and Historical Perspectives on the Developmental Consequences of Education'. *Human Development* 48:195–216.

Cole, Michael, J. Gay, J.A. Glick and D.A. Sharp, eds. 1971. *The Cultural Context of Learning and Thinking: An Exploration in Experimental Anthropology*. New York: Basic Books.

Cole, Michael, and Sylvia Scribner. 1974. *Culture and Thought*. New York: John Wiley & Sons.

Colish, Marcia. 1997. *Medieval Foundations of the Western Intellectual Tradition: 400–1400*. New Haven: Yale University Press.

Collins, H.M. 1985. *Changing Order: Replication and Induction in Scientific Practice*. London: Sage.

Counihan, Marian. 2008. 'Looking for Logic in All the Wrong Places: An Investigation of Language, Literacy and Logic in Reasoning'. Institute for Logic, Language and Computation, University of Amsterdam (ILLC Dissertation Series DS-2008–10).

Cousin, D.R. 1948. 'Propositions'. *Proceedings of the Aristotelian Society* 49:151–70.

Crowell, Steven G. 2010. 'Transcendental Logic and Minimal Empiricism: Lask and McDowell on the Unboundedness of the Conceptual'. In *Neo-Kantianism in Contemporary Philosophy*. Edited by Rudolf A. Makkreel and Sebastian Luft. Bloomington: Indiana University Press, 150–76.

D'Angour, Armand. 2011. *The Greeks and the New: Novelty in Ancient Greek Imagination and Experience*. Cambridge: Cambridge University Press.

Davidson, Donald. 1980. *Essays on Actions and Events*. Oxford: Oxford University Press.

Davidson, Donald. 1989. 'A Coherence Theory of Truth and Knowledge'. In *Truth and Interpretation: Perspectives on the Philosophy of Donald Davidson*. Edited by Ernest LePore. Oxford: Blackwell, 307–19.

Davidson, Donald. 1990. *Plato's* Philebus. New York: Routledge.

Davidson, Donald. 1999. 'Spinoza's Causal Theory of the Affects'. In *Desire and Affect: Spinoza as Psychologist. Papers presented at the Third Jerusalem Conference (Ethica III)*. Edited by Yirmiyahu Yovel. New York: Little Room Press, 95–112.

Davidson, Donald. 2001. *Inquiries into Truth and Interpretation*. Oxford: Oxford University Press.

Davidson, Donald. 2005a. *Truth and Predication*. Cambridge, MA: Harvard University Press.

Davidson, Donald. 2005b. *Truth, Language, and History*. Oxford: Clarendon Press.

de Bruin, Boudewijn. 2015. *Ethics and the Global Financial Crisis: Why Incompetence is Worse than Greed*. Cambridge: Cambridge University Press.

De Cruz, Helen. 2016. 'Numerical Cognition and Mathematical Realism'. *Philosophers' Imprint* 16 (16):1–13.

de Waal, Frans. 2005. 'Intentional Deception in Primates'. *Evolutionary Anthropology: Issues, News, and Reviews* 1 (3):86–92.

DeBrabander, Firmin. 2007. *Spinoza and the Stoics*. London: Continuum.

Deleuze, Gilles. 1981. *Spinoza: Practical Philosophy*. Translated by Robert Hurley. San Francisco: City Lights Books.

Deleuze, Gilles. 1988. *Bergsonism*. Translated by Hugh Tomlinson and Barbara Habberjam. New York: Zone Books.

Deleuze, Gilles. 1990a. *Expressionism in Philosophy: Spinoza*. Translated by Martin Joughin. New York: Zone Books.

Deleuze, Gilles. 1990b. *The Logic of Sense*. Translated by Mark Lester and Charles Stivale. New York: Columbia University Press.

Deleuze, Gilles. 1991. *Empiricism and Subjectivity*. Translated by Constantin Boundas. New York: Columbia University Press.

Deleuze, Gilles. 1993. *The Fold: Leibniz and the Baroque*. Translated by Tom Conley. London: Athlone.

Deleuze, Gilles. 1994. *Difference and Repetition*. Translated by Paul Patton. New York: Columbia University Press.

Deleuze, Gilles. 1998. 'Spinoza and the Three "Ethics"'. In *The New Spinoza*. Edited by Warren Montag and Ted Stolze. Minneapolis: University of Minnesota Press.

Deleuze, Gilles. 2001. *Pure Immanence*. Translated by Anne Boyman. New York: Zone Books.

Deleuze, Gilles. 2004. *Desert Islands and Other Texts 1953–1974*. Translated by Michael Taormina. New York: Semiotext(e).

Deleuze, Gilles. 2015. *What is Grounding?* Translated by Arjen Kleinherenbrink. Grand Rapids, MI: &&& Publishing. Transcription of lecture notes attributed to Pierre Lefebvre.

Deleuze, Gilles, and Félix Guattari. 1977. *Anti-Oedipus: Capitalism and Schizophrenia*. Translated by Mark Seem, Robert Hurley and Helen R. Lane. Minneapolis: University of Minnesota Press.

Deleuze, Gilles, and Félix Guattari. 1987. *A Thousand Plateaus: Capitalism and Schizophrenia*. Translated by Brian Massumi. Minneapolis: University of Minnesota Press.

Deleuze, Gilles, and Félix Guattari. 1994. *What is Philosophy?* Translated by Hugh Tomlinson and Graham Burchell. New York: Columbia University Press.

Della Rocca, Michael. 2011. 'Primitive Persistence and the Impasse Between Three-Dimensionalism and Four-Dimensionalism'. *Journal of Philosophy* 108 (11):591–616.

Della Rocca, Michael. 2013. 'Taming of Philosophy'. In *Philosophy and its History*. Edited by Mogens Lærke, Justin E.H. Smith and Eric Schliesser. Oxford: Oxford University Press.

Della Rocca, Michael. 2017. 'Playing With Fire: Hume, Rationalism, and a Little Bit of Spinoza'. In *Oxford Handbook of Spinoza*. Edited by Michael Della Rocca. Oxford: Oxford University Press.

Descartes, René. 1996 [1641]. *Meditations on First Philosophy*. Translated by John Cottingham. Cambridge: Cambridge University Press.

Devitt, Michael. 1980. '"Ostrich Nominalism" or "Mirage Realism"?' *Pacific Philosophical Quarterly* 61 (4):433–9.

Dewey, John. 1941. 'Propositions, Warranted Assertibility, and Truth'. *The Journal of Philosophy* 38 (7):169–86.

Dillon, John M., and A.A. Long, eds. 1988. *The Question of 'Eclecticism': Studies in Later Greek Philosophy*. Berkeley: University of California Press.

Donald, Merlin. 1991. *Origins of the Modern Mind: Three Stages in the Evolution of Culture and Cognition*. Cambridge, MA: Harvard University Press.

Dreyfus, Hubert L. 2005. 'Overcoming the Myth of the Mental: How Philosophers Can Profit from the Phenomenology of Everyday Expertise'. *Proceedings and Addresses of the American Philosophical Association* 79:47–65.

Ducasse, C. J. 1944. 'A Symposium on Meaning and Truth, Part II Propositions, Truth, and the Ultimate Criterion of Truth'. *Philosophy and Phenomenological Research* 4 (3):317–40.

Duffy, Simon B., ed. 2006. *Virtual Mathematics: The Logic of Difference*. London: Clinamen.

Dummett, Michael. 1959. 'Wittgenstein's Philosophy of Mathematics'. *The Philosophical Review* 68 (3):324–48.

Dummett, Michael. 1991. *The Logical Basis of Metaphysics*. Cambridge, MA: Harvard University Press.

Durkheim, Émile. 1965 [1915]. *The Elementary Forms of Religious Life*. Translated by Joseph Ward Swain. New York: Basic Books.

Eichengreen, Barry. 2008. *Globalizing Capital: A History of the International Monetary System*. Princeton: Princeton University Press.

Elden, Stuart. 2013. *The Birth of Territory*. Chicago: University of Chicago Press.

Elliott, Kevin C., and Ted Richards, eds. 2017. *Exploring Inductive Risk: Case Studies of Values in Science*. Oxford: Oxford University Press.

Euclid. 1908. *The Thirteen Books of Euclid's Elements, Vol. I (Books I, II)*. Translated by Sir. Thomas L. Heath. Cambridge: Cambridge University Press.

Fama, Eugene F. 1970. 'Efficient Capital Markets: A Review of Theory and Empirical Work'. *The Journal of Finance* Papers and Proceedings of the Twenty-Eighth Annual Meeting of the American Finance Association:383–417.

Fichte, J.G. 1982. *The Science of Knowledge*. Translated by Peter Heath and John Lachs. Cambridge: Cambridge University Press.

Field, Hartry. 2001. *Truth and the Absence of Fact*. Oxford: Oxford University Press.

Fine, Arthur. 1998. 'The Viewpoint of No-One in Particular'. *Proceedings of the American Philosophical Association* 72(2):7–20.

Fine, Gail. 1993. *On Ideas: Aristotle's Criticism of Plato's Theory of Forms*. Oxford: Clarendon Press.

Fink, Eugen. 1995. *Sixth Cartesian Meditation: The Idea of a Transcendental Theory of Method*. With Notations by Edmund Husserl. Translated by Ronald Bruzina. Bloomington: Indiana University Press.

Finnegan, Ruth. 1973. 'Literacy versus Non-literacy: The Great Divide?' In *Modes of Thought, Essays on Thinking in Western and Non-Western Societies*. London: Faber and Faber.

Fisher, Irving. 1932. *Booms and Depressions*. New York: Adelphi.

Fisher, Irving. 1933. 'The Debt-Deflation Theory of Great Depressions'. *Econometrica* 1 (4):337–57.

Flandreau, Marc, Carl-Ludwig Holtfrerich and Harold James, eds. 2003. *International Financial History in the Twentieth Century: System and Anarchy*. Cambridge: Cambridge University Press.
Foucault, Michel. 1972. *The Archaeology of Knowledge*. Translated by Rupert Swyer. New York: Random House.
Foucault, Michel. 1973. *The Order of Things*. New York: Vintage.
Foucault, Michel. 1980. *Power/Knowledge: Selected Interviews & Other Writings, 1972–1977*. Translated by Colin Gordon, Leo Marshall, John Mepham and Kate Soper. Edited by Colin Gordon. New York: Pantheon.
Foucault, Michel. 2008. *The Birth of Biopolitics: Lectures at the Collège de France*. Translated by Graham Burchell. London: Palgrave Macmillan.
Foucault, Michel. 2013. *Lectures on the Will to Know: Lectures at the Collège de France*. London: Palgrave Macmillan.
Frege, Gottlob. 1960 [1884]. *The Foundations of Arithmetic*. Translated by J.L. Austin. New York: Harber & Brothers.
Frege, Gottlob. 1984 [1891]. 'Function and Concept'. In *Collected Papers on Mathematics, Logic, and Philosophy*. Edited by Brian McGuinness. Oxford: Blackwell.
Frege, Gottlob. 1997. *The Frege Reader*. Edited by Michael Beaney. Oxford: Blackwell.
French, Steven. 2011. 'Metaphysical Underdetermination: Why Worry?' *Synthese* 180 (2):205–21.
Fricker, Miranda. 2007. *Epistemic Injustice: Power and the Ethics of Knowing*. Oxford: Oxford University Press.
Friedman, Milton. 1966. 'The Methodology of Positive Economics'. In *Essays in Positive Economics*. Chicago: University of Chicago Press, 3–43.
Galbraith, John Kenneth. 2009. *The Great Crash 1929*. New York: Mariner Books.
Garber, Daniel. 2009. *Leibniz: Body, Substance, Monad*. Oxford: Oxford University Press.
Garfinkel, Harold. 1967. *Studies in Ethnomethodology*. Englewood Cliffs: Prentice-Hall.
Gaskin, Richard. 1997. 'Fregean Sense and Russellian Propositions'. *Philosophical Studies: An International Journal for Philosophy in the Analytic Tradition* 86 (2):131–54.
Gauthier, David. 1986. *Morals by Agreement*. Oxford: Oxford University Press.
Geach, Peter Thomas. 1980. *Reference and Generality*. Ithaca: Cornell University Press.
Gellner, Ernest. 1983. *Nations and Nationalism*. Oxford: Blackwell.
Gellner, Ernest. 1998. *Language and Solitude: Wittgenstein, Malinowski and the Habsburg Dilemma*. Cambridge: Cambridge University Press.
Gibbons, S., and C. Legg. 2013. 'Higher-Order One-Many Problems in Plato's *Philebus* and Recent Australian Metaphysics'. *Australasian Journal of Philosophy* 91 (1):119–38.
Gillespie, Sam. 2001. 'Placing the Void: Badiou on Spinoza'. *Angelaki* 6 (3):63–77.
Gillespie, Sam. 2008. *The Mathematics of Novelty: Badiou's Minimalist Metaphysics*. Melbourne: re.press.
Gillett, Carl, and Bradley Rives. 2005. 'The Nonexistence of Determinables: Or, a World of Absolute Determinates as Default Hypothesis'. *Nous* 39 (3):483–504.
Ginzburg, Carlo. 1989. *Clues, Myths and the Historical Method*. Baltimore: Johns Hopkins University Press.
Ginzburg, Carlo. 1993. 'Microhistory: Two or Three Things That I Know About It'. *Critical Inquiry* 20 (1):10–35.
Ginzburg, Carlo. 2012. *Threads and Traces: True, False, Fictive*. Berkeley: University of California Press.
Girouard, Mark. 1990. *The English Town: A History of Urban Life*. New Haven: Yale University Press.
Glick, James. 1975. 'Cognitive Development in Cross-cultural Perspective'. In *Review of Child Development Research*. Edited by J. Horowitz. Chicago: Chicago University Press.
Glock, Hans-Johann. 2008. 'The Development of Analytic Philosophy: Wittgenstein and

After'. In *The Routledge Companion to Twentieth-Century Philosophy*. Edited by Dermot Moran. New York: Routledge, 76–117.

Gödel, Kurt. 1947. 'What is Cantor's Continuum Problem?' *The American Mathematical Monthly* 54 (9):515–25.

Goldgar, Anne. 2007. *Tulipmania: Money, Honor, and Knowledge in the Dutch Golden Age*. Chicago: University of Chicago Press.

Goodman, Nelson. 1983. *Fact, Fiction, and Forecast*. 4th ed. Cambridge, MA: Harvard University Press.

Gordon, Peter. 2012. *Continental Divide: Heidegger, Cassirer, Davos*. Cambridge, MA: Harvard University Press.

Graeber, David. 2001. *Toward an Anthropological Theory of Value*. New York: Palgrave.

Graeber, David. 2015. 'Radical Alterity is Just Another Way of Saying "Reality": A Reply to Eduardo Viveiros de Castro'. *Journal of Ethnographic Theory* 5 (1):1–41.

Grice, H.P. 1957. 'Meaning'. *Philosophical Review* 66:377–88.

Grice, H.P. 1989. 'Logic and Conversation'. In *Studies in the Way of Words*. Cambridge, MA: Harvard University Press, 22–40.

Grice, H.P., and P.F. Strawson. 1956. 'In Defense of a Dogma'. *The Philosophical Review* 65 (2):141–58.

Grice, Paul. 1991. *The Conception of Value*. Oxford: The Clarendon Press.

Guala, Francesco. 2006. 'Has Game Theory Been Refuted?' *The Journal of Philosophy* 103 (5):239–63.

Guérin, Daniel. 2005 [1980]. *No Gods, No Masters*. Translated by Paul Sharkey. Oakland: AK Press.

Hacking, Ian. 1975. 'All Kinds of Possibility'. *Philosophical Review* 84 (3):321–37.

Hacking, Ian. 1979. 'What is Logic?' *Journal of Philosophy* 76 (6):285–319.

Hacking, Ian. 1993. 'Working in a New World: The Taxonomic Solution'. In *World Changes*. Edited by Paul Horwich. Cambridge, MA: Harvard University Press, 275–310.

Hall, Stuart. 1996 [2006]. 'The Problem of Ideology'. In *Stuart Hall: Critical Dialogues*. Edited by Kuan-Hsing Chen and David Morley. New York: Routledge, 24–45.

Halmos, Paul R. 1974. *Naive Set Theory*. New York: Springer-Verlag.

Hardin, Russell. 2007. *David Hume: Moral and Political Theorist*. Oxford: Oxford University Press.

Harlow, Harry F. 1959. 'Learning Set and Error Factor Theory'. In *Psychology: A Study of a Science*. Edited by Sigmund Koch. New York: McGraw-Hill, 492–537.

Harsanyi, John C. 1966. 'A General Theory of Rational Behavior in Game Situations'. *Econometrica* 34 (3):613–34.

Hartmann, Nicolai. 2012 [1942]. *New Ways of Ontology*. Westport, CT: Greenwood Press.

Haslanger, Sally. 2012. *Resisting Reality: Social Construction and Social Critique*. New York: Oxford University Press.

Haslanger, Sally. 2017. 'Racism, Ideology, and Social Movements'. *Res Philosophica* 94 (1):1–22.

Havelock, Eric. 1963. *Preface to Plato*. Cambridge, MA: Harvard University Press.

Hawking, Stephen. 2012. *The Grand Design*. New York: Bantam.

Hayek, Friedrich August von. 1945. 'The Use of Knowledge in Society'. *The American Economic Review* 35 (4):519–30.

Hayek, Friedrich August von. 1948a. 'The Meaning of Competition'. In *Individualism and Economic Order*. Edited by Friedrich August von Hayek. Chicago: University of Chicago Press.

Hayek, Friedrich August von. 1948b. *Individualism and Economic Order*. Chicago: University of Chicago Press.

Hayek, Friedrich August von. 1978. *New Studies in Philosophy, Politics, Economics and the History of Ideas*. New York: Routledge.

Heidegger, Martin. 1959. *An Introduction to Metaphysics*. Edited by Ralph Manheim. New Haven: Yale University Press.

Heidegger, Martin. 1984 [1928]. *Metaphysical Foundations of Logic*. Bloomington: Indiana University Press.
Heidegger, Martin. 1997. *Kant and the Problem of Metaphysics*. Translated by Richard Taft. Bloomington: Indiana University Press.
Hilbert, David. 2013 [1917/18]. *David Hilbert's Lectures on the Foundations of Arithmetic and Logic, 1917–1933*. New York: Springer.
Hilbert, David, and Wilhelm Friedrich Ackerman. 1999 [1928]. *Principles of Mathematical Logic*. Providence: American Mathematical Society.
Hilson, Mary. 2008. *The Nordic Model: Scandinavia Since 1945*. London: Reaktion Books.
Hintikka, Jaakko. 1996. 'Knowledge Acknowledged: Knowledge of Propositions vs. Knowledge of Objects'. *Philosophy and Phenomenological Research* 56 (2):251–75.
Hirata, Satoshi. 'Tactical Deception and Understanding of Others in Chimpanzees'. In *Cognitive Development in Chimpanzees*. Edited by Tetsuro Matsuzawa, Masaki Tomonaga and Masayuki Tanaka. New York: Springer, 265–78.
Hobsbawm, Eric. 1990. *Nations and Nationalism Since 1780*. Cambridge: Cambridge University Press.
Hobsbawm, Eric, and Terence Ranger, eds. 1983. *The Invention of Tradition*. Cambridge: Cambridge University Press.
Hochschild, Arlie. 2016. *Strangers In Their Own Land: Anger and Mourning On the American Right*. New York: The New Press.
Holt, Edwin B., Walter T. Marvin, W.P. Montague, Ralph Barton Perry, Walter B. Pitkin and Edward Gleason Spaulding. 1910. 'The Program and First Platform of Six Realists'. *The Journal of Philosophy, Psychology and Scientific Methods* 7 (15):393–401.
Holt, Edwin B., Walter T. Marvin, W.P. Montague, Ralph Barton Perry, Walter B. Pitkin and Edward Gleason Spaulding. 1912. *The New Realists*. New York: Macmillan Company.
Hook, Sidney. 1930. 'A Personal Impression of Contemporary German Philosophy'. *The Journal of Philosophy* 27 (6):141–60.
Horwich, Paul, ed. 1993. *World Changes*. Cambridge, MA: Harvard University Press.
Hsu, Carolyn L. 2007. *Creating Market Socialism: How Ordinary People Are Shaping Class and Status in China*. Durham, NC: Duke University Press.
Huber, Joseph. 2017. *Sovereign Money: Beyond Reserve Banking*. London: Palgrave Macmillan.
Hughes, Joe. 2008. *Deleuze and the Genesis of Representation*. London: Continuum.
Hume, David. 1978 [1739]. *A Treatise of Human Nature*. Edited by L.A. Silby-Bigge. Oxford: Clarendon Press.
Hume, David. 1985 [1741–2]. *Essays, Moral, Political, and Literary*. Edited by Eugene Miller. Indianapolis: Liberty Fund.
Hume, David. 2005 [1748]. *An Enquiry Concerning Human Understanding*. Edited by Tom Beauchamp. Oxford: Oxford University Press.
Hume, David. 2007 [1739]. *A Treatise of Human Nature*. Oxford: Oxford University Press.
Humphrey, Caroline, and Stephen Hugh-Jones. *Barter, Exchange and Value: An Anthropological Approach*. Cambridge: Cambridge University Press.
Husserl, Edmund. 1969. *Formal and Transcendental Logic*. Edited by Dorion Cairns. The Hague: Martinus Nijhoff.
Husserl, Edmund. 1970. *The Crisis of European Sciences and Transcendental Phenomenology*. Translated by David Carr. Evanston: Northwestern University Press.
Husserl, Edmund. 1980. *Ideas III: Phenomenology and the Foundations of the Sciences*. Translated by Ted E. Klein and William E. Pohl. Boston: Martinus Nijhoff.
Husserl, Edmund. 1988 [1931]. *Cartesian Meditations*. Translated by Dorion Cairns. Boston: Martinus Nijhoff.
Husserl, Edmund. 1998. *The Paris Lectures*. Translated by Peter Koestenbaum. Dordrecht: Kluwer Academic Publishers.
Husserl, Edmund. 2001 [1901]. *Logical Investigations, vol. 1*. New York: Routledge.

Hylton, Peter. 1993. *Russell, Idealism and the Emergence of Analytic Philosophy*. Oxford: Oxford University Press.
Ingham, Geoffrey. 2004. *The Nature of Money*. Cambridge: Polity Press.
Ingham, Geoffrey. 2008. *Capitalism*. Cambridge: Polity Press.
Innes, A. Mitchell. 1913. 'What is Money?' *Banking Law Journal*, May:377–408.
Innes, A. Mitchell. 1914. 'The Credit Theory of Money'. *Banking Law Journal*, January:151–68.
Inwood, Stephen. 1998. *A History of London*. New York: Carroll & Graf Publishers.
Jackson, Frank. 1982. 'Epiphenomenal Qualia'. *The Philosophical Quarterly* 32 (127):127–36.
Jackson, Frank. 1986. 'What Mary Didn't Know'. *The Journal of Philosophy* 83 (5):291–5.
Jackson, Frank. 2007. 'Colour for Representationalists'. *Erkenntnis* 66 (1/2) Perspectives on Colour Perception):169–85.
Jakobson, Roman. 1987 [1922]. *Language in Literature*. Translated by Krystyna Pomorska and Stephen Rudy. Cambridge, MA: Harvard University Press.
Jakobson, Roman. 1990. *On Language*. Edited by Linda R. Waugh and M. Monville-Burston. Cambridge, MA: Harvard University Press.
Judt, Tony. 2011. *Ill Fares the Land*. New York: Penguin Books.
Kacelnik, Alex. 2006. 'Meanings of Rationality'. In *Rational Animals?* Edited by Susan Hurley and Matthew Nudds. Oxford: Oxford University Press, 87–106.
Kahneman, Daniel. 2003. 'A Psychological Perspective on Economics'. *The American Economic Review* 93 (2):162–8.
Kahneman, Daniel. 2011. *Thinking, Fast and Slow*. New York: Farrar, Straus and Giroux.
Kahneman, Daniel, and Amos Tversky. 1983. 'Extensional Versus Intuitive Reasoning: The Conjunction Fallacy in Probability Judgment'. *Psychological Review* 90 (4):293–315.
Kakutani, Michiko. 2018. *The Death of Truth: Notes on Falsehood in the Age of Trump*. New York: Tim Duggan Books.
Kant, Immanuel. 1965 [1781/1787]. *Critique of Pure Reason*. Translated by Norman Kemp Smith. New York: St. Martin's Press.
Kant, Immanuel. 1983. *Perpetual Peace and Other Essays*. Indianapolis: Hackett.
Kant, Immanuel. 2004 [1783]. *Prolegomena to any Future Metaphysics*. Translated by Gary Hatfield. Cambridge: Cambridge University Press.
Kant, Immanuel. 2014 [1783]. *Prolegomena to Any Future Metaphysics*. Cambridge: Cambridge University Press.
Katzav, Joel, and Kristi Vaesen. 2017. 'On the Emergence of American Analytic Philosophy'. *The British Journal for the History of Philosophy* 25 (4):772–98.
Keynes, John Maynard. 1921. *A Treatise on Probability*. London: Macmillan and Company.
Keynes, John Maynard. 1930. *A Treatise of Money*. New York: Harcourt, Brace and Company.
Keynes, John Maynard. 1931. *Essays in Persuasion*. London: Macmillan and Company.
Keynes, John Maynard. 1936. *The General Theory of Employment, Interest, and Money*. London: Palgrave.
Kierkegaard, Søren. 1968. *Concluding Unscientific Postscript*. Translated by David F. Swenson and Walter Lowrie. Princeton: Princeton University Press.
Kindleberger, Charles. 2005. *Manias, Panics, and Crashes: A History of Financial Crises*. Hoboken: John Wiley & Sons.
Kirk, G.S., and J.E. Raven. 1984. *The Presocratic Philosophers: A Critical History with a Selection of Texts*. Cambridge: Cambridge University Press.
Knight, Frank H. 1921. *Risk, Uncertainty and Profit*. New York: Sentry Press.
Knight, Frank H. 1922. 'Ethics and the Economic Interpretation'. *The Quarterly Journal of Economics* 36 (3):454–81.
Knight, Frank H. 1923. 'The Ethics of Competition'. *The Quarterly Journal of Economics* 37 (4):579–624.
Knight, Frank H. 1952. 'Institutionalism and Empiricism in Economics'. *The American Economic Review* 42 (2):45–55.

Kremer, Michael. 1992. 'The Multiplicity of General Propositions'. Noûs 26 (4):409–26.
Kuhn, Thomas. 1993. 'Afterwords'. In *World Changes*. Edited by Paul Horwich. Cambridge, MA: Harvard University Press, 311–41.
Labov, William. 1966. *The Social Stratification of English in New York City*. Washington, DC: Center for Applied Linguistics.
Labov, William. 1972. 'The Logic of Nonstandard English'. In *Language in the Inner City: Studies in the Black English Vernacular*. Philadelphia: University of Pennsylvania Press, 201–40.
Labov, William. 1994. *Principles of Linguistic Change: Internal Factors*. New York: Blackwell.
Labov, William. 2000. *Principles of Linguistic Change: Social Factors*. New York: Blackwell.
Labov, William. 2007. 'Transmission and Diffusion'. *Language* 83 (2):344–87.
Labov, William, and Joshua Waletzky. 1967. 'Narrative Analysis: Oral Versions of Personal Experience'. In *Essays on the Verbal and Visual Arts*. Edited by June Helm. Seattle: University of Washington Press, 12–44.
Laruelle, François. 2000. 'Identity and Event'. *Pli* 9:174–89.
Laruelle, François. 2010 [1986]. *Philosophies of Difference*. Translated by Rocco Gangle. London and New York: Continuum.
Laruelle, François. 2013 [1996]. *Principles of Non-Philosophy*. Translated by Nicola Rubczak and Anthony Paul Smith. London: Bloomsbury.
Latour, Bruno. 1986. 'The Powers of Association'. In *Power, Action and Belief: A New Sociology of Knowledge?*. Edited by John Law. New York: Routledge & Kegan Paul, 268–80.
Latour, Bruno. 1993. *We Have Never Been Modern*. Translated by Catherine Porter. Cambridge, MA: Harvard University Press.
Latour, Bruno. 1999. *Pandora's Hope: Essays on the Reality of Science Studies*. Cambridge, MA: Harvard University Press.
Latour, Bruno. 2000. 'On the Partial Existence of Existing and Nonexisting Objects'. In *Biographies of Scientific Objects*. Edited by Lorraine Daston. Chicago: University of Chicago Press, 247–69.
Latour, Bruno, and Shirley S. Strum. 1987. 'Redefining the Social Link - from Baboons to Humans'. *Social Science Information* 26 (4):783–802.
Latour, Bruno, and Stephen Woolgar. 1986. *Laboratory Life: The Construction of Scientific Facts*. Princeton: Princeton University Press.
Lautman, Albert. 2011. *Mathematics, Ideas and the Physical Real*. Translated by Simon B. Duffy. London: Continuum.
Learner, Edward E. 1983. 'Let's Take the Con Out of Econometrics'. *The American Economic Review* 73 (1):31–43.
Lefebvre, Henri. 1991 [1974]. *The Production of Space*. Translated by Donald Nicholson-Smith. Oxford: Blackwell.
Lefebvre, Henri. 1996. *Writings on Cities*. Translated by Eleonore Kofman and Elizabeth Lebas. Oxford: Blackwell.
Lefebvre, Henri. 2003 [1970]. *The Urban Revolution*. Translated by Robert Bononno. Minneapolis: University of Minnesota Press.
Lehoux, Daryn. 2012. *What Did the Romans Know? An Inquiry into Science and Worldmaking*. Chicago: University of Chicago Press.
Leibniz, G.W.F. 1956. *Philosophical Papers and Letters, Vol. 2*. Chicago: University of Chicago Press.
Leibniz, G.W.F. 1973. *Philosophical Writings*. Edited by G.H.R. Parkinson. New York: Dent.
Leibniz, G.W.F. 1996 [1704]. *New Essays on Human Understanding*. Cambridge: Cambridge University Press.
Leibniz, G.W.F. 2016. *The Leibniz–Arnauld Correspondence*. Translated by Stephen Voss, *The Yale Leibniz*. New Haven: Yale University Press.
Lepinay, Vincent-Antonin. 2007. 'Economy of the Germ: Capital, Accumulation and Vibration'. *Economy and Society* 36 (4):526–48.

Lewis, David. 1970. 'Anselm and Actuality'. *Noûs* 4 (2):175–88.
Lewis, David. 1983. 'New Work for a Theory of Universals'. *Australasian Journal of Philosophy* 61:343–77.
Lewis, David. 1984. 'Putnam's Paradox'. *Australasian Journal of Philosophy* 62:221–36.
Lewis, David. 1986a. *On the Plurality of Worlds*. New York: Wiley-Blackwell.
Lewis, David. 1986b. *Philosophical Papers II*. New York: Oxford University Press.
Lewis, David. 1986c. 'Against Structural Universals'. *Australasian Journal of Philosophy* 64 (1):25–46.
Lewis, David. 1991. *Parts of Classes*. New York: Wiley-Blackwell.
Lewis, David. 1994. 'Humean Supervenience Debugged'. *Mind* 114 (412):473–90.
Lewis, David. 1999a. *Papers in Metaphysics and Epistemology*. Cambridge: Cambridge University Press.
Lewis, David. 1999b. 'Many, But Almost One'. In *Papers in Metaphysics and Epistemology*. Cambridge: Cambridge University Press, 164–82.
Lewis, David. 2002. *Convention: A Philosophical Study*. New York: Wiley-Blackwell.
Liberman, Kenneth. 2013. *More Studies in Ethnomethodology*. Albany: State University of New York Press.
Locke, John. 1988 [1689]. *Two Treatises of Government*. Cambridge: Cambridge University Press.
Long, A.A., and D.N. Sedley, eds. 1987. *The Hellenistic Philosophers*. 2 vols. Translations of the principal sources with philosophical commentary. Cambridge: Cambridge University Press.
López de Sa, Dan. 2014. 'Lewis vs Lewis on the Problem of the Many'. *Synthese* 191:1105–17.
Luce, R. Duncan, and Howard Raiffa. 1957. *Games and Decisions*. New York: John Wiley & Sons.
Luria, Aleksandr. 1976. *Cognitive Development: Its Cultural and Social Foundations*. Cambridge, MA: Harvard University Press.
Lynch, Michael P. 2005. *True to Life: Why Truth Matters*. Cambridge, MA: The MIT Press.
Lynch, Michael P. 2009. *Truth as One and Many*. Oxford: Clarendon Press.
McCauley, Robert N., and Joseph Henrich. 2006. 'Susceptibility to the Müller-Lyer Illusion, Theory-Neutral Observation, and the Diachronic Penetrability of the Visual Input System'. *Philosophical Society* 19 (1):79–101.
McDaniel, Kris. 2009. 'Structure-Making'. *Australasian Journal of Philosophy* 87 (2):251–74.
McDaniel, Kris. 2017. *Fragmentation of Being*. Oxford: Oxford University Press.
McDowell, John. 1994. *Mind and World*. Cambridge, MA: Harvard University Press.
McDowell, John. 2004. 'Reply to John MacFarlane'. *Theoria* 70 (2–3):266–70.
McDowell, John. 2007. 'What Myth?' *Inquiry* 50 (4):338–51.
MacFarlane, John. 2004. 'McDowell's Kantianism'. *Theoria* 70:250–65.
MacFarlane, John. 2005. 'Making Sense of Relative Truth'. *Proceedings of the Aristotelian Society* 105:305–23.
MacFarlane, John. 2012. 'The Origins of Logical Hylomorphism', at <https://johnmacfarlane.net/origins.pdf>.
McIntyre, Lee. 2018. *Post-Truth*. Cambridge, MA: The MIT Press.
McTaggart, J. Ellis. 1908. 'The Unreality of Time'. *Mind* 17 (68):457–74.
Mader, Mary Beth. 2012. *Sleights of Reason: Norm, Bisexuality, Development*. Albany: State University of New York Press.
Madva, Alex. 2016. 'Why Implicit Attitudes are (Probably) Not Beliefs'. *Synthese* 193 (8):2659–84.
Mares, Edwin. 2010. 'Logic and Metaphysics: Dummett Meets Heidegger'. In *Postanalytic and Metacontinental: Crossing Philosophical Divides*. Edited by Jack Reynolds, James Chase, James Williams and Edwin Mares. London: Continuum Books, 53–70.
Marmodoro, Anna, and David Yates, eds. 2016. *The Metaphysics of Relations*. Oxford: Oxford University Press.

Marshall, Alfred. 1890. *Principles of Economics*. New York: Macmillan.
Marshall, Peter. 2010 [1992]. *Demanding the Impossible: A History of Anarchism*. Oakland: PM Press.
Mason, Richard. 2000. *Before Logic*. Albany: State University of New York Press.
Medin, Douglas L. 1989. 'Concepts and Conceptual Structure'. *American Psychologist* 44:469–81.
Meillassoux, Quentin. 2010. *After Finitude*. Translated by Ray Brassier. London: Continuum.
Meillassoux, Quentin. 2012. 'Iteration, Reiteration, Repetition: A Speculative Analysis of the Meaningless Sign'. Spekulative Poetik, Freie Universität, Berlin, 20 April 2012.
Mercier, Hugo, and Dan Sperber. 2011. 'Why Do Humans Reason? Arguments for an Argumentative Theory'. *Behavioral and Brain Sciences* 34:57–111.
Mercier, Hugo, and Dan Sperber. 2017. *The Enigma of Reason*. Cambridge, MA: Harvard University Press.
Miller, Jon. 2015. *Spinoza and the Stoics*. Cambridge: Cambridge University Press.
Miller, Peter, and Michael Power. 2013. 'Accounting, Organizing, and Economizing: Connecting Accounting Research and Organization Theory'. *The Academy of Management Annals* 7 (1):557–605.
Mills, Charles W. 1997. *The Racial Contract*. New York: Cornell University Press.
Mills, Charles W. 2005. '"Ideal Theory" as Ideology'. *Hypatia* 20 (3):165–84.
Minsky, Hyman P. 2008. *Stabilizing an Unstable Economy*. New York: McGraw Hill.
Montes, Leonidas, and Eric Schliesser, eds. 2006. *New Voices on Adam Smith*. London: Routledge.
Moore, A.W. 1990. *The Infinite*. New York: Routledge.
Moore, A.W. 2012. *The Evolution of Modern Metaphysics: Making Sense of Things*. Cambridge: Cambridge University Press.
Moore, G.E. 1899. 'The Nature of Judgment'. *Mind* 8 (30):176–93.
Moore, G.E. 1903. 'The Refutation of Idealism'. *Mind* 12 (48):433–53.
Moore, Joseph. 1999. 'Propositions without Identity'. *Noûs* 33 (1):1–29.
Nagel, Ernest. 1936a. 'Impressions and Appraisals of Analytic Philosophy in Europe. I'. *The Journal of Philosophy* 33 (1):5–24.
Nagel, Ernest. 1936b. 'Impressions and Appraisals of Analytic Philosophy in Europe. II'. *The Journal of Philosophy* 33 (2):29–53.
Nagel, Ernest. 1938. 'Review of *Determinismus und Indeterminismus in der Modernen Physik* by Ernst Cassirer'. *Philosophy of Science* 5 (2):230–32.
Nagel, Ernest. 1941. 'A Review of Philosophical Essays in Memory of Edmund Husserl, ed. by Marvin Farber'. *The Journal of Philosophy* 38 (11):301–6.
Nagel, Ernest. 1961. *Structure of Science: Problems in the Logic of Scientific Explanation*. New York: Harcourt, Brace & World.
Needham, Paul. 2009. 'Reduction and Emergence'. *Philosophical Studies* 146 (1):93–116.
Neurath, Otto. 2004. *Otto Neurath: Economic Writings, Selections 1904–1945*. Translated by Robert S. Cohen, Marie Neurath, Christoph Schmidt-Petri and Thomas E. Uebl. New York: Kluwer Academic Publishers.
Nietzsche, Friedrich. 1966 [1886]. *Beyond Good and Evil*. Translated by Walter Kaufmann. New York: Vintage Books.
Nietzsche, Friedrich. 1996 [1879]. *Human, All-Too-Human: A Book for Free Spirits*. Translated by R.J. Hollingdale. Cambridge: Cambridge University Press.
North, Michael. 2013. *Novelty: A History of the New*. Chicago: University of Chicago Press.
Nozick, Robert. 1998 [1974]. *Anarchy, State, and Utopia*. New York: Basic Books.
Olson, David R. 1977. 'From Utterance to Text: The Bias of Language in Speech and Writing'. *Harvard Educational Review* 47:257–81.
Olson, David R. 1994. *The World on Paper: The Conceptual and Cognitive Implications of Writing and Reading*. Cambridge: Cambridge University Press.

Oppy, Graham. 2006. *Philosophical Perspectives on Infinity*. Cambridge: Cambridge University Press.
Parfit, Derek. 1984. *Reasons and Persons*. Oxford: Oxford University Press.
Parsons, Terence, and Peter Woodruff. 1994. 'Worldly Indeterminacy of Identity'. *Proceedings of the Aristotelian Society* 95:171–91.
Paul, L.A. 2015. 'What You Can't Expect When You're Expecting'. *Res Philosophica* 92 (2):1–23.
Peart, Sandra J., and David M. Levy. 2008. *The Street Porter and the Philosopher: Conversations on Analytical Egalitarianism*. Ann Arbor: University of Michigan Press.
Peden, Knox. 2014. *Spinoza Contra Phenomenology: French Rationalism from Cavaillès to Deleuze*. Stanford: Stanford University Press.
Penn, Derek, and D.J. Povinelli. 2016. 'The Comparative Delusion: the 'Behavioristic'/'Mentalistic' Dichotomy in Comparative Theory of Mind Research'. In *Agency and Joint Attention*. Edited by H.A. Terrace and J. Metcalfe. Oxford: Oxford University Press, 62–81.
Piketty, Thomas. 2014. *Capital in the Twenty-First Century*. Cambridge, MA: Belknap Press.
Pixley, Jocelyn, and G.C. Harcourt, eds. 2013. *Financial Crises and the Nature of Capitalist Money: Mutual Developments from the Work of Geoffrey Ingham*. London: Palgrave Macmillan.
Plato. 2006. *Philebus*. Translated by Harold North Fowler and W.R.M. Lamb. *Loeb Classical Library*, Vol. 164. Cambridge, MA: Harvard University Press.
Polanyi, Karl. 2001 [1944]. *The Great Transformation: The Political and Economic Origins of Our Time*. New York: Beacon Press.
Popkin, Richard. 1952. 'David Hume and the Pyrrhonian Controversy'. *The Review of Metaphysics* 6 (1):65–81.
Potter, Michael. 2004. *Set Theory and its Philosophy*. New York: Oxford University Press.
Potter, Michael. 2008a. 'The Birth of Analytic Philosophy'. In *The Routledge Companion to Twentieth Century Philosophy*. Edited by Dermot Moran. New York: Routledge, 43–75.
Potter, Michael. 2008b. *Wittgenstein's Notes on Logic*. Oxford: Oxford University Press.
Povinelli, D.J., J.M. Bering, and S. Giambrone. 2000. 'Toward a Science of Other Minds: Escaping the Argument by Analogy'. *Cognitive Science* 24:509–41.
Price, Huw. 2009. 'Metaphysics after Carnap: The Ghost Who Walks?' In *Metametaphysics: Essays on the Foundations of Ontology*. Edited by David Chalmers, David Manley and Ryan Wasserman. Oxford: Oxford University Press, 320–46.
Price, Huw, Simon Blackburn, Robert B. Brandom, Paul Horwich and Michael Williams. 2013. *Expressivism, Pragmatism and Representationalism*. Cambridge: Cambridge University Press.
Prior, Arthur N. 1948. 'Facts, Propositions and Entailment'. *Mind* 57 (225):62–8.
Putnam, Hilary. 1967. 'Mathematics without Foundations'. *The Journal of Philosophy* 64 (1):5–22.
Putnam, Hilary. 1977. 'Realism and Reason'. *Proceedings and Addresses of the American Philosophical Association* 50 (6):483–98.
Quine, W.V. 1966. *The Ways of Paradox and Other Essays*. Cambridge, MA: Harvard University Press.
Quine, W.V. 1970. *The Web of Belief*. New York: McGraw-Hill.
Quine, W.V. 1980. *From a Logical Point of View: Nine Logico-Philosophical Essays*. Cambridge, MA: Harvard University Press.
Quine, W.V. 2013 [1960]. *Word and Object*. Cambridge, MA: The MIT Press.
Quine, W.V.O. 1980 [1948]. 'On What There Is'. In *From a Logical Point of View*. Cambridge, MA: Harvard University Press, 1–19.
Radulescu, Alexandru. 2016. 'Three Views on Propositions: King, Soames and Speaks'. *Analysis* 76 (3):1–9.
Ramsey, F.P. 1990a [1925]. 'Universals'. In *F.P. Ramsey: Philosophical Papers*. Edited by D.H. Mellor. Cambridge: Cambridge University Press, 8–30.

Ramsey, F.P. 1990b [1927]. 'Facts and Propositions'. In *F.P. Ramsey: Philosophical Papers*. Edited by D.H. Mellor. Cambridge: Cambridge University Press, 34–51.
Ramsey, F.P., and G.E. Moore. 1927. 'Symposium: Facts and Propositions'. *Proceedings of the Aristotelian Society, Supplementary Volumes* 7:153–206.
Rankin, K.W. 1969. 'The Duplicity of Plato's Third Man'. *Mind* 78 (310):178–97.
Rawls, John. 1955. 'Two Concepts of Rules'. *Philosophical Review* 64 (1):3–32.
Rawls, John. 1971. *A Theory of Justice*. Cambridge, MA: Harvard University Press.
Reinhart, Carmen M., and Kenneth S. Rogoff. 2011. *This Time is Different: Eight Centuries of Financial Folly*. Princeton: Princeton University Press.
Richard, Mark. 2008. *When Truth Gives Out*. Oxford: Oxford University Press.
Roberts, Robert C. 1996. 'Propositions and Animal Emotion'. *Philosophy* 71 (275):147–56.
Romer, Paul. forthcoming. 'The Trouble With Macroeconomics'. *The American Economist*.
Rorty, Richard. 1979. *Philosophy and the Mirror of Nature*. Princeton: Princeton University Press.
Rosen, Gideon. 1995. 'Armstrong on Classes as States of Affairs'. *Australasian Journal of Philosophy* 73 (4):613–25.
Rothbart, M., and M. Taylor. 1992. 'Category Labels and Social Reality: Do We View Social Categories as Natural Kinds?' In *Language, Interaction and Social Cognition*. Edited by G. Semin and K. Fielder. London: Sage, 11–36.
Runciman, W.G., and Amartya Sen. 1965. 'Games, Justice and the General Will'. *Mind* 74 (296):554–62.
Russell, Bertrand. 1900. *A Critical Exposition of the Philosophy of Leibniz*. Cambridge: Cambridge University Press.
Russell, Bertrand. 1903. *The Principles of Mathematics*. Cambridge: Cambridge University Press.
Russell, Bertrand. 1905. 'On Denoting'. *Mind* 14 (56):479–93.
Russell, Bertrand. 1907. 'On the Nature of Truth'. *Proceedings of the Aristotelian Society* 7:28–49.
Russell, Bertrand. 1910. 'Explanations in Reply to Mr. Bradley'. *Mind* 19 (75):373–8.
Russell, Bertrand. 1914. 'The Relation of Sense-Data to Physics'. *Scientia* 16:1–27.
Russell, Bertrand. 1915. 'The Ultimate Constituents of Matter'. *Monist* 25 (3):399–417.
Russell, Bertrand. 1917a. 'On Scientific Method in Philosophy'. In *Mysticism and Logic and Other Essays*. London: George Allen & Unwin Ltd.
Russell, Bertrand. 1917b. *Mysticism and Logic and Other Essays*. London: George Allen & Unwin Ltd.
Russell, Bertrand. 1919. 'On Propositions: What They Are and How They Mean'. *Proceedings of the Aristotelian Society, Supplementary Volumes* 2:1–43.
Russell, Bertrand. 1923. 'Vagueness'. *Australasian Journal of Philosophy and Psychology* 1:84–92.
Russell, Bertrand. 1940. *An Inquiry into Meaning and Truth*. London: Allen & Unwin.
Russell, Bertrand. 1950. *Unpopular Essays*. New York: Simon and Schuster.
Russell, Bertrand. 1959. *My Philosophical Development*. New York: Simon and Schuster.
Russell, Bertrand. 1970. *Logic and Knowledge: Essays 1901–1950*. Oakville: Capricorn Books.
Russell, Bertrand. 1996 [1928]. *Sceptical Essays*. London: Routledge.
Russell, Bertrand. 2001 [1912]. *The Problems of Philosophy*. Oxford: Oxford University Press.
Ryle, Gilbert. 1929. 'Are There Propositions?' *Proceedings of the Aristotelian Society* 30:91–126.
Ryle, Gilbert. 1946. 'Knowing How and Knowing That'. *Proceedings of the Aristotelian Society* 46:1–16.
Sabl, Andrew. 2012. *Hume's Politics: Coordination and Crisis in the History of England*. Princeton: Princeton University Press.
Sandbrook, Richard. 2014. *Reinventing the Left in the Global South: The Politics of the Possible*. Cambridge: Cambridge University Press.
Sartre, Jean-Paul. 1960 [1936]. *The Transcendence of the Ego*. Translated by Forrest Williams and Robert Kirkpatrick. New York: Farrar, Straus and Giroux.
Sassoon, Donald. 1998. *One Hundred Years of Socialism: The West European Left in the Twentieth Century*. New York: The New Press.

Sawyer, R. Keith. 2005. *Social Emergence: Societies as Complex Systems*. Cambridge: Cambridge University Press.
Sayer, Andrew. 2011. *Why Things Matter to People: Social Science, Values and Ethical Life*. Cambridge: Cambridge University Press.
Schacht, Hjalmar. 1967. *The Magic of Money*. Translated by Paul Erskine. London: Oldbourne.
Schaffer, Jonathan. 2010. 'Monism: The Priority of the Whole'. *Philosophical Review* 119 (1):31–76.
Schaffer, Jonathan. 2012. 'Necessitarian Propositions'. *Synthese* 189 (1):119–62.
Schelling, Thomas. 1963. *The Strategy of Conflict*. Cambridge, MA: Harvard University Press.
Schlick, Moritz. 1939 [1930]. *Problems of Ethics*. Translated by David Rynin. New York: Prentice-Hall.
Schliesser, Eric. 2010. 'Friedman, Positive Economics, and the Chicago Boys'. In *The Elgar Companion to the Chicago School of Economics*. Edited by Ross B. Emmett. Cheltenham: Edward Elgar, 175–95.
Schliesser, Eric. 2012. What Happened to Knightian (and Keynesian) Uncertainty Post WWII? A Philosophic History. *SSRN*, at <https://papers.ssrn.com/sol3/papers.cfm?abstract_id=2033117>.
Schliesser, Eric. 2017. *Adam Smith: Systematic Philosopher and Public Thinker*. Oxford: Oxford University Press.
Schliesser, Eric. 2018. 'Hume on Affective Leadership'. In *Hume's Moral Philosophy and Contemporary Psychology*. Edited by P.A. Reed and R. Vitz. New York: Routledge, 311–33.
Schmitt, Bernard. 2014. 'The Formation of Sovereign Debt: Diagnosis and Remedy: Troika's Historical Error: The Duplication of Countries' External Debts'. *SSRN*, at <https://papers.ssrn.com/sol3/papers.cfm?abstract_id=2513679>.
Schmitt, Carl. 2006 [1922]. *Political Theology: Four Chapters on the Concept of Sovereignty*. Chicago: University of Chicago Press.
Schmitt, Carl. 2008a [1932]. *The Concept of the Political*. Chicago: University of Chicago Press.
Schmitt, Carl. 2008b [1938]. *The Leviathan in the State Theory of Thomas Hobbes: The Meaning and Failure of a Political Symbol*. Translated by George Schwab. Chicago: University of Chicago Press.
Schmitt, Carl. 2014 [1921]. *Dictatorship*. Cambridge: Polity Press.
Schofield, Malcom. 1986. 'Cicero For and Against Divination'. *Journal of Roman Studies* 76 (76):47–64.
Schofield, Malcom. 1991. *The Stoic Idea of the City*. Cambridge: Cambridge University Press.
Schumpeter, Joseph A. 1939. *Business Cycles: A Theoretical, Historical, and Statistical Analysis of the Capitalist Process*. New York: McGraw-Hill.
Schumpeter, Joseph A. 1954. *Economic Doctrine and Method: An Historical Sketch*. New York: Oxford University Press.
Schutz, Alfred. 1967. *The Phenomenology of the Social World*. Translated by George Walsh and Frederick Lehnert. Evanston: Northwestern University Press.
Scribner, Sylvia. 1977. 'Modes of Thinking and Ways of Speaking: Culture and Logic Reconsidered'. In *Thinking: Readings in Cognitive Science*. Cambridge: Cambridge University Press, 483–500.
Scribner, Sylvia. 1997. *Mind and Social Practice: Selected Writings of Sylvia Scribner*. Cambridge: Cambridge University Press.
Seaford, Richard. 2004. *Money and the Early Greek Mind: Homer, Philosophy, Tragedy*. Cambridge: Cambridge University Press.
Searcy, William A., and Stephen Nowicki. 2005. *The Evolution of Animal Communication: Reliability and Deception in Signaling Systems*. Princeton: Princeton University Press.
Segall, Marshall, D. Campbell and M.J. Herskovits. 1966. *The Influence of Culture on Visual Perception*. New York: Bobbs-Merrill.

Sellars, John. 2003. *The Art of Living: The Stoics on the Nature and Function of Philosophy*. London: Bloomsbury.
Sellars, Wilfrid. 1949. 'Acquaintance and Description Again'. *Journal of Philosophy* 46 (16):496–504.
Sellars, Wilfrid. 1950. 'Quotation Marks, Sentences, and Propositions'. *Philosophy and Phenomenological Research* 10 (4):515–25.
Sellars, Wilfrid. 1955. 'Vlastos and "The Third Man"'. *Philosophical Review* 64 (3):405–37.
Sellars, Wilfrid. 1997 [1956]. *Empiricism and the Philosophy of Mind*. Cambridge, MA: Harvard University Press.
Sewell, William H., Jr. 2005. 'The Concept(s) of Culture'. In *Practicing History: New Directions in Historical Writing after the Linguistic Turn*. Edited by Gabrielle M. Spiegel. New York: Routledge, 76–95.
Shapin, Steven, and Simon Schaffer. 1985. *Leviathan and the Air-Pump: Hobbes, Boyle and the Experimental Life*. Princeton: Princeton University Press.
Sherman, David K., and Geoffrey L. Cohen. 2006. 'The Psychology of Self-Defense: Self-Affirmation Theory'. *Advances in Experimental Social Psychology* 38:183–242.
Simmel, Georg. 1910. 'How is Society Possible?' *The American Journal of Sociology* 16 (3):372–91.
Simmel, Georg. 1957. 'Fashion'. *The American Journal of Sociology* 62 (6):541–58.
Simmel, Georg. 1978. *The Philosophy of Money*. New York: Routledge and Kegan Paul Ltd.
Smith, Adam. 1776. *An Inquiry into the Nature and Causes of the Wealth of Nations*. London: Printed for William Strahan and Thomas Cadell.
Smith, Adam. 1976 [1759]. *The Theory of Moral Sentiments*. Indianapolis: Liberty Fund.
Smith, Daniel W. 2012. *Essays on Deleuze*. Edinburgh: Edinburgh University Press.
Smith, John Maynard. 1982. *Evolution and the Theory of Games*. Cambridge: Cambridge University Press.
Somers-Hall, Henry. 2012. *Hegel, Deleuze, and the Critique of Representation*. Albany: State University of New York Press.
Somers-Hall, Henry. 2022. *Judgment and Sense in Modern French Philosophy: A New Reading of Six Thinkers*. Cambridge: Cambridge University Press.
Sraffa, Piero. 1960. *Production of Commodities: Prelude to a Critique of Economic Theory*. Cambridge: Cambridge University Press.
Staley, Kent W. 2017. 'Decisions, Decisions: Inductive Risk and the Higgs Boson'. In *Exploring Inductive Risk: Case Studies of Values in Science*. Edited by Kevin C. Elliott and Ted Richards. Oxford: Oxford University Press, 37–57.
Stanley, Jason. 1996. 'Truth and Metatheory in Frege'. *Pacific Philosophical Quarterly* 77:45–70.
Stanley, Jason. 2001. 'Knowing How'. *Journal of Philosophy* 98:411–44.
Stanley, Jason. 2015. *How Propaganda Works*. Princeton: Princeton University Press.
Stanley, Jason, and John W. Krakauer. 2013. 'Motor Skill Depends on Knowledge of Facts'. *Frontiers in Human Neuroscience* 7:1–11.
Stasavage, David. 2003. *Public Debt and the Birth of the Democratic State: France and Great Britain, 1688–1789*. Cambridge: Cambridge University Press.
Stasavage, David. 2015. *States of Credit: Size, Power, and the Development of European Polities*. Princeton: Princeton University Press.
Steele, Claude M. 1988. 'The Psychology of Self-Affirmation: Sustaining the Integrity of the Self'. In *Advances in Experimental Social Psychology*. Edited by L. Berkowitz. New York: Academic Press, 261–302.
Stenning, Keith, and Michiel van Lambalgen. 2008. *Human Reasoning and Cognitive Science*. Cambridge, MA: The MIT Press.
Stewart, Dugald. 1792. *Elements of the Philosophy of the Human Mind*. London: Printed for Andrew Strahan, and Thomas Cadell; and William Creech, Edinburgh.
Stewart, M.V. 1973. 'Tests of the "Carpentered World" Hypothesis by Race and Environment in America and Zambia'. *International Journal of Psychology* 8:83–94.

Stone, Abraham. 2006. 'Heidegger and Carnap on the Overcoming of Metaphysics'. In *Martin Heidegger*. Edited by Stephen Mulhall. London: Ashgate, 217–44.

Strawson, Galen. 2002. 'David Hume: Objects and Power'. In *Reading Hume on Human Understanding: Essays on Hume's First Enquiry*. Edited by Peter Millican. Oxford: Oxford University Press, 231–57.

Strawson, Galen. 2009. *Selves*. Oxford: Oxford University Press.

Strawson, P.F. 1950. 'On Referring'. *Mind* 59 (235):320–44.

Strawson, P.F. 1957. 'Propositions, Concepts and Logical Truths'. *The Philosophical Quarterly* 7 (26):15–25.

Streeck, Wolfgang. 2014. *Buying Time: The Delayed Crisis of Democratic Capitalism*. Translated by Patrick Camiller. London: Verso.

Streeck, Wolfgang. 2016. *How Will Capitalism End? Essays on a Failing System*. London: Verso.

Sudnow, David. 1978. *Ways of the Hand*. Cambridge, MA: Harvard University Press.

Tarski, Alfred. 1944. 'The Semantic Conception of Truth: And the Foundations of Semantics'. *Philosophy and Phenomenological Research* 4 (3):341–76.

Taylor, A.E. 1916. 'Parmenides, Zeno, and Socrates'. *Proceedings of the Aristotelian Society* XVI.

Todorov, Tzvetan. 1977. *The Poetics of Prose*. Translated by Richard Howard. Ithaca: Cornell University Press.

Todorov, Tzvetan. 1982. *Symbolism and Interpretation*. Translated by Catherine Porter. Ithaca: Cornell University Press.

Tomasello, Michael. 1999. *The Cultural Origins of Human Cognition*. Cambridge, MA: Harvard University Press.

Traverso, Enzo. 2003. *The Origins of Nazi Violence*. Translated by Janet Lloyd. New York: The New Press.

Tuomela, Raimo. 2009. 'Collective Intentions and Game Theory'. *The Journal of Philosophy* 106 (5):292–300.

Turing, Alan. 1937. 'On Computable Numbers, With an Application to the Entscheidungsproblem'. *Proceedings of the London Mathematical Society* 42:230–65.

Uexküll, Jakob von. 2010 [1934]. *A Foray into the Worlds of Animals and Humans: With a Theory of Meaning*. Translated by Joseph D. O'Neil. Minneapolis: Posthumanities Press.

Ullman-Margalit, Edna. 1977. *The Emergence of Norms*. Oxford: Oxford University Press.

Unger, Peter. 1980. 'The Problem of the Many'. *Midwest Studies in Philosophy* 5:411–67.

van Fraassen, Bas C. 1966. 'Singular Terms, Truth-Value Gaps, and Free Logic'. *Journal of Philosophy* 63:481–95.

Vanderschraaf, Peter. 2008. 'Game Theory Meets Threshold Analysis: Reappraising the Paradoxes of Anarchy and Revolution'. *The British Journal for the Philosophy of Science* 59 (4):579–617.

Varoufakis, Yanis. 1993. 'Modern and Postmodern Challenges to Game Theory'. *Erkenntnis* 38 (3):371–404.

Viveiros de Castro, Eduardo. 2014. *Cannibal Metaphysics*. Translated by Peter Skafish. Minneapolis: Univocal Publishing.

Vlastos, Gregory. 1937. 'Organic Categories in Whitehead'. *The Journal of Philosophy* 34 (10):253–62.

Vlastos, Gregory. 1954. 'The Third Man Argument in the Parmenides'. *Philosophical Review* 63 (3):319–49.

Vygotsky, Lev Semenovich. 1972. 'Spinoza's Theory of the Emotions in Light of Contemporary Psychoneurology'. *Soviet Studies in Philosophy*:36–81.

Vygotsky, Lev Semenovich. 1986. *Thought and Language*. Translated by Alex Kozulin. Cambridge, MA: The MIT Press.

Weber, Max. 1961. *General Economic History*. New York: Collier.

Weber, Max. 1968. *Economy and Society*. New York: Bedminster Press.

Weinberg, Steven. 1977. 'The Search for Unity: Notes for a History of Quantum Field Theory'. *Daedalus* 106 (4):17–35.
Werner, Richard A. 2014. 'How Do Banks Create Money, and Why Can Other Firms Not Do the Same? An Explanation for the Coexistence of Lending and Deposit-taking'. *International Review of Financial Analysis* 36:71–7.
Whiten, A., and R.W. Byrne. 1988. 'Tactical Deception in Primates'. *Behavioral and Brain Sciences* 11 (2):233–44.
Williams, Donald C. 1953a. 'On the Elements of Being: I'. *The Review of Metaphysics* 7 (1):3–18.
Williams, Donald C. 1953b. 'On the Elements of Being: II'. *The Review of Metaphysics* 7 (2):171–92.
Williams, James. 2004. *Gilles Deleuze's Difference and Repetition: A Critical Introduction*. Edinburgh: Edinburgh University Press.
Williams, James. 2016. *A Process Philosophy of Signs*. Edinburgh: Edinburgh University Press.
Williamson, Timothy. 1996. *Vagueness*. London: Routledge.
Wilson, Jessica. 1999. 'How Superduper Does a Physicalist Supervenience Need to Be?' *The Philosophical Quarterly* 49 (194):33–52.
Wilson, Jessica. 2013. 'A Determinable-Based Account of Metaphysical Indeterminacy'. *Inquiry* 56 (4):359–85.
Wilson, Jessica M. 2011. 'Non-reductive Realization and the Powers-based Subset Strategy'. *The Monist (Issue on Powers)* 94 (1):121–54.
Wilson, Jessica M. 2012. 'Fundamental Determinables'. *Philosophers' Imprint* 12 (4).
Wilson, Mark. 1982. 'Predicate Meets Property'. *The Philosophical Review* 91 (4):549–89.
Wilson, Mark. 1985. 'This Thing Called Pain'. *Pacific Philosophical Quarterly* 66 (3–4):227–67.
Wilson, Mark. 2004. 'Theory Façades'. *Proceedings of the Aristotelian Society* 104:273–88.
Wilson, Mark. 2006. *Wandering Significance: An Essay on Conceptual Behavior*. Oxford: Oxford University Press.
Winston, Patrick Henry. 2011. 'The Strong Story Hypothesis and the Directed Perception Hypothesis'. Advances in Cognitive Systems: Papers from the 2011 AAAI Fall Symposium.
Winston, Patrick Henry. 2014. 'The Genesis Story Understanding and Story Telling System: A 21st Century Step toward Artificial Intelligence'. *Center for Brains, Minds & Machines* 19:1–12.
Wittgenstein, Ludwig. 1958 [1935]. *The Blue and Brown Books*. London: Blackwell.
Wittgenstein, Ludwig. 1974 [1933]. *Philosophical Grammar*. Translated by Anthony Kenny. Oxford: Blackwell.
Wittgenstein, Ludwig. 1976 [1922]. *Tractatus Logico-Philosophicus*. Edited by D.F. Pears and Bernard McGuinness. London: Routledge and Kegan Paul.
Wittgenstein, Ludwig. 1979 [1935]. *Wittgenstein's Lectures, Cambridge, 1932–1935*. New York: Prometheus Books.
Wittgenstein, Ludwig. 1983 [1937–1944]. *Remarks on the Foundations of Mathematics*. Edited by G.H. von Wright, R. Rhees and G.E.M. Anscombe. Cambridge, MA: The MIT Press.
Wittgenstein, Ludwig. 2009 [1953]. *Philosophical Investigations*. Edited by G.E.M. Anscombe. Oxford: Blackwell.
Wray, L. Randall, and A. Mitchell Innes, eds. 2004. *Credit and State Theories of Money: The Contributions of A. Mitchell Innes*. Cheltenham: Edward Elgar.
Wright, Crispin. 1983. *Frege's Conception of Number*. Aberdeen: Aberdeen University Press.

Index

Adorno, Theodor, 13, 148–58, 161, 182, 191, 201
antinomies, 82–4
Armstrong, D.M., 13, 101–7, 108–14, 124
Austin, J.L., 72–3

Bell, Winthrop, 133
Bergson, Henri, 161, 201
Bourdieu, Pierre, 66–72
Bradley, F.H., 11, 16, 28–33, 38–9, 41–9, 56, 66, 132, 180, 192, 204
Brandom, Robert, 167

Cairns, Dorion, 133–5
Cantor, Georg, 175
Carlsen, Magnus, 171
Carnap, Rudolf, 7–9, 10, 136–7, 139, 160–4, 171, 175, 182–90, 200, 205–6
Cavaillès, Jean, 64
Chang, Hasok, 128–9
coffee tasting, 152, 155–7

Davidson, Donald, 14, 18, 137, 165, 175, 193–8
Deleuze, Gilles, 3, 11, 30, 53–64, 72, 76–80, 92–3, 117–19, 144–5, 147–8, 161, 178, 191
and Guattari, Félix, 72–6, 198, 202
Della Rocca, Michael, 11, 33, 43–9, 56, 139, 162–3, 189, 192–3
Demos, Raphael, 133
Dennett, Daniel, 1

Descartes, René, 54–5, 60, 168
determinable/determinate, 114, 116–17, 119–23
Dilthey, Wilhelm, 141–2
Dreyfus, Hubert, 13, 169–74, 187–8
Dummett, Michael, 160

Eleatic principle, 116–17
emergence, problem of, 17, 112–13, 115–16
Ethnomethodology, 155–7
Euclid, 179

Faraday, Michael, 67
Farber, Marvin, 133
Field, Hartry, 186
Fine, Gail, 21, 25, 31–2
Frege, Gottlob, 96–7, 100–1, 126, 132, 170

Garfinkel, Harold, 155–7
Gödel, Kurt, 177

Habitus, 68–9
Hartmann, Nicolai, 17
Hawking, Stephen, 6
Haydn, Joseph, 16,
Hegel, G.W.F., 23, 34, 70, 148–9, 154–5
Heidegger, Martin, 7, 23, 135–7, 138–9, 141–2, 148–50, 160
Hilbert, David, 178–9
Hook, Sidney, 132–5, 137
Hume, David, 4–6, 11, 28, 46–7, 52, 55, 83–5, 104, 106, 138, 165–6, 175, 193, 202–3, 204

INDEX

Humean supervenience, 109–11
Husserl, Edmund, 131–42, 144–5, 147–8, 153, 156, 158, 171, 202–3

incorporeal transformation, 72–3

Kant, Immanuel, 1–2, 3–5, 7–9, 34, 54, 81–100, 139, 169, 204, 206
Kripke, Saul, 137

Lautman, Albert, 64
learning, 76–7
Leibniz, G.W.F., 12, 48, 51–64, 97
Lewis, David, 13, 17, 48, 101–14, 124–5, 137, 140–4, 177–8, 182, 187
Liberman, Kenneth, 155–7
Locke, John, 43

McDowell, John, 13, 165, 167, 168–77, 195
MacFarlane, John, 174–7
Maxwell, James Clerk, 67
Meillassoux, Quentin, 178–82, 183, 200–1
Merleau-Ponty, Maurice, 170
Minsky, Marvin, 170
Moore, G.E., 35–7, 41, 44, 46, 132, 139, 163, 193
music, 151

Nagel, Ernest, 8, 135–6, 164–5, 171
Natorp, Paul, 133
Neo-Kantian, 144, 148
Neurath, Otto, 165
new, problem of the, 15, 22
Nietzsche, Friedrich, 151, 153
Nozick, Robert, 43

one and many, problem of, 18,

Parfit, Derek, 47–8
Parmenides, 19–20
Perry, Ralph Barton, 132–3
Philebus, 24–6, 49, 65, 95, 112–13, 150, 162
Plato, 2–3, 7, 19–28, 32–3, 49, 62–3, 65–6, 95–6, 150, 158, 162, 201
  Ideas, 78–9, 81, 158
Price, Huw, 14, 165, 182–90, 205–6
Primacy of the determinate, 10–11, 107, 111–12, 114, 119–23, 126, 197–8, 200–1, 204
Principle of Sufficient Reason, 39, 42–3, 49, 59, 180
Problematic Idea(s), 7, 9–10, 13–14, 33, 61, 64, 66, 79–80, 90, 95, 97–8, 107, 114, 121–2, 125–6, 143, 147–8, 153, 157–8, 197–200, 204–5
protocol sentences, 163–4

Quine, W.V.O., 44–5, 137, 165, 182–91, 192–4

Rawls, John, 43
relations, problem of, 16,
relevance questions, 6
Rorty, Richard, 195
Russell, Bertrand, 1–2, 11, 34–5, 37–41, 44, 46, 50–3, 58–9, 70–1, 87–9, 139, 163, 170, 175, 180, 193, 204
Ryle, Gilbert, 173

Sartre, Jean-Paul, 140–1
Schlick, Moritz, 165
Schutz, Alfred, 156
Sellars, Wilfrid, 22, 65, 165–8
Sider, Theodore, 48
singletons, 107–8, 140–4
Skinner, B.F., 166
Smith, Dan, 56–7
Spinoza, Benedict, 11–12, 193

Stanley, Jason, 173–4
Stewart, Dugald, 127
Stone, Abraham, 136–7

Tarksi, Alfred, 196
Third Man Argument, 12, 19–27, 28, 30–2, 34–6, 41, 48, 62, 66, 95, 100–1, 105, 162, 192
Transcendental empiricism, 143–5, 147–8
transcendental illusion, 98, 99–100
tropes (theory of), 103

Uexküll, Jakob von, 118

vitalism, 161–2
Vlastos, Gregory, 19, 20,

Weimar Republic (and hyperinflation), 74–5
Weinberg, Steven, 67–8
Whitehead, Alfred North, 98
Wilson, Jessica, 17, 116–23, 125
Wilson, Mark, 125–31, 146–8, 153, 157–8, 161, 170, 189–90
Wittgenstein, Ludwig, 42, 166

EU representative:
Easy Access System Europe
Mustamäe tee 50, 10621 Tallinn, Estonia
Gpsr.requests@easproject.com

www.ingramcontent.com/pod-product-compliance
Lightning Source LLC
Chambersburg PA
CBHW070347240426
43671CB00013BA/2434